European Economic Interaction and Integration
(formerly East–West European Economic Interaction)

Workshop Papers
Series Editor: Philipp Rieger

The Vienna Institute for Comparative Economic Studies organises a series of international workshops concerned with problems of European economic interaction and integration guided by an International Steering Committee consisting of:

Carlo Boffito, Milan
Oleg Bogomolov, Moscow
Bernard Cazes, Paris
John P. Hardt, Washington
András Inotai, Budapest
Norbert Kloten, Stuttgart
Karel Kouba, Prague
Kazimierz Laski, Vienna

Friedrich Levcik, Vienna
Jože Mencinger, Ljubljana
Philipp Rieger (Chairman), Vienna
Christopher T. Saunders, Brighton, UK
Witold Trzeciakowski, Warsaw
Dragomir Vojnić, Zagreb
Todor Vulchev, Sofia

The present volume is based on Workshop Session XIV held in Mariánské Lázně (Marienbad), CSFR, 1992.

D1486331

The Role of Competition in Economic Transition

Edited by

Christopher T. Saunders
Visiting Fellow, Science Policy Research Unit
University of Sussex, UK

150th YEAR

M

St. Martin's Press

in association with
THE VIENNA INSTITUTE
FOR COMPARATIVE ECONOMIC STUDIES

Research Director: Prof. Dr. Kazimierz Laski
Administrative Director: Dr. Ingrid Gazzari

First published in Great Britain 1993 by
THE MACMILLAN PRESS LTD
Houndmills, Basingstoke, Hampshire RG21 2XS
and London
Companies and representatives
throughout the world

A catalogue record for this book is available from the British Library.

ISBN 0–333–59034–1

Printed in Great Britain by
Antony Rowe Ltd, Chippenham, Wiltshire

Sponsored by The Commission of the European Communities'
Stimulation Plan for Economic Science (S.P.E.S.)

First published in the United States of America 1993 by
Scholarly and Reference Division,
ST. MARTIN'S PRESS, INC.,
175 Fifth Avenue,
New York, N. Y. 10010

ISBN 0–312–09151–6

Library of Congress Cataloging-in-Publication Data
The Role of Competition in Economic Transition/
edited by Christopher T. Saunders.
p. cm.
Based on the 14th Workshop on European Economic
Interaction and Integration, held in April, 1992 at Mariánské Lázně
(Marienbad), CSFR.
Includes bibliographical references and index.
ISBN 0–312–09151–6
1. Post-communism—Europe, Eastern—Congresses. 2. Post
—communism—Central Europe—Congresses. 3. Europe, Eastern–
–Economic policy—1989– —Congresses. 4. Central Europe—Economic
policy—Congresses. I. Saunders, Christopher Thomas. II. Workshop
on European Economic Interaction and Integration (14th : 1992: Mariánské
Lázně, CSFR)
HC244.R584 1993
338.947—dc20   92–38065
                                                          CIP

PREFACE

The Vienna Institute for Comparative Economic Studies (WIIW) was a pioneer in organising international Workshops on East-West economic relations. The present volume is based on the proceedings of the Fourteenth Workshop held since 1975. It was conducted, under the title "The Role of Competition in Economic Transition and Integration", from 27 to 30 April 1992 at Mariánské Lázne (Marienbad) in Czechoslovakia. The thirty participants came from eleven countries (Austria, Croatia, Czechoslovakia, France, Great Britain, Hungary, Italy, Japan, Poland, Russia and the USA). Representatives of UN/ECE and the EC Commission also attended.

In *Part One*, headed "Competition: Theories and Conditions", the theoretical framework of competition is dealt with. A sketch of the evolution of economists' concepts of competition is followed by an outline of the international setting and the relevant policies and institutions, especially in the EC. The two papers presented and the subsequent discussion disclose, in varying degrees, realistic – even sceptical – views of the economic benefits of unqualified competition. The simple virtues of perfect competition, taken for granted by classical economists, are superseded by a more pragmatic approach based on what happens in the real world, here described as a world of "adult" or "mature" or "workable" competition. It was, however, suggested that some advocates of economic reform in Central and Eastern Europe (CEE) seem to put excessive weight on the micro-economic approach, believing that mere enforcement of competition and privatisation, would constitute a panacea, a cure-all.

Part Two, headed "Eastern Approaches", spotlights some of the difficulties encountered by CEE countries, both in creating competition internally and in facing it externally in the process of transformation. Liberalisation of trade in 1989-1991, badly prepared in some of these countries and meeting increasing difficulties in the wake of economic decline, may even lead to a reversal of the liberalisation process.

According to experiences of most CEE countries, privatisation of state enterprises by itself has not led to a more responsive, more competitive behaviour of the firms. The prevailing view, however, was that various elements of competition should be implemented simultaneously: privatisation with breaking down monopoly positions; gradual trade liberalisation; strengthening of small- and medium-sized competitors; and legal and institutional requirements for controlling competition rules.

Part Three, "Views from the West", mainly devoted to competition policies within the European Communities, led to discussions focused on the following issues:

– The feasibility of European Monetary Union (EMU): There was agreement that not only the 12 EC countries but also most EFTA countries could adopt the conditions required by the end of the decade. The problems still extant were dealt with in some detail.

– Regional problems in a more integrated Europe: It was recognised that with continuing integration there will arise critical reactions to centralist tendencies. In particular, the importance of regions will tend to increase.

– The dynamics of change: A lively debate centred on the issue as to whether the dynamics of change within Europe might not force the Community off its current path. CEE countries who want to become members will first have to develop their new market economy structures. But access is primarily a political, not an economic issue; though in reality the economic gap creates hindrances on both sides.

Part Four: "A Role for International Action?" In his contribution the author of the last chapter points to New Zealand's experience in moving from a highly controlled to a liberalised and open economy.

ACKNOWLEDGEMENTS

The Vienna Institute for Comparative Economic Studies, organiser of the Workshop sessions under the guidance of the International Steering Committee, is greatly indebted to the *Commission of the European Communities,* which, under the Commission's SPES Programme (Stimulation Plan for Economic Science), had sponsored this Workshop and granted generous financial support. The papers and ensuing discussions were edited with accustomed skill by Professor C.T. *Saunders,* assisted by Eva *Strobl.* The text was efficiently typeset and prepared for printing by Renate *Szumilowski.* We are grateful, as always, for valuable cooperation to Mr. T.M. *Farmiloe* of the Macmillan Press Ltd.

Philipp Rieger
Chairman of the Workshop

TABLE OF CONTENTS

PART IV – A ROLE FOR INTERNATIONAL ACTION?

EDITOR'S INTRODUCTION

Christopher Saunders[*]

In a previous volume in this series[1], the whole range of transition problems in the former socialist countries was discussed by writers from both East and West Europe. The present volume concentrates largely on one aspect of the economy – *competition*, its role in western economic theory and practice and the process of introducing (or restoring) it in Eastern Europe[2]. The contributors discuss competition between the actors (economic agents in the jargon) within an economy and the ways and institutions by which governments endeavour, with varying success, to create or support competitive structures. But it is also clear that competitive policy is intended to improve international competitiveness and can, in particular, influence the future development of transactions between East and West and the place of Eastern Europe in the future world economy.

For most Eastern European contributors, competition in the market is closely linked with private (i.e. non-state) ownership of the means of production and thus with *privatisation* of state enterprises as part of the transition process. The most common experience is that good progress has been made in privatising small-scale business and in encouraging new entrepreneurs especially in the service sectors (accompanied, it must be said, by proliferation of unrecorded or "black" markets). Much less has so far been done to privatise the great state enterprises; most of them exercise more or less of a monopoly in their own fields, have become powerful centres of economic and political influence, and have the opportunity to hinder the establishment of a competitive environment. To some

---

[*] Science Policy Research Unit, University of Sussex, Brighton, UK.

[1] C.T. Saunders (ed.), *Economics and Politics of Transition*, Macmillan, 1992, based on papers written in 1990.

[2] Political geography: for brevity and familiarity I am using the term "Eastern Europe" to cover the whole group of countries belonging to the former CMEA normally including USSR plus Yugoslavia – now variously known as Central and Eastern Europe, Transition countries etc. References to USSR, Germany, Yugoslavia depend on the context and on the time referred to.

participants the ownership of resources is less important than the creation of competition: breaking-up state monopolies into largely autonomous business units (what the management experts describe as "profit centres"), publicly owned but competing with each other and with the private sector, might in some circumstances prove a practicable "middle way" (which, it is admitted, some writers dismiss as unhelpful).

It is, certainly, coming to be realised in both East and West that in the real world there is no such thing as a standard market economy. Western industrial countries could almost all be described as mixed economies, the balance between state authority and market forces varying greatly in both space and time. The extent to which the state should – or, indeed, can – take part in economic management is likely to remain controversial and it is reasonable to envisage a variety of experimental solutions. At present there is much discussion of what the former socialist countries reshaping their societies could learn from the West. Is it inconceivable that out of the transition process in the East new forms may emerge from which the West could derive useful lessons?

Some words of President Václav Havel (quoted by *Charrier* at the end of Chapter 9) seem apposite: "The market economy ... is not and cannot be for me ... an ideology ... I find it fairly ridiculous, and also rather dangerous, that for many people ... the market economy should become a cult object".

* * *

For the reader's convenience, notes follow taking some selected points from the rich material in the chapters and in comments thereon. The chapters were discussed at a workshop held in Mariánské Lázně, CSFR, in April 1992; revisions were made subsequently but in view of the rush of events the reader must remember that the book reflects the analyses and expectations of mid-1992.[3]

---

[3] The editor acknowledges summaries made at the workshop by *Inotai, Gács* and *Walterskirchen*.

Part I   Competition: theories and conditions

The simple virtues of perfect competition have been found a useful basis for theoretical constructs in much of classical economics, associated with *homo oeconomicus* as a motivisation system. Yet, in the view of *Bienaymé* (Ch. 1), the theory applies in the real world only where certain rather exceptional conditions apply, such as a wide dispersion of market power. He regards the modern capitalist economy as predominantly a world of "adult" or "workable" competition, as distinct from the "pure and perfect competition" of some intellectual discourse. Thus the large business corporations "encompass many more dimensions than rational economic calculus ... or the search for strict optimal solutions" in their strategic decisions. This implies the need for a pragmatic stance of public policy towards the place of competition in the dynamics of the economy. While competition must be safeguarded because of the opportunities for choice which it offers, it must also be recognised that the contemporary world economy requires a more variegated approach than any attempt to reproduce the business structures of a, perhaps mythical, past age of perfect competition and free markets. Analysis of economies of scale, where they exist, and the implications of technological advance, must come into play, as must the integration of political economy with other social disciplines.

Rouam (Ch. 2), from the Commission of the EC, moves from general concepts of competition to the institutional problems of the efforts to create and administer international (or supra-national) rules for protecting competition where business practices concern the interests of more than one country. (This theme is taken up again in *Mayes*, (Ch. 13)). The purpose is not only to reconcile national systems of regulation when problems of territorial jurisdictions arise, but also to promote a competitive environment in the countries concerned. The most important system is that established in the EC by the Treaty of Rome administered by the Commission and subject to the European Court of Justice. A considerable body of case law has by now been created, based on the examination and control of firms believed to hold "dominant positions" in the EC market (or a substantial part of it), extending to the review of state subsidies and other aids to firms which might be regarded as distorting competition. *Rouam* also describes other international actions for protecting competition, such as that contained in the Free

Trade Agreements between the EC and the EFTA countries. Similar rules may apply in the new arrangements for the European Economic Area (EC plus EFTA)[4]; the important point here is the procedure of the "one-stop shop" for the allocation of cases between the EC and the EFTA Surveillance authority, the decision of either authority (being based on common rules) applying to all member states concerned. It is recognised that in the formulation of common rules, those already established by the EC have carried the greater weight. Negotiations to introduce similar rules in agreements between the EC and Hungary, Poland and Czecho-slovakia raise doubts about the application of the principles when state mono-polies and various state aids to industry come into question.

In commenting on Chapters 1 and 2, *Williamson* asks for a clearer focus on how competition could be important for East Europe. He suggests that the key point should be the need for competition to operate, e.g. through incentives, in a "socially beneficial way". While urging privatisation for small-scale enterprise, he is dubious about privatising large enterprises, feeling that it may be preferable to deconcentrate them first. On the application of western-style rules to East Europe, *Mayes* points out that although the EC negotiations have been somewhat one-sided, yet international agreements would not necessarily rule out the formation of separate national systems of regulation.

Part II   Eastern approaches

These chapters deal with the experience and prospects of two countries, Czechoslovakia (three chapters on different aspects), and Hungary, both countries which have made significant advances in establishing a competitive climate; Russia, where the reform process has made limited and much disturbed progress; and Croatia, where, as in the rest of the now tragically divided Yugoslavia, radical changes in the economic system originated more than thirty years ago.

The results of the first years of transition must be assessed in the light of the associated violent inflation and the collapse of production, employment, trade and, in some cases, living standards throughout the area. Policy-makers have

---

[4]   The agreements on the EEA should be ratified and in force in 1993.

had to combine urgent measures to stabilise disequilibrated economies with longer-term objectives of reorganisation and reconstruction.

Czechoslovakia: Bělehrádek (Ch. 3), chairman of the Czech Competition Office, regards the creation of a new competitive environment as resting on the pillars of freedom of (most) prices, internal convertibility, extensive freedom of imports and privatisation. Privatisation began in 1991 with small-scale business; most retailing and some other services should be in private ownership at end-1992. The author gives useful data on the composition of the private sector by legal form and by branch. Privatisation of large-scale industry presented, as elsewhere, much more difficulty. In total, the private sector is estimated to contribute only about 3 per cent of industrial output (about 8 per cent of GNP as a whole). A campaign to privatise large-scale industry is planned but the author recognises the serious obstacles to reducing the market power of the great state enterprises (observing that "the respective ministries are not very helpful"). The other aspect of the government's competition policy is, indeed, that of restraining misuse of dominant market positions (cartels, mergers, unfair business practices, tied sales etc.) especially by the big enterprises. *Flassik* (Ch. 5), chairman of the Federal Competition Office of the CSFR, summarises some of the 45 cases decided by his Office in its first year. Like *Bělehrádek*, he notes the resistance shown by some managements accustomed to the former acceptance by officials of monopolistic practices. He also regrets that many small businesses dis-advantaged by the unfair practices of the large enterprises on which they depend have failed to support use of the laws to indict such practices. However it seems that efforts to promote competition are now beginning to secure acceptance. Special problems arise in applying legal powers to joint venture arrangements with foreign firms which sometimes expect to receive special privileges beyond those justified by the general need to encourage foreign investors. *Hrnčíř* (Ch. 4) takes a broad view of Czechoslovak experience and objectives. New policies and legal structures have seen general stabilisation, and new legislation has provided for privatisation. What has been lacking is an adequate response by economic agents to the new possibilities. In spite of a stream of active policies on the macro-economic level, managements have tended to exhibit a certain inertia, and a continuing reliance for help on the state, derived from inherited patterns of behaviour. Over-optimistic expectations that liberalisation and privatisation would quickly release the springs of enterprise and competition have hardly been fulfilled. *Hrnčíř* also discusses the impact on incentives of the new competition from imports, on which the reformers had placed much hope. The results have been weak, partly because of the poor marketing and distribution system, but also because low labour costs and lack of finance for innovation have led to continuing reliance on down-market exports. He feels that if the problems of modernisation are to be regarded as only temporary there is a case for short-term protection and support to "revitalise" the economy.

Hungary, as *Pogácsás* and *Stadler* (Ch. 6), from the Hungarian Competition Office, report, had the advantage of an early start in 1968 with its New Economic Mechanism. By 1991 the shortage economy was over (surpluses arising in most sectors), a competitive environment was slowly emerging, and liberalisation of prices and foreign trade was nearly complete. But these favourable features were accompanied in the early 1990s by the collapse of demand affecting CMEA trade, as well as by weaker markets in the West. Growth of competition was promoted by establishment of the Competition Office (significantly transformed from the long-established Price Control Office) with rather wide powers to investigate and restrain abuses of dominant market positions. The authors emphasise that the policy is administered pragmatically (as in CSFR): in some cases, restrictions on competition imposed by enterprises may be justified by promotion of technology or by reinforcing export capacity. Policy is also concerned with the implications for competition of the privatisation (organised by the State Property Agency) of state enterprises; new company laws have provided for various legal forms of which the joint-stock company is the most frequently adopted. The breaking up of state enterprises into smaller units, while retaining state ownership, has been encouraged; yet the degree of concentration, according to the authors, has changed very little. The "big old companies" still dominate much of the economy. At the same time entrepreneurial activity has boomed, the number of economic units rising from 13,500 in 1988 to 47,000 in 1991. It is observed, too, that foreign investors account for over half of the state proceeds from privatisation (and, incidentally, that these investors look whenever possible for state firms which have established dominant and stable market shares).

Russia: After three generations of the Soviet economy and society, its radical transformation presents quite unique problems, probably unprecedented in

6

history. The previous economy as described by *Yevstigneyev* (Ch. 7), of the Moscow Institute of International Economics and Politics, was a complex of monopolistic structures, vertical and horizontal, from the centre down to the individual enterprise – with management at each level operating through an elaborate bargaining process. In one of three product groups, the biggest enterprise accounted for 90 per cent of total output. Now, the concept of competition "has at least returned to our economic science". Government action to promote competition include laws for the formation of different legal forms to replace state monopolies and also provide for the issue of vouchers for shares in privatised business (a mechanism of privatisation in which the author has little confidence). Yet 70 per cent of employment is still in the public sector (data for 1991 and for the former USSR). As elsewhere, privatisation has been mainly in small business (useful statistics are given). Many big enterprises resist commercialisation or deconcentration, preferring to rely, as in the past, on state aids. The transition is further complicated by the need to adapt nation-wide enterprises to the political break-up. The author feels that far more privatisation is essential to create a competitive economy and that the "idea of a third way ... and all other attempts to combine plan and market lead to deadlock". The shifts in applying the economic strategy of *perestroika*, against a disturbed political background, do not encourage confidence in an early resolution of the deadlock.

Croatia: *Lang* and *Vojnić* (Ch. 8), writing from Zagreb, concentrate on the development of the newly formed Croatia, but include interesting comparisons with the other republics (as they then were) of Yugoslavia. Their historical analysis stresses in particular the consistently low productive returns from the heavy capital investments in the relatively rich regions of Croatia and Slovenia as well as in the rest of the Federation. This low factor productivity is reflected, in their Cobb-Douglas type exercise, in a very low residual factor which they take to indicate deficient technical progress. Preparations, and some progress, have been made for restructuring, before and despite the fighting and movements of peoples. Thus opportunities have been opened for further privatisation; because of the different system of social ownership from that in other East European countries, and because of more elements of market economy and private enterprise, the starting-point for privatisation also differs. At the time of writing, of course, the overwhelming preoccupation must be the restoration of a degree of normal life

7

in the face of material devastation and the flood of refugees added to the break-down of the Federal constitution and the disruption of commercial relations with the rest of Yugoslavia and the outside world. Despite the 40 per cent drop in output during the civil war, and all the obviously unfavourable conditions for looking ahead, the authors venture tentative statistical projections for Croatia, envisaging a recovery to pre-war levels of production, but not before 1996. The projection, they stress, depends on substantial international support, both in investment and in opening markets. They hope that continuing movement towards the market economy will accompany and, indeed, promote the recovery.

In comments on the chapters dealing with East Europe, *Inotai* remarks that Hungary and Czechoslovakia, and also Poland, have been able to increase their market shares in exports to the west, particularly to Germany, to some extent offsetting the fall in CMEA trade. *Gács* fears that rushed liberalisations may lead to a subsequent reversal of direction. *Mayes* stresses the importance of an effective system of investigation and rules to establish respect for competition agencies. He also pointed to the experience of New Zealand in moving from a highly controlled to a liberalised and open economy in the 1980s (see also references to New Zealand in Ch. 13).

The reader may notice that the discussions of privatisation barely mention the effects on the extensive networks of social activities (housing, medical services, catering and food supplies) which have long been run by the larger state enterprises and which could be regarded as supplements to cash wages and salaries. Will these services continue to be provided by competing private enterprises, or will the costs fall on the state, or be added to cash wages – or will the services disappear?

With Czechoslovakia and Hungary, Poland (although not the subject of a special study in this volume[5]) is the former communist country making significant progress towards the market economy. The urgent need to cope with inflation, shortages, general disequilibrium and a massive debt delayed the ambitious programme of rapid attack on all fronts – the "big bang", characteristic of the

---

[5]   The previous volume in this series included three studies on Polish reforms written in 1990. (C.T. Saunders (ed.), op cit.). For more recent information, the editor is grateful to Dr. George Blazyca (University of Paisley, Scotland).

Polish reform policy. The economy was largely stabilised; most shortages of consumer goods disappeared at the cost of much higher prices only partly offset by pay rises.

A programme of privatisation was begun in 1989, the intention being to privatise half of the State's assets within three years. As elsewhere, small-scale privatisation proceeded quite fast; few of the big state enterprises were tackled, although some were "commercialised" in the form of joint-stock companies, the state holding the shares. By 1992, it is estimated, only about 15 per cent of all state enterprises had been privatised (about 10 per cent of state employment). Later legislation is intended to accelerate the process: investment funds, holding shares in a mix of 4-600 leading state firms, are planned; "coupons" giving title to shares in these funds will be issued to the public at a minimal price.

Part III   Views from the west

These chapters recount the experience of four western countries – Austria, France, Italy and Japan – all of which have long but differing histories of extensive government intervention in what are dominantly competitive market economies but with substantial public sectors.

France: In the view of *Charrier* (Ch. 9), of the French Conseil de la Concurrence, French competition policy has stressed not only law and institutions but also the behaviour of economic agents. The function of law should be to punish abuses rather than to monitor strict criteria (such as specific market shares). Thus competition is regarded pragmatically as "only one way of achieving economic efficiency"; the author points to Italy where high levels of economic efficiency have been reached without, until 1990, a legally enforced competition law. He raises the issue of possible conflict between promotion of competition and the vigorous industrial policy which, with indicative planning, characterised French economic strategy for at least two or three decades after WW II. *Charrier* records however the substantial recent operations of the Competition Council and gives examples of the 6-800 cases a year with which it has dealt. In early post-war years, price control was a main instrument of policy. The author feels that governments, as in France, should retain enabling powers to adopt price controls, even if only in specific cases of abuse. On industrial policy he looks to a shift towards a

Community programme with a wider scope than the present EC programmes for technical cooperation (such as Esprit in the field of information technology).

Japan: In reporting Japan's experience (in 1945-1970), *Inagawa* (Ch. 10) ventures a certain, if highly qualified, analogy between the present transition in East Europe and the emergence of Japan after 1945 from a highly controlled war economy into drastic restructuring and rapid growth. During, as before, WW II the Japanese economy was dominated by the small number of great family conglomerates – the Zaibatsu – working closely with government. Among the first acts of the American occupation authorities after the war was the order to break up these power centres. In that sense, a new element of competition was introduced; but, as the author points out, the structure continued to be subject to strong government controls combined with an elaborate corporative organisation of enterprises, designed to maintain an organic system of consensual decision-making. The main government instrument was a vigorous industrial policy, based on selective promotion ("fostering") of chosen industries by investment, technical aid and protection. The object, as now in East Europe, was to catch up with the west. The corporative structure encouraged cooperation between firms e.g. by a no doubt cautious exchange of information, but not to the extent of subduing the competitive urge of managements. The result is described by *Inagawa* as "fierce competition between private firms in a protected domestic market". Anti-trust action was pursued but as one aspect of industrial policy rather than as an end in itself. The chapter ends in 1970, after which both fast growth and the active intervention of government began to fade away. The author suggests, however, that Japan can offer to East Europe generous funds, technical transfers and help in building up, e.g. by joint ventures, the infrastructure of distribution, communications and banking, and also management training.

Austria: Traditionally, as *Kramer* (Ch. 11) recalls, Austria has been regarded as a land of cartels: competition policy has meant "protecting from competition rather than protecting competition". Such judgements now need some modification in the light of the liberalisation and opening of the economy. The resulting substantial gains in competitiveness have been marked in manufacturing industries. But some other sectors have continued to be well sheltered by subsidy or protection – for example, agriculture and some of the many state monopolies. Cartel legislation is described by the author as "permissive", influenced by the "inclination of the

10

bureaucracy to act in the interest of domestic producers"; strong vested interests have had political as well as economic influence. Consequently, *Kramer* suggests, a pronounced dual economy has been formed; despite increasingly competitive industry, sheltered sectors remain and are largely responsible for the high level of domestic costs and prices.

Italy: Like Austria, Italy inherited from the earlier period of industrialisation a powerful state sector with, in the view of *Boffito* and *Martinelli* (Ch. 12), a strong influence on the rapid growth and industrial modernisation of the post-war years. In the increasingly difficult 1970s, the load on the state-owned conglomerates (pressures from workers, the private sector and the government) became excessive; it led to efforts to rationalise and to some, not fully successful, attempts to privatise. In considering the relevance of Italian experience to the problems of transition, the authors take the view that the public sector should continue to play a positive role in production – subject to breaking up of monopoly positions, to managerial autonomy, and to a balance between profits "and the social goal of defending employment, with priority for profitability in the long-run"; and the state-owned firm should be considered a temporary solution for the transition period.

Commenting on *Inagawa*, *Inotai* agrees that some interesting similarities exist between Japan and East European economies which are also latecomers to the industrial world. But he is sceptical of much of her treatment of Japan as a model. In particular he does not agree that Japan's specialisation in high-technology and capital-intensive industries would be appropriate for East Europe, where a general modernisation of all industry is more needed. But the major difference is that Japan has had access to a huge flow of funds for restructuring – and East Europe has not. Nor, in present circumstances is it likely to be practicable for East European countries, even if they wished, to emulate Japan's early policy of import-substitution as an instrument of development.

Part IV A role for international action?

Finally, *Mayes* (Ch. 13), coordinator of a UK-based research initiative on the Single European Market, concentrates on the future of the European institutions. The legal and institutional changes already in progress, or in preparation, have implications for prospective new members of the Community. Such changes – the Single European Act, the Maastricht Treaty on European Union (when fully ratified), the European Economic Area Agreement – have been framed without much consideration of their consequences for Eastern Europe (for more about these developments see *Rouam*, in Ch. 2 of this volume). Indeed *Mayes* expects that developments in Eastern Europe will "lead to a substantial rethink on the part of the Community". He discusses in some detail the various actions, institutions and proposals for the future of the EC itself and its possible extension; he gives special attention to the arrangements for monetary union involving the project for a European Central Bank independent of national governments and, ultimately, for a single currency. This also involves the highly controversial requirement of "convergence" of the member economies. Adhesion to the EC of the EFTA countries may not present great difficulties, but extension to some or all of East Europe – leading to a Community of twenty or more member states – is likely to demand substantial changes in institutions and performance. *Mayes* refers to the strong feeling that such a Community will have to take the form of a "variable geometry" Europe with member countries committed to varying areas of common action.

Commenting on this chapter, *Walterskirchen* notes (a) agreement that adhesion of EFTA countries is likely to set the limit to widening the EC within its present structure or that now planned; (b) that political resistance to centralisation of power in the EC may well lead (on the now accepted, if not yet defined, principle of subsidiarity) to greater powers for regional authorities within national states.

PART I – COMPETITION: THEORIES AND CONDITIONS

Chapter 1

COMPETITION IN THEORY AND IN THE EVOLVING REAL WORLD

Alain Bienaymé[*)]

We shall take it for granted that the growth rate of GDP per head affords, in the long run, the best yardstick we can think of for measuring economic progress. It measures the outcome of steady increases in labour productivity. It expresses in figures the growing purchasing power of national income which we will in turn assume to be positively and closely linked with consumer welfare. Now, what kind of relationships exist between economic progress and competition in a supra-national setting?

Strangely enough, market competition was recognised as playing a specific role as a major factor in economic evolution rather late in this century. This is for two reasons. One was stressed by Schumpeter (1954, p. 545). Referring to the classics from Adam Smith to John Stuart Mill, he wrote: "Competition was an institutional assumption rather than the result of certain market conditions. And

---

[*)]   Professor; University of Paris-Dauphine.

so firmly were they convinced that the competition case was the obvious thing, familiar to all, that they did not bother to analyse its logical content. In fact the concept usually was not even defined." The other reason is that when competition began to be explored in its ins and outs, the mainstream economists concentrated analysis on price determination in the short run, much more than economic evolution in the long run. This resulted from the big impulse given by the neo-classical school: in its most abstract side, which emphasised the law of great numbers and "mass effects of the action of all households and all firms in markets" and on prices (ibid., p. 972); and in its more pragmatic side which points, with Alfred Marshall and J. Chamberlin, to adulterations and deviations fostered by the monopolistic propensities shown by actual business behaviour. Chamberlin first coined the phrase "pure competition" in order to define the concept opposed to his own concept of monopolistic competition. But the role of competition in the process of economic evolution could not be thoroughly discussed until economists began to show their concern for stagnation, growth and development, which was not until the late 1930s.

Today, market competition is generally considered by most economists and governments in industrialised countries (if not by businesses doomed to be taken over or to disappear) as the most efficient set of market conditions when com-pared with any alternative structures: private monopolies, centrally planned self-sufficient economies, barter economies. But the presumption has to be defined and analysed and may be falsified in some cases.

1.1 The conditions of perfect competition

One cannot fully understand how competition actually works as an agent of economic progress if one fails first to clarify the meaning of pure and perfect competition (PPC), both its essence and its limitations on the one hand, and its prerequisite of property rights on the other.

PPC is a set of axioms defining how market prices are determined in conditions which exclude any influences other than natural scarcity of goods deriving from the intensity of demand relative to the difficulty of supply. It defines a type of society where any disturbance originating from a discretionary centre of power (big businesses, public administration, monopsonies) is banished – just as Olympic records require good weather conditions. The important good weather

conditions for PPC are the following:
- Monoproduct suppliers working under fast increasing unit costs.
- A uniform rationality model in which every individual aims at maximising the satisfaction to be derived from a limited budget.
- An economy where power is dispersed among an infinity of suppliers and demanders.
- Free information flows about market conditions and about the best production techniques available and, in the most extreme case, certainty (transparency).
- Freedom of contract and multilateral trade supported by commercial law.
- Freedom of entry and exit (fluidity).
- An optimal market structure, minimising costs and prices, defined by the triplet: number of firms (n), their sizes (s), and the size of market (M), where n is close to infinite, s is small compared to M and highly concentrated close to the average size $\bar{s}$ (small standard deviation of s).

Economic suppliers behave like clones. They adapt their quantities supplied to the market price (anonymously fixed by mass effect) in order not be outsold. Market fluidity and multilateralism prevent them from squeezing any profit from clients. The prices are thus stuck to the minimum long-term average costs in the long run, and those average costs are supposed to be minimised in a given state of the arts. The assumption of certainty implies that the equilibrium price comprises only factor prices multiplied by the quantity of factors used. Consumer welfare is thus maximised: the consumer gets the most from his budget. And in a pure exchange economy (Boulding 1941, Bienaymé 1992), exchange results from the free agreement of the two partners on mutually advantageous terms of trade.

A major condition for this freedom of agreement is a clear-cut definition of property rights. As Telser (1982) puts it, competition is related to a situation in which individuals are able and willing to exchange property rights. Property rights in an economically efficient society concern consumer goods, capital goods, labour force and working time, cash in hand, deposits, equity in businesses, natural resources, royalties, patents and trade marks. The law protects property holders in such a way that every individual has an incentive to build up property rights.

15

In the simplest PPC market structure, all transactions in property rights are made at the same time and place, in what one might call an open-air economy where everybody knows how to find the best opportunities and where supply and demand are equated – ignoring those uncompetitive suppliers and those customers too short of money who are eliminated on the right side of the market-equilibrium position. The main message of PPC is that economic games through freedom of exchange are positive-sum games and give the highest conceivable rewards *hic et nunc*.

1.2 Workable competition in adult capitalism

In fact, transactions are rarely made at one and the same time and place with all the economic agents perfectly well-informed on the best opportunities. And in order to understand the sequence of transactions and transitions which allows us to speak of economic changes and progress, we have to realise that economic activity is a time-consuming process. Thus beyond the peculiar market structure postulated by PPC, industrial economists point out important facts which explain more directly the dynamism of capitalist economies. If indeed we consider competition as an observable phenomenon rather than an axiom of pure economics, we must admit that transactions happen every day under irregularly but constantly changing conditions in supply, demand and, upstream, in production, technology, tastes and incomes. These changes are time-consuming in that they involve three main features of time: irreversibility through accumulation, novelty, uncertainty. They open wide possibilities for different patterns of behaviour. The volatility of the economic environment, the asymmetry of information, the extent of risk aversion or venture affinity and spirit of entrepreneurship, all work together towards shaping idiosyncratic behaviour patterns. For example, the business strategies of Volkswagen, Renault, Fiat and Toyota may differ widely on such issues as marketing policies, new car modelling, product diversification of foreign investment, although they are confronted by rather similar issues in the automobile industry.

One major condition of what may be called "workable competition" which is considered worth safeguarding nowadays is the following. Economic growth is the outcome of a kind of rivalry between independent suppliers who are mutually ignorant of each others' detailed actions and reactions. Competition is a risky but rewarding job for the survivors. Between the absolute transparency postulated in PPC, which would actually send to sleep the suppliers and demanders on the one hand, and an extreme turmoil like war where nobody dares to take any initiative whatsoever, there is a broad area of workable uncertainty which is favourable to innovation, to the search for information and to the design of new tactics and strategies. The courts and councils in charge of enforcing antitrust regulation are always checking whether this condition is met.

If markets work differently from one industry to another, this is due not only to patterns of business behaviour under uncertainty; but it is also an outcome of modern technology. PPC works under a very peculiar hypothesis according to which the average production cost is minimised only with a large number of suppliers, each of them knowing very well what is the best production technique. But if technology determines cost functions under which the average cost decreases when the number of suppliers falls, an oligopoly, or even a monopoly in a small country, may be a more efficient market structure than PPC. And the substitute for the small country is obviously a wider free-trade area. This techno-logical argument can be split into its static component (economies of scale) and its dynamic component (experience curves (Boston Consulting Group 1971)). It may be completed by the fact that most sophisticated manufactured goods are complex systems, the production of which require a shrewd combination of several different technologies: economies of scope and complementarity can be reaped if the company masters these technologies and their proper coordination.

This raises the issue of multiproduction and the famous "make or buy" choice on which every producer has to decide. On the other hand, the theory of scope economies and the integration theories elaborated by Chandler (1990), Coase (1937) and Williamson (1975), express the idea that production and transaction costs may decrease when the business corporation diversifies its product mix and expands upstream and downstream. This area of expansion is not infinite: costs of bureaucratic coordination increase with scope and with the number of techno-logies combined within the manufactured goods and sophisticated systems (satellites, surgical units, armaments, and even automobiles etc.).

These technologies:

(a) may not be fully mastered by the main producer,

(b) do not automatically reach a minimum average cost at the same scale of operation.

Thus the industrial organisation of a country is partly shaped by the technological constraints which underlie widespread practices – such as subcontracting, franchising, agreements, R and D cooperation contracts – which blurr the boundaries of the firm (Bienaymé, 1988).

Finally, competition is consistent with a monopoly situation if several conditions are met:

–   The existence of sufficiently close substitutes for the monopoly goods.

–   The existence of active customers ready to protest or to change their buying habits.

–   The "contestability" of the market, which means freedom of entry and exit: i.e. relatively low costs of entry and exit so that the market remains open to hit and run strategies (Baumol et al., 1982). Both the long-run international trade policy under the GATT and the creation and successive extensions of the European Community, have greatly helped to increase the contestability and openness of the markets within industrialised countries.

1.3 Pure and workable competition compared

Thus from uncertainty and technical progress there arises a kind of workable competition which does not crunch prices at every instant so much as help to foster long-term productivity growth: This in turn contributes through foreign competition to keep down relative prices of the most internationally traded goods. But the game is played by rivals which, unlike the individual anonymous suppliers playing on the PPC stage, are a few stars wearing the name of big, and sometimes gigantic organisations.

Competition in a pure market economy, where the market is the only organisation to play a role under the State antitrust authority, is not the same game as competition in mature or "adult" capitalism where sizeable organisations effect market coordination in a wholly different way (Bienaymé, 1992), at least in three respects:

(a) In PPC the uncompetitive individual has no way out other than to disappear from the market supply side – and eventually come back with more efficient techniques; in mature capitalism, each business struggles for its own survival, to keep its strategic autonomy by finding an expansion path which reconciles its financial autonomy (through cash flow and equity) with the maintenance of satisfying market shares. The goal of the player is not so much to survive by minimising prices as to survive by maximising quality for price under financial constraints. This second kind of competition is much more ambiguous than the binary "stay or disappear" kind of competition under PPC. Nelson and Winter (1982) have demonstrated that workable competition allows for the survival of apparently inefficient suppliers if the following conditions are met:

(i)   The efficient leaders have neither the incentive nor the funds to increase their output capacity to out-sell the least efficient rivals.

(ii)   The potential outsiders are unwilling or unable to find the techniques which could out-perform the less efficient survivors.

(b)   PPC organises a head-on competition between suppliers confronting each other on the product market. In adult capitalism, competition involves the whole organisation as such: this means that each business has to compete not only for a market share, but also in the choice of product portfolio and market segmentation; it must compete not only downstream in selling goods, but also upstream in buying strategic materials, in hiring skilled and talented engineers or salesmen, and in borrowing costly funds. It must also compete on the labour market, in order to remain attractive. Finally, it must build an image and a reputation, and keep good relations with public administration, local authorities, trade unions, public opinion, ecological pressure groups, various lobbies etc. Thus the business corporation is rather a different kind of animal from the individual supplier in PPC. From this we can infer that a market for, say, dairy products or electronics may appear to be crowded with 3, 4 or even 10 big independent rivals, between them holding 80 per cent of the whole market; they may, nevertheless, live quite a quiet life, each having chosen a niche in which to enjoy a high degree of market power. Such a situation needs to be monitored by the anti-trust authorities if active competition policy is regarded as an effective substitute for State *dirigisme* or price control.

(c)   The third big difference between PPC or pure market transactions à la Boulding on the one side, and adult capitalism on the other, is a complete split of the decision process into two categories. In PPC there are open market-wide operations where prices, quantities etc. are more or less openly determined. In adult capitalism the decision process takes place within the cocoon: who decides what? who makes what? what are the decision rules and procedures? This latter kind of underground economy, nurtured by organisation systems, supports the specialisation of roles in hierarchical and informal arrangements. But since the ultimate aim of every organisation is to survive in the long run, the biggest difference is that a supplier in a pure market economy can take instant decisions; but in a business corporation, dependent on many investors, both operating decisions and strategic decisions inspired by long-term aims, must generally be subject to administrative procedures. Thus criticism of "market myopia" by supporters of state intervention derives from a misinterpretation: in most important industries the business corporations in fact pursue long-term goals with horizons beyond those of the average elected politician in a democratic country. Perseverance is a major quality of successful business leadership.

Thus on some occasions apparent violations of free competition rules may be mitigated by long-term considerations and by the fierceness of global competition. Strategic decisions, whether articulated with some sophistication by business planning teams or simply crafted through day-to-day action (Mintzberg 1989), take on a particular complexity. They encompass many more dimensions than rational economic calculus and they involve something other than the search for strict optimal solutions. They bear often on fuzzy problems which need first to be clarified and then gradually structured. They involve many different goals which have to be reconciled in order to keep the cohesion of the staff. So conflicting views may be expressed about some marketing practices which clearly violate the free market and the rules of fair competition but which could be understood, if not accepted, if placed in their appropriate strategic perspective.

1.4 Market power and the Treaty of Rome

Workable competition is thus a deep-seated factor in explaining economic change in that it takes into account uncertainty, technology and organisations and exhibits their consequences on the operations, structures and equilibrium of the market.

The market power of strong businesses requires therefore that public authorities should play a vigorous role through enforcement of antitrust regulations. If we limit ourselves to the supranational legal framework, we can summarise the basic principles of antitrust regulation as follows. They derive from the Common Market spirit which inspired the first stage of European Union and still remain valid. European authorities see to it that trade practices do not create distortions in intra-community exchanges.

The main thrust of the Treaty of Rome is the promotion and safeguarding of competition. Business corporations work with their own capital assets, know-how and brands, but they should not behave as if they also had proprietary rights over their clients and markets. A free market economy is an economic system in which the market and the buyers remain free to select the best suppliers, the best companies in which to invest, and the best managers to appoint – even including the undertaking of hostile takeover bids. Free and fair competition is protected by the Treaty of Rome and defined by Articles 85, 86 and 90 ff. Article 85 forbids business agreements affecting trade between member states presumed to impede efficient competition: price restrictions, market-sharing agreements, restrictions on supply and artificial obstacles to competitive tendering for public contracts are all prohibited. Article 85 (3) however allows that in certain limited circumstances the partners to such agreements may be able to show positive advantages. They must clarify the expected outcome and must prove in respect of specific elements of their agreement:
–   that the agreement is an essential condition of the expected benefits;
–   that the agreement leaves open other areas for competition between the partners:
–   that the benefits will be fairly shared between the partners and with their customers;
–   and that the agreement is subject to a time limit.

Article 86 forbids abuse of market dominance; this implies that market dominance must first be established in order to show that the business concerned has taken undue advantage of its position.

Articles 85 and 86 are enforced a posteriori, i.e. after specific activities have been brought under attack and complaints filed. But the EC Commission may also take preventive action: under a 1989 regulation, prospective partners to a merger must apply for authorisation if their combined sales exceed ECU 5 billion

21

and if at least two of the partners have sales each exceeding ECU 250 million.

In Articles 90 ff., subsidies and other state aids are to be terminated as incompatible with the common market if they are regarded as distorting competition and diverting trade flows in a substantial area of the EC.

Moreover the EC as such is an active member of the GATT. Although allowing for the possibility of subsidising a few key industries in order to maintain a level playing ground in competition with the US, Japan, or LDCs, the EC and EFTA members agree that free trade provides the most efficient rules of the game. Between the EC and the US, however, there is controversy about industrial subsidies. The US officially rejects any subsidy whatsoever, public or private, which allows dumping prices and cross-subsidises some goods at the expense of customers for others. The US takes that position on the basis of PPC as the ideal, first-best solution. The EC replies that world trade is in practice impeded by all sorts of market imperfections (monopoly power, State subsidies, bilateral agreements, information asymmetries ...) and that public subsidies may be legitimate in limited and specific circumstances when the terms of trade are too obviously unequal. One might add that if cross-subsidising was absolutely forbidden, the majority of big industrial companies would have to refrain from a deeply entrenched habit, justified for example by the product portfolio-matrix theory of the Boston Consulting Group (1971). But on the whole, the US argument still stands, for two reasons.

(a) The European arguments state correctly that public intervention through "industrial policy" may be explained as an endeavour to escape from third-best solutions (for example, autarky, isolation) to a second-best solution (for example, subsidising export industry). But these solutions remain different in principle from the first-best solution: that is, a Pareto-efficient solution, which requires free trade in order to reach the *optimum optimorum*. Economic palliatives should not be confused with a Pareto solution.

(b) The other reason why Europe should be cautious in considering subsidies to "key" industries on purely economic grounds is that the selection of key industries relies on a fuzzy notion of what is a key industry. It remains entirely at a government's discretion to choose the key industries to be subsidised. Considerations of security may offer plenty of justifications for protecting agriculture and food, energy, computers and chips, biotechnology and so on. This may

develop into a costly over-bidding between States competing with each other to defend their old ailing industries as well as to improve their chances in the race towards future national comparative advantages. The notion of a key industry is boundless and dangerously encourages States in an everlasting, sisyphean task wasting public funds and tax payers' money. Some economists seem nevertheless to argue strongly in favour of subsidising new high-tech industries open to substantial economies of scale. The case of the Brazilian aircraft industry seems to make sense: the State helps the industry to conquer quickly a substantial global market-share by supporting part of the R and D costs. But this so-called strategic and nationalistic industrial policy may be subject to three flaws:
– the government may be inaccurately informed about competitors' costs;
– the risks of reprisals;
– the risk of creating overcapacity and of overestimating the size of the world market.

At least in a peaceful world, free trade and free competition apparently remain an efficient solution. For developing countries struggling to upgrade their own industries, economic cooperation and dialogue through international machinery such as GATT or EC-ACP cooperative agreements, is the good solution.

1.5 The limits of competition-promoting policies

So free competition has to be safeguarded by public national and supra-national regulations. But these regulations should remain open to revision or, at least, flexible in implementation. Because technology is changing fast in several industries, precise regulations rapidly become obsolete. So-called natural monopolies which were technologically justified twenty years ago are losing their justification today and should be open to competition. There is no need for each country to own its own public monopoly of air transport. Nor is there a need for a State to hold total control over a public monopoly such as a TV and radio broadcasting network. Nor is there any absolute necessity to entrust public authorities with water distribution, highway construction or refuse collection and processing. Technological progress and organisational innovations very often reduce the minimum efficient size of operations and make it economically advantageous to privatise production units and submit them to free competition.

These advantages of private competition spring from the fact that private companies under competition are motivated by experience and by quality in price/maximisation and innovation. Furthermore private accountancy rules add some rigour to management.

If the State wants to keep informed, a light regulation insisting on a minimal set of rules may be devised to safeguard collective interests.

Last but not least, free competition in the real world raises different issues from free competition in an ideal and peaceful world. Economists then enter into competition with sociologists, historians and political scientists and are exposed to the criticism of public opinion. On what grounds?

If we may assume general agreement that economic and technical progress is a valuable goal, does it mean that competition in a borderless world will be necessary and sufficient to promote economic welfare everywhere, and equally enough, and to foster global understanding?

Free competition and open trade appear to have brought economic welfare to a substantial part of the West and also seem (according to the World Bank's 1991 report) to have enhanced productivity growth in most of those South-East Asian and other countries which have macro-economic free trade policies (e.g. Mexico, Colombia, Chile). Yet objections are made on historical grounds.

First, gradualism may be considered a better solution. After all, the Zollverein took 70 years to open the German market (1818-1888) and the common market appears now as the first step on a long path of liberalisation.

Second, competition does not exclude alliances in a cooperative multinational setting. The spirit of freedom today consists, for each country, in belonging to several clubs in order not to be enslaved to any one in particular.

Third, competition enhances good and economically efficient activities. But at the same time there is social concern for those national industries which are eliminated. In France, for example, the motorbike, piano-factoring and natural salt industries have almost totally disappeared "thanks to" free competition; with them, much experience and craftsmanship has been lost. The increasing numbers of white-collar employees stuck to their computer-screens will not replace them. At least we must recognise, in the Schumpeterian tradition, the multiple destructive effects of economic evolution through innovation. This raises a burning issue, especially in cultural and communication activities.

Fourth, in some cases which deserve to be studied more deeply, voice and protest may bring more efficient solutions than exit and consumer votes (as Hirschman (1970) showed more than twenty years ago).

Fifth and finally, if Adam Smith thought that competition was the best way to curb the rapaciousness of human beings and to stimulate wealth-creating activities, modern technology, monopoly power and modern cultural trends raise a number of new ethical problems which cannot be solved only, or even mainly, by free competition (Pope John Paul II, 1991). This illustrates some of the limitations of pure economic instruments, and the need to increase mutual interaction between political economy and other social disciplines.

References

Baumol, W., Panzar, Willig (1982), *Contestable Markets and theory of industry structures*, New York, Harcourt Brace Jovanovic Inc.

Bienaymé, A. (1973), *La croissance des entreprises*, Tome 2, Paris, Bordas.

‒ (1988), "Technology and the nature of the firm", *Revue d'Economie Politique*, December.

‒ (1992), *Le capitalisme adulte*, in print, Paris, P.U.F.

Boston Consulting Group (1971), *Perspective on Experience*, Boston, USA.

Boulding, K. (1941), *Economic Analysis*, Fourth edition 1966, London, Harper and Row.

Chamberlin, J. (1933), *The Theory of Monopolistic Competition*, Cambridge (Mass), Harvard University Press.

Chandler, A. (1990), *Scale and Scope*, Harvard University Press.

Coase, R. (1937), "The nature of the firm", *Economica No. 4*.

Gelinier, O. (1991), *L'éthique des affaires, halte à la dérive*, Paris, Seuil.

Hirschman, A.O. (1970), *Exit, Voice and Loyalty: Response to Decline in Firms, Organisations and States*, Harvard University Press.

John Paul II (1991), Encyclical, *Centesimus Annus*.

Marshall, A. (1890), *Principles of Economics*, London.

Mintzberg, H. (1989), *On Management: Inside the Strange World of Organisations*, New York, Free Press.

Nelson, R. and Winter (1982), *An Evolutionist Theory of Economic Change*, Harvard University Press.

Schumpeter, J.A. (1954), *History of Economic Analysis*, Oxford University Press, third printing 1959.

Smith, A. (1759), *Theory of Moral Sentiments*, Oxford University Press, Edit. 1976-1981.

− (1776), *An Inquiry into the Nature and Causes of the Wealth of Nations*, Oxford University Press, Edit. 1976-1981.

Telser, L.G. (1982), "Competition", in *Encyclopedia of Economics,* Greenwald, D. (ed.), New York, McGraw-Hill.

Williamson, O. (1975), *Markets and Hierarchies: Analysis and Antitrust Implication*", New York, Free Press.

Chapter 2

COMPETITION IN A SUPRA-NATIONAL SETTING

Claude Rouam[*]

The purpose of this paper is to address an issue which is both important and difficult: Are supra-national rules necessary for the application of competition policy in a supra-national setting today?

Everyone would agree that the process of globalisation of world economies continues and that companies operate across borders not only through trade, but also by establishing their own research, production and distribution facilities in many countries. The effects of their business decisions are liable to be felt in more than one jurisdiction.

The essence of any competition policy is to ensure the best possible operation of the market – which is not necessarily a national one – by protecting the competition system from abuses, so that consumers may be offered the best choice of goods and services at the lowest price. From an EC point of view, other objectives are to promote market integration, to facilitate cross-border trade and, more generally, economic progress.

It has become evident to us all that markets are expanding, or the world is shrinking in economic terms. An item on the agenda is therefore to define how regulations should develop to reflect this fact of life. For trade, an answer – at least partially satisfactory – has been given by the GATT rules, as is demonstrated by their progressive implementation and their extension to new areas, including services, as provided in the Punta del Este Declaration. But what do international rules for trade mean if competition is not dealt with in a similar way? This is the issue I would like to address, by expressing a few ideas on unilateral, bilateral, regional or multinational rules in this area.

---

[*] Deputy Head of Unit, Directorate General for Competition, Commission of the European Communities. The views expressed are entirely personal and do not necessarily reflect the policies of the Commission.

2.1 Unilateral actions

Unilateral approaches to competition are the most common ones, since competition depends mainly on national legislation. There are cases of restrictive business practices (for instance distribution agreements) where the negative effects are felt on a national market, or even on a part of it, giving room for unilateral action by national antitrust authorities. But there are also cases where operations with international effects are dealt with unilaterally, and these are more important for this discussion.

In this respect, the *EC Merger Control* is a cornerstone of EC competition policy and plays a unique role in ensuring success in completion of the internal market.

The principles of the EC policy (as contained in Regulation 4064/89) are, in summary:

(a)   to establish a clear allocation between Community-wide mergers for which the Commission is responsible, and those whose main impact is in the territory of a Member State for which the national authorities are responsible;

(b)   to define mergers having a Community dimension on the basis of certain criteria, namely:

–   a threshold of a least ECU 5 billion for the aggregate world-wide turnover of all the undertakings concerned. For financial institutions and insurance companies, more specific criteria are laid down;

–   a threshold of at least ECU 250 million for the aggregate Community-wide turnover of each of at least two of the undertakings concerned;

–   a transnationality criterion under which Community control does not apply if each of the undertakings concerned achieves two thirds of its turnover within one and the same Member State.

The basic concept is that of *dominant position*. The creation or strengthening of a dominant position will be declared incompatible with the common market if effective competition is impeded to a significant extent, whether within the common market as a whole, or in a substantial part thereof. The assessment process takes into account various aspects of competition. These include the structure of the markets concerned, actual and potential competition (from inside and outside the Community), the market position of the undertakings concerned, the scope for choice on the part of third parties, barriers to entry, the interests of consumers, and technical and economic progress. This list is used when assessing the impact of a merger on competition.

It can easily be concluded that neither the domicile of companies nor their "nationality" will prevent the EC Commission from applying Regulation 4064/89. For example, this Regulation has been applied to mergers between two Japanese banks[1] and between a Japanese and an American company[2]. It must be stressed that if the Commission adopts a negative decision in respect of a merger of, for instance, two non-EC companies, even though the Commission's jurisdiction is limited to the EC territory, the feasibility of the project as a whole will probably disappear. International cooperation between antitrust agencies consequently takes on dramatic importance in such cases, in order to avoid large scale operations being decided upon without appropriate consultations. This of course does not mean that antitrust agencies in each jurisdiction concerned must reach identical conclusions, since substantive rules and market conditions may vary. To protect legal certainty for economic agents, international cooperation is needed when unilateral approaches are taken.

The United States is well known for giving an extraterritorial dimension to implementation of its competition rules. The limits of this extraterritoriality have been explained, for example, in the *Antitrust Guidelines for International Operations* published by the Department of Justice in 1988. It is not my purpose to examine the scope of this extraterritorial enforcement which might undercut the sovereignty of foreign authorities. (I suggest as an example of this issue the description in Rosenthal (1990) of the case of the Institute Mérieux dealt with by the Federal Trade Commission.)

I only want to point out that we have here an illustration of the unilateral approach to international transactions which is still very much in evidence today. I understand that the American Bar Association – through its Special Committee on International Antitrust – has recently expressed views in favour of import cartels being subject to antitrust enforcement by the exporting nations. Such a proposal

---

[1] Kyowa – Saitama.

[2] Matsushita – MCA.

could mean that unilateral enforcement of competition rules might become a weapon in the context of the current debate on trade relations between the US and Japan.

Even more recently (3 April 1992) the US Department of Justice announced that it may take antitrust law enforcement action in US courts to challenge business activities outside the US that restrict US exports, provided that those activities would have violated US antitrust law if they had occurred in the US, but *regardless* of whether they caused direct injury to US consumers. This is obviously a change in US policy, being tantamount to the adoption of a unilateral enforcement policy.

2.2 Bilateral agreements

Even though unilateralism has been dominant for a long time in the field of competition, some examples of *bilateral approaches* deserve to be described. My examples will be related to the EC's experience in this respect.

A first example is the bilateral approach of the *Free Trade Agreements* (FTAs) concluded in the early 1970s between the *EC and the EFTA countries*. At that time EFTA states were not interested in membership, but their traditional links with the Community made both partners recognise that one of the aims of these agreements should be "to contribute, by the removal of barriers to trade, to the harmonious development and expansion of world trade". Article 23 of these Agreements states that cartels and concerted practices, abuses of dominant positions and public aids are not compatible with a proper functioning of the Agreements, since these activities may affect trade between the Contracting Parties.

If one of the Contracting Parties considered the activities to be incompatible with these rules, it may request consultations on the basis of Article 27 (in the respective "Joint Committees"). Contracting Parties may adopt "appropriate measures" if no mutually acceptable solution has been found.

This is an example of a bilateral approach, but unfortunately it must be said that in reality it has been of little help. Furthermore, the rules and procedures provided for in the FTA's do not preclude the application of the EC's Competition rules, if a given practice is incompatible with both an FTA and the EC rules. In the "Woodpulp case" this was confirmed by the EC Court regarding the EC's FTA with Finland. This is probably one of the reasons why a totally different approach has been chosen in creating the European Economic Area. We will come to this later under the heading "regional approach".

A more recent example of bilateralism can be found in the *European Agreements* signed on 16 December 1991 between the Community and, respectively, Hungary, Poland and the Czech and Slovak Federal Republic. These agreements contain far-reaching rules especially in the field of competition. There are provisions identical to Articles 85 and 86, as well as 92, of the Treaty of Rome. These provisions do not only cover cartels, abuses of dominant position and State aids, but also state monopolies and companies to which special or exclusive rights have been granted. The parties have likewise agreed that competition rules will be interpreted in accordance with EC rules.

Furthermore, the agreements require that a special Association Council will adopt implementing rules for competition within three years. In the meantime there are specific interim procedures regarding state aids. The actual application of competition rules will be dealt with by the parties – the three states and the Community. It should also be noted that the agreement has opened a process of dialogue and consultation, which is most important.

The European Agreements are examples of bilateral agreements which contain substantive standards for competition rules, their gradual implementation being adapted to the situation of new democracies. Nevertheless, I would like, in this respect, to stress that these competition rules will apply to enterprises involved in international trade. In practice, this will include companies now operating in the new democracies such as General Motors, Fiat or Air France, to take but a few examples of investments recently made in Central and Eastern European countries. Obviously, as the number of international investments and investors increases so will the need for more competition rules.

It is certainly too early to assess the functioning of these agreements. But, it can be stressed that the Contracting Parties agreed on the need to have at their disposal specific competition rules between the Community and the respective country. One reason is the fact that existing legislation, based on the "effect doctrine", is not sufficient to deal with all restrictive business practices (e.g. for anticompetitive practices which create access barriers to an external market, domestic competition rules are useless); moreover, traditional antitrust rules are not sufficient to ensure that competition is not distorted (e.g. state aids and state monopolies).

Last but not least, the *EC-US Agreement* (September 1991) is an example of bilateralism. The aim of this agreement was to establish closer cooperation and better understanding between EC and US competition authorities, and to lessen the possibility or impact of differences between the parties in application of their competition laws. Without going into detail concerning this agreement, I would like to stress a few points.

The agreement helps to prevent conflicts through cooperation and communication of differences between the parties. Each party will continue to act on the basis of its own rules but at the same time the agreement establishes machinery to facilitate consideration of issues of mutual concern.

Three elements of this agreement may be cited:

– Article II, Notification: "Each party shall notify the other whenever its competition authorities become aware that the enforcement activities will affect important interests of the other party."

– Article III, Exchange of Information: "The parties agree that it is in their common interest to share information that will for example facilitate effective application of their respective competition laws (...)."

– Article IV, Cooperation and Coordination: "The competition authorities of each party will render assistance to the competition authorities of the other party in their enforcement activities."

Furthermore, this agreement is also an important tool helping both parties to deal in concert with common challenges in their struggle against restrictions on competition and liberalisation of trade. Here, again, it is certainly too early to draw conclusions. There is no doubt, however, that this agreement is an important attempt to use bilateral cooperation with a new meaning, thanks in particular to the concept of positive comity which is an innovation in the field of cooperation between antitrust agencies. Positive comity allows one party to the agreement to request the other party to take positive steps to remedy a situation which affects the requesting party. Nothing in the agreement limits the discretion of the second authority to decide whether to take enforcement action.

2.3 Regional agreements

One of the most striking features of the world economy in this second part of the 20th century is that relationships of supremacy and domination have begun to give way to cooperation. This cooperation is to a great extent *regional*. A few examples follow.

Opting for a system of free competition was from the start a cornerstone in the building of the *European Community*, but this example is so well known that I need only mention it.

Another a regional approach is the draft *North American Free Trade Zone Agreement* (NAFTA), involving US, Canada and Mexico, which will create a continent-wide integrated market. As far as I know, specific competition rules are not part of this Agreement. Competition rules are also not included in the Canada-US Free Trade Agreement even though such provisions could certainly be useful.

The Free Trade Area between *Australia and New Zealand* may also be mentioned. This agreement has as its objectives to develop closer economic relations between the two countries through a mutually beneficial expansion of free trade. Further the agreement develops trade under conditions of fair competition and aims gradually to eliminate, under an agreed timetable, barriers to trade. Australia and New Zealand simultaneously adopted measures to eliminate dumping in the trans-Tasmanian market. Instead they will regulate trade between them through harmonised competition laws. Further, the competition authorities in each country have power to investigate companies in the other country, and the decisions of each tribunal are enforceable in the other country.

The European Economic Area – EC and EFTA

But the main example of "regionalism" which I want to elaborate, and which certainly deserves analysis, is the project for creation of the *European Economic Area* (EEA). The main issues of a supra-national approach arise in this Agreement: establishment of common rules, allocation of cases, cooperation for enforcement. We may recall that the objective of the EEA is the creation of an area (of 19 countries and about 370 million consumers) in which the free movement of goods, services, people and capital would be fully realised.

From the very beginning of the negotiations, it was recognised that the competition rules should be identical throughout the EEA, but should be implemented on the basis of a so-called *two pillar model* by which the same substantive rules (in practical terms, the rules existing for the time being in the Community) would be applied by the EC Commission as well as by an independent EFTA Surveillance Authority.

The two pillar model actually means that surveillance and enforcement of competition will be carried out by the two authorities. They will act on the basis of the second important principle, the "*one stop shop*", which means that each individual case will be handled either by the EC Commission or by the EFTA Surveillance Authority and the decisions of both of these bodies will be valid throughout the EEA. The EFTA Surveillance Authority will have the same powers as the Commission already has under EC and ECSC rules.

Once agreement had been reached on this double issue of "a two pillar model with a one stop shop principle", the discussions focused on the difficult question of the allocation of individual cases between the Commission and the EFTA Surveillance Authority. The Community, in particular after the Court's opinion of December 1991, made clear that it was impossible for it to give up the responsibilities it had under the EEC and ECSC Treaties. It was therefore agreed that the Community will keep all its existing competences (which are even extended, for instance in the field of merger control); on the other hand the EFTA Surveillance Authority would be in charge of State aids in EFTA countries, state monopolies in EFTA countries, mergers with an EFTA dimension (beyond the scope of EC Regulation 4064/89), abuses of dominant position which take place on the EFTA territory only, and cartels affecting trade exclusively between EFTA states, or between one EC Member State and (an) EFTA state(s) (provided that 33 per cent at least of the EEA turnover of the companies in question takes place on the EFTA territory). In addition there are so-called *de minimis* cases (from the EC point of view) arising from trade between the Contracting Parties.

A necessary condition for the proper functioning of the Agreement is close cooperation between the Commission on one side and the EFTA Surveillance Authority on the other. Competition experts know quite well that excellent rules are useless if implementing rules are inadequate; the competition provisions of the EEA Agreement include administrative assistance for enforcement. Enforce-

34

ment is an indispensable component of a competition policy if an antitrust agency wants to be more than a toothless dog. The EEA Agreement had therefore to cover cooperation in the crucial field of investigations (especially when they take place in the territory of the authority which is not competent to deal with a given case) and for the recovery of fines. This cooperation is of paramount importance and probably represents one of the most difficult issues in international agreements of this kind.

This far-reaching example of regional cooperation can certainly serve for further reflection on supra-national rules on competition. It illustrates the complexity of the deal, which was possible – or which will be possible after the initialling and the ratification of the Agreement – because the EFTA states could agree to "import" most EC rules as part of the package giving them access to the EC internal market.

2.4 Multilateral possibilities: OECD, UNCTAD, GATT

Multilateral approaches could also be useful in order to promote convergent policies towards abusive or restrictive practices which may distort international trade, to avoid conflicts between antitrust agencies and to promote similar commitments to tackle restrictive practices. At present, the OECD, UNCTAD and GATT could all claim predominant responsibility in this respect.

OECD has particular importance since it embraces nearly all industrialised market economies, and has progressively developed a specific expertise. OECD has, in particular, a Committee dealing with Competition Law and Policy which has been for many years a unique forum for exchange of views between antitrust agencies of Western countries. OECD has had a leading role in establishing cooperation through, in particular, the adoption and implementation of a 1986 Recommendation on "Cooperation between Member Countries on restrictive business practices (RBP) affecting international trade"; up to now, the main challenge for OECD has arisen from disputes regarding extraterritorial jurisdiction.

These traditional functions are not the only ones and OECD has recently developed new projects to provide technical assistance for non-OECD countries which are ready to adopt competition rules. OECD is also supporting a greater convergence of the policies of its member countries.

What can be expected from the OECD – in addition to its traditional activities – is certainly more action in favour of strict implementation by all its member countries of existing competition rules. This seems more useful than the definition of new over-ambitious rules which would create overlapping in most industrialised countries, and which would not be applicable to third countries, increasing therefore the gap between competition-oriented economies and the others.

Let me quote Sir Leon Brittan (1992b):

"The most serious trade and investment distortions resulting from the application or lack of application of domestic laws and policies must be targeted and remedied individually, in one way or another, as a matter of urgency. Broader thoughts or plans for the future should not be allowed to delay action which must be taken now if confidence in the benefits of an open trading system is not to be undermined".

What can be expected from *UNCTAD?* UNCTAD's work in the antitrust field is carried out by an Intergovernmental Group of Experts concerned with restrictive business practices. UNCTAD has contributed to the promotion of a competitive spirit – inspired to a large extent by the provisions of the Treaty of Rome – based on the "Set of multilaterally agreed equitable principles and rules for the control of restrictive business practices". This traditional reference in UNCTAD's work is not a set of binding rules, but has been considered as a useful basis for the adoption of domestic legislation by some developing countries. Debates in the Intergovernmental Group of Experts have sometimes been controversial about adding new elements to the Set, and developing countries have regularly insisted on the need to provide for better international control of RBPs. A new consensus is emerging. I think of the work recently carried out by UNCTAD VIII in Cartagena de Indias, which was not concerned with defining supra-national rules but with making developing countries benefit as widely as possible from the experience of developed countries in the field of competition. Technical assistance is therefore the key word to describe UNCTAD's priorities in the field of RBPs.

The pending *GATT* negotiations, based on the mandate defined in Punta del Este, do not include specific actions for an international treatment of anticompetitive business behaviour. It is questionable whether it makes sense to agree on a commitment in favour of free trade without a similar commitment in favour of corresponding competition rules to ensure fair trading conditions! There will probably be opportunities for reflection after the conclusion of the Uruguay Round.

This message was delivered recently by Sir Leon Brittan when he mentioned the possibility of developing minimum rules and enforcement standards to be respected by signatory governments of the GATT Agreement. He also suggested that a rule might be devised whereby governments would have to show that they had used their best endeavours to prevent or punish illegal behaviour such as price fixing.

It must be noted that these proposals would not create supra-national rules superseding those prevailing, e.g. in the EC, nor establish supra-national authorities to enforce commonly agreed principles. But they would make effective and operational a consensus that seems acceptable for most countries involved in international trade. It would therefore be a significant step forward.

2.5 Concluding remarks

The time when domestic competition policies ignore the international setting is certainly over, and that must definitely be considered positive progress. It would be simplistic, however, to conclude that supra-national rules – or even commonly agreed, binding international rules – can for the time being constitute a credible alternative.

The situation is much more complex, for which there are good reasons:
–   Unilateral action – as in other areas of economic legislation or policy – remains a basic feature of competition policies, but multilateral fora can usefully prevent it from being detrimental to foreign partners, thanks for instance to exchange of views or consultations, as in OECD or UNCTAD. Multilateralism could also serve to promote commonly agreed minimum standards, and here GATT might play a constructive role in the future. Multilateralism has also found a new importance through technical assistance provided by developed countries to developing countries and economies in transition.
–   Bilateral cooperation, probably the most flexible approach, is certainly the most appropriate solution for establishing close links between partners, such as the EC and the US where harmonisation of rules is not feasible (differences between competition policies on the two sides of the Atlantic are well-known) but where one partner cannot ignore the other's views. The conclusion of the EC-US Agreement was indeed facilitated by the need to

avoid contradictory approaches, in particular towards mergers. The reference to positive comity for the first time as part of the international setting is clearly a significant breakthrough.

– The flexibility of bilateral cooperation takes into account the differences between the EC and its Central and Eastern European partners to the European Agreement. In this case harmonisation along EC standards has been reached.

– Regional approaches to competition rules depend on the degree of economic integration envisaged. It is not surprising that the EFTA countries made little progress toward a common competition policy on the basis of the Stockholm Convention, nor that the NAFTA Agreement seems very cautious in this respect. On the other hand, the planned European Economic Area will represent the most homogenous model, since the 19 countries will have the same rules, the "one stop shop" principle and close cooperation in enforcement.

References

Brittan, L. (1991), "Competition Policy in the Light of the Agreement Creating the European Economic Area", Walras Conference, 8 November.

– (1992a), "A Framework for International Competition", World Economic Forum, Davos, 3 February.

– (1992b), "Competition Policy and International Relations", CEPS, Brussels, 17 March.

Ehlermann, C.D. (1992), "Antitrust Issues in an International Dimension", University of Chicago, 31 January.

Jakob, Th., "Wettbewerbspolitik im Europäischen Wirtschaftsraum" (to be published).

Rosenthal, D. (1990), "The Potential for Jurisdictional Conflicts in Multi-state International Merger Transactions", Fordham University.

Rouam, Cl. (1992), "L'Espace Economique Européen: un horizon nouveau pour la politique de concurrence?", *Revue du Marché Commun*, January.

COMMENTS ON PART I:

John Williamson*⁾

The task taken on by *Bienaymé* (Ch. 1), of providing a theoretical framework
to shape our thoughts on the role of competition in the economies in transition,
is a daunting one. It brings *Bienaymé* quickly to the ancient issue of appraising
the usefulness of the model of perfect competition that has mesmerised so many
economists for so many years. I share his distaste for the profession's traditional
addiction to this model, but I am not entirely comfortable with either his demolition
job or his attempt to provide an alternative.

Perfect competition is useful for two purposes: as an intellectual reference
point, and as an institutional description of some markets (mainly for primary
commodities and financial assets). Note that perfect competition offers a model
of a *market* rather than of a society (although the "fundamental theorem of welfare
economics", the proposition that ubiquitous perfect competition implies Pareto
optimality, does indeed apply to society, or at least the economy, as a whole).

One certainly does not need all nine of *Bienaymé*'s axioms in order to use
the perfectly competitive model of a single market. The key requirement is his
third axiom, that there be many suppliers and demanders. The second axiom
(individual maximising behaviour) and the fifth (concerning the legal environment)
are perhaps also necessary, although these are rather weak conditions. But the
first axiom (increasing costs) is a requirement for the third one rather than an
independent factor. Neither the fourth axiom ("free information flows on market
conditions and on the best production techniques available and ... certainty/
transparency"), nor the requirement that transactions take place simultaneously,
seem at all necessary, for they are surely violated in markets that I would describe
as preeminently perfectly competitive, like fish auctions or the foreign exchange
market. Freedom of entry and exit is necessary to conclude that profits will be
zero (after imputing back to the responsible scarce factor the extra output
resulting from any firm-specific advantages), but profits will also be zero if that

---

*⁾   Senior Fellow, Institute for International Economics. Copyright 1992, Institute for International
Economics, Washington DC, All rights reserved.

condition is satisfied in an industry with Chamberlinian monopolistic competition. The seventh axiom essentially repeats the third. Hence it seems to me that *Bienaymé* has much exaggerated the conditions that must be satisfied before one can exploit the model of perfect competition.

Nevertheless, the more important fact is that, even with my far less demanding conditions for perfect competition, almost all industrial products and almost all services are sold under conditions that cannot be modelled adequately as perfectly competitive. I cannot see that much is gained by asserting that all will be well provided there is "workable competition". I much prefer to follow up the thought suggested by my favourite sentence in *Bienaymé*'s paper, the one which defines " a free market economy [as] an economic system in which ... the buyers [are] free to select ... the best suppliers ...". The key idea is that the possibility of *choice* disciplines the sellers. Hence a "competitive" firm is one that is chosen by many buyers. Large firms engage in the multidimensional striving described so well in the paper in order to persuade purchasers to choose their products. Those effects are not dependent upon the presence of a near-infinite number of alternative suppliers, but they certainly are dependent on there being more than one, and larger numbers are better than smaller.

Let me sketch some of the implications that seem to follow from this definition of competition.

(i)   An increase in market size – due, for example, to the elimination of trade barriers – will increase the range of choice faced by buyers, and thus increases competition.

(ii)   Potential choice can also discipline sellers, thus justifying the attention paid to free entry (or "contestability") in the literature.

(iii)   One still has the paradox that excessively successful competition that wipes out the competitors can destroy competition, which is especially dangerous where contestability is absent (large civil airliners come to mind as a possible example).

(iv)   Subject to the preceding qualification and an absence of externalities, I would argue that this definition justifies Adam Smith's presumption that self-serving behaviour will have socially beneficial results if and only if competition exists. Of course, this presumption cannot be proved mathematically (except under universal perfect competition). But those of us who regard the essence of economics as being a series of robust empirical propositions tend to feel that the bulk of the profession places altogether too much value on the elaboration of rigorous mathematical proofs.

Rouam's paper (Ch. 2) did not strike me as an economist's paper, for its principal concern is with assigning jurisdiction over competition policy rather than with the content of what is being enforced. The sort of questions that came to my mind as I read the paper were: what happens if the EC denies two Japanese banks permission to merge their European operations? What is implied by exporters policing import cartels? What is the content of the competition agreements that the EC reached with Czechoslovakia, Hungary and Poland? Toward what is the OECD promoting convergence? Such questions are suggested but not answered.

I have only one substantive challenge to offer, which concerns the proposition that the case for free trade fails "without a similar commitment in favour of corresponding competition rules to ensure fair trading conditions". Perhaps it is true that such rules are politically necessary to keep the producer lobbies at bay, but the only economic case for requiring competition rules to accompany free trade is the fear that in their absence temporary predatory pricing might permit establishment of a monopoly position with the power to engage in permanent exploitation of consumers. Such permanent exploitation is possible only where there is a lack of contestability, which perhaps helps explain why it is not easy to think of cases where such exploitation has actually occurred. Nevertheless, the danger provides one strand of the case for a global anti-trust policy, along with elimination of the excuse for engaging in competitive rent-grabbing as recommended by the strategic trade policy school. With a global anti-trust policy in place, one could relax at the possibility of (for example) all the cars in the world being produced by firms with headquarters in Japan.

Why competition

One failing of both Chh. 1 and 2 is that they do not focus much on whether and why competition is of importance to the European economies in transition. To my mind, the key point is exactly that competition is necessary if markets are to create incentives to act in a socially-beneficial way. Privatisation is useful to sharpen incentives. But – as some of Mrs. Thatcher's privatisations unaccompanied by increased competition (which benefited managerial salaries rather than the consumers) have shown – competition is crucial if the incentives are to yield social benefits.

What is the evidence that justifies one in giving such salience to (nonperfect) competition, given that no logical proof is possible and that one is instead claiming this to be a robust empirical proposition? Let me cite two areas from my own field of international economics where the importance of competition has become increasingly clear. The first is the success of outward orientation in promoting development: one of the key differences between a strategy of import substitution and the alternative strategy of outward orientation is that the former creates a series of national monopolies sheltered against foreign competition, while the latter sends firms out to compete on the world market. The other relates to the benefits of economic integration, which have turned out to be far greater than the initial attempts to measure Harberger triangles suggested would be conceivable. It is now generally accepted that this is because integration permits the reconciliation of economies of scale with the maintenance of competition.

An obvious next question concerns the policies needed to promote the development of competition in the economies in transition. One is demonopoli-sation. Small-scale privatisation can be of direct help in this regard, which provides a strong reason for pushing ahead and not getting bogged down in restitution. But privatisation of large enterprises is not likely to help, and indeed competition policy would suggest that it might be preferable to deconcentrate before pri-vatising. The other policy involves opening the economy to foreign competition, which requires early establishment of current account convertibility and trade liberalisation. Such liberalisation may reasonably be tempered by enough transi-tional protection to avoid simultaneous mass bankruptcies, but it should be real enough to provide at least a measure of discipline on domestic producers.

The key role that I have argued should be assigned to competition should not be taken to imply that competition is a panacea. On the contrary, it will lead to wrong results in the presence of externalities, and so the creation of a compe-titive environment needs supplementing by measures to internalise externalities. Furthermore, under the best of circumstances competition leads to efficiency rather than equity, and so concerns on the latter score need to be addressed separately. Once again, however, competition should be supplemented rather than supplanted. If I believed that there was a case in equity for preserving a

French motorbike or salt-making industry – something that in fact strikes me as about as convincing as the case of Bastiat's candle-makers against the unfair competition of the sun – I would do it by organising a competitive tender for the lowest subsidy needed to induce a specified level of output rather than by excluding imports.

In short, I hope that the main message of these studies is that, while privatisation is needed to sharpen incentives, a competitive environment is the key to ensuring that the incentives are such as to encourage agents to act in the social interest.

Alain Bienaymé

Responding to some comments on my Chapter 1, I would make the following observations.

If Perfect Competition (PC) in a pure market economy such as Walras depicted discards the issue of social justice, it is mainly because (unlike Ricardo's theory of rent) suppliers and sellers are so numerous and so small that inequality of resources does not raise a critical issue. Moreover the assumption of perfect information and equal access of producers to the best known techniques of production entails as a consequence that every competitor uses roughly the same production method and the same set of cost parameters linked to it.

If PC remains an intellectual construct, well suited to some clearly defined situations, it rarely gives a fair account of how markets really work and how bargains are actually made. The PC model helps to raise relevant issues such as the costs of information processing, or the free trade solution as a device to enlarge the market size to fit the average or median size of production units. But we need also other tools of analysis to cope with real behaviour and to give a clear understanding of business games and strategies.

"Workable competition" emphasises the role of quality, innovation and the dynamics of unit costs. It leads to different expressions of the cost-price relationship, in highly competitive industries at least. Instead of deriving the price from a cost-plus formula, the producer may chose to fix *ex ante* the price of his new product at a level which indicates to the market how he intends to sell his

43

product: the targeted segment of clientèle, the channels of distribution, the quality signals, the built-in services etc. Then, if the market grows as expected, the unit costs will descend the cost curves, thanks to experience and scale effects. They will hence generate the cash-flow needed to prepare the next generation of products.

Industrial output often results from highly sophisticated combinations of technologies. The boundaries of the networks of companies which all contribute to the delivery of end-products depend on a mix of competition and cooperation which is influenced by policy decisions on procurement, subcontracting, R and D agreements, mergers and capital arrangements such as joint ventures. This increases the difficulty of implementing antitrust regulation; the antitrust authorities are obliged in their investigations to ponder to what extent observed practices impair potential competition as well as actual competition, and restrict unduly the consumer's choices.

The impact of competition on economic evolution is positive in that it fast enhances labour productivity. But the incidence on GDP per head is slower because increased competition, especially in countries which have to catch up with modern production techniques, sharply raises unemployment during a first stage which can last for several years. Moreover, competition does not spontaneously cope with external costs and external economies nor with the risks of natural resources depletion. Thus free trade and free competition should not prevent the public authorities from intervening through new marketing devices (auction sales for pollution rights, taxation, subsidies and/or regulation) in order to reconcile economic growth with other social needs. Competition is a wealth-generating mechanism; in so far it breaks sharply with basic equality between individuals, competition has to be somewhat mitigated through taxation and regulation.

Some general comments on the concept of competition

Deep transformations have affected the concept of competition throughout the history of capitalism. They derive partly from the observation of the core practices of business companies and partly from the pervasive trends towards internationalisation and globalisation of Western economies. Several aspects of this transformation may be singled out.

(a)   The concept of perfect competition (PC) was and is entirely focused on the instant maximisation of consumer welfare. By contrast, "workable competition" draws attention to the real and dynamic conditions of production within and between organisations fighting and bargaining for their own survival. If, on the whole, in the long run, consumers become more affluent than they would have been in a Walrasian competition, long-lasting profits and monopoly rents permanently postpone welfare maximisation.

(b)   The concept of perfect competition sets the mathematical definition of an optimal market structure which, although actually established only under very restrictive conditions, has long been considered as the unique optimal structure. But the concept of workable competition, at least in mature capitalist countries, stresses three important features of real economic life:

(i)   The technically efficient production functions may justify in many industries the survival of only a limited number of plants and companies.

(ii)   The business strategies which are constrained by uncertainty display a wide span of responses which are well beyond the reach of pure economic rationality and of the "one best way" it dictates.

(iii)   Moreover, the culture of workable competition requires a frame of mind to which all suppliers are not spontaneously prepared. Beyond the material product they wish to sell, efficient suppliers have to consider the services which are really offered to their clients, the real needs which they should aim to satisfy. Even in industrialised societies where economic actors have keenly grasped the importance of services the business entrepreneurs are unequally prone to see to it. Those who are more dedicated to open competition could if they wished outperform the less efficient suppliers. But in the process of economic life the latter may survive and even be well off if they are lucky enough to take advantage of a protected "niche". Workable competition almost inevitably breaks the theoretical equality of situations postulated in a non-Ricardian perfect competition model, i.e. in a rentless world.

(c)   PC conveys the ideal of an optimal society in which economic decisions would be entirely freed from political interference, totally subject to rational choices and unbiased by any imbalance of power whatsoever.

Workable competition opens instead wide possibilities to market power, lobbying influences and political interference. It is a self-destroying process and has to be continuously watched over by appropriate independent institutions such as antitrust courts and commissions. Otherwise powerful corporations which derive their influence from their former efficiency might misuse their domination at the expense of their present economic performance. Pure market power may thus become easily detrimental to consumer welfare. So the mission delegated by the country to antitrust institutions is to ensure that large firms will still bear their fruit in terms of economies of scale, scope and experience, without restricting unduly the span of choices open to the partners and to the final consumer.

(d)   We have thus discovered that economic efficiency requires a type of competition which is not any more correlated with the greatest possible number of suppliers and sellers, nor with a total transparency of market conditions. Nor is workable competition any more linked with short-term endless price-minimisation behaviour.

(e)   Finally in a world where markets and transactions are not the only way for coordinating economic activities, economic efficiency depends also on the structural set of organisations through which a country chooses to stimulate, to regulate and to channel economic initiatives. The banking system and the anti-trust authorities play therefore a decisive role in this respect.

David G. Mayes[*]

It is clear from *Rouam*'s paper (Ch. 2) that the European Commission feels that it has already set the framework for fair competition across Europe by its current (and planned) legislation and the form of the European Economic Area (EEA) Agreement. Between them, these set out the rules for an "internal market" that would run across Europe. The Commission would be concerned with any large-scale mergers that affected its jurisdiction and with anti-competitive actions which discriminated against firms from another member state or country within the market. These discriminatory actions would include restrictive practices by

---

[*]   Professor; National Institute of Economic and Social Research, London.

firms as well as state aids and other forms of discrimination by government as regulator or purchaser.

In the EEA case the comparable jurisdiction is extended outside the EC by a new court. It would appear likely that East European countries wishing to join in such a market with the EC would also have to adhere to these rules. The EEA negotiations were very one-sided. In effect the EFTA countries had to agree to the outstanding EC legislation relating to the internal market and indeed also make a contribution towards a cohesion fund to provide assistance for the least-favoured regions of the Community.

The form of internal competition policy permitted within this framework is largely unspecific provided that it is compatible with the EC rules. Thus participating countries can take harsher or laxer views about national or smaller mergers and acquisitions to which subsidiarity applies. Thus there is no reason for the East European countries to seek to change their planned competition policies in the face of these requirements for an integrated European market. The changes will need to come in the opening of these countries to foreign competition from the EC and from each other, both in investment and in freedom of establishment (as well as in trade in goods and services). This progressive approach should fit with the programme of transition. But whether such a one-sided form of agreement will be congenial remains to be seen.

PART II – EASTERN APPROACHES

Chapter 3

COMPETITION POLICY AND PRIVATISATION IN CZECHOSLOVAKIA

Stanislav Bělehrádek[*]

A major task in Czechoslovakia is to create a competitive environment. The previous economic development under socialist rule ignored competition. The enterprises in manufacturing, services, shops, transport and so on were regarded as dominant or monopolistic participants in the relevant market and their position on the market was justified by efforts to maximise their efficiency. This efficiency was never achieved, because the lack of competition led to small, or no interest in further development. Productivity and product quality were constantly dropping. Total state regulation of prices, the various systems of state subsidies to enterprises, together with a heavy tax burden, resulted in poor economic management, obsolete technologies, etc.

In preparing and establishing the market and a competitive environment, several necessary measures were adopted:

---

[*]   Chairman, Czech Office for Economic Competition (AMO), Brno, CSFR.

- the currency was devalued and internal convertibility introduced;
- foreign trade was partly liberalised by lowering import duties and customs fees;
- prices were freed for approximately 90 per cent of products; prices of the remaining 10 per cent are being gradually decontrolled now.

These measures created the conditions for easing the entry of foreign products to the Czechoslovak market, in competition with some domestic products. An agreement was signed between Czechoslovakia and the EC, and another between Czechoslovakia and the European Free Trade Area is ready. We expect that these agreements, together with privatisation, will promote economic growth and will have a major influence on the evolution of a competitive environment. This should be reflected in better quality, variety and prices. Both agreements are advantageous for Czechoslovakia and we expect an annual profit of approximately Kcs 5 billion.

We started small-scale privatisation in 1991. Almost all retail shops, except department stores, and smaller service enterprises were privatised by public auctions. We hope to finish the small-scale privatisation in 1992. Basically, the whole commercial network will then be in private ownership.

Big-scale privatisation started in 1992, and in its first stage concerned almost 3,000 medium-sized and large companies from all branches of Czechoslovak industry. In the second stage, which is supposed to end by the beginning of 1993, more companies will be privatised, bringing the private sector to more than 90 per cent of the economy. The remaining enterprises will not be privatised until after five years. We now expect that in some key companies, which will be hard to privatise, the state will retain ownership of a part of the company in the form of shares.

The private sector represented in 1990 and 1991 only a small part of the economy. Since 1990 a number of laws promoting entrepreneurial activities, and legalising entry of foreign capital, have been passed. Changes affecting in 1992 two-thirds of the coverage of state statistical records make national economic comparisons even more difficult than before. Currently only estimated data for 1991 are available. Exact data must await the processing of tax records for 1991. Only then will we know how many entrepreneurs were active and in what areas, how many of them have ceased activity, etc. The least exact data in the 1991

50

statistics are those concerning the number of people employed by private firms. The interpretation of 1991 laws allowed companies to register employees as "private entrepreneurs" (e.g. shop assistants as shopowners, artisans as owners of building companies). The laws have been partly amended and this ambiguity is no longer possible.

Most of the public interest in entrepreneurship was related to Law No. 105/1990 (concerning enterprises run by physical persons, registration with the Registrar of Companies being optional). This law was later replaced by legal provisions in the Commercial Code and the Business Code (under which registration with the Registrar of Companies was not required).

The size of the private sector in CSFR

The Czechoslovak Bureau of Statistics recorded 1,060 entrepreneurs at the end of 1991 (in Slovakia it was only about a quarter of that figure). Most of them are engaged in small-scale crafts and repair work (20 per cent), business activities (20 per cent), small-scale building activities (17 per cent), commercial and technical services (10 per cent).

		January 1991	January 1992	Growth
Total		26,275	73,382	47,101
of which:	commercial companies	–	20,571	20,571
	joint-stock companies	658	2,511	1,853
	private entrepreneurs[a]	1,787	9,607	7,820

Table 3.1

Number of registered private companies and entrepreneurs

a) Registered under Law 105/91.

A few statistics (*Tables 3.1 to 3.4*), even though not exact, demonstrate the shift in the development of the national economy and the evolution of a competitive environment. While the number of entrepreneurs and separate legal entities was negligible in 1990, a rapid increase occurred in 1992 (*Tables 3.1 and 3.2*).

Table 3.2

Composition of joint-stock and commercial companies
as of 1 January 1992

Joint-stock companies		2,511
of which:	private	1,159
	cooperative	28
	foreign (100 per cent)	97
	with foreign participation	531
	combined ownership	
	(state-private-coop.)	100
	state	596
Commercial companies		20,571
of which:	public commercial companies	2,349
	limited liability companies	18,030
	limited partnerships	190
	partnerships limited by shares	2

In *industry*, the largest number of entrepreneurs was found in metal-working and machine-tools (including maintenance and repair activities). In spite of the large number, the share of total industrial performance is quite small (*Table 3.3*). But probably not all the registered entrepreneurs are in fact operating; and some of them are just part-timers. The importance of the private sector in the economy does not reflect the number of entrepreneurs – approximately 17 per cent of them achieved only about 2.7 per cent of the total output.

In *construction*, the private sector accounted for about Kcs 10.6 billion out of the Kcs 40 billion total gross product of the sector.

In *agriculture*, the number of private farms bigger than 2 ha grew from 1,201 to 5,118 but accounted for only 0.5 per cent of total agricultural land. The average size of farms rose from 0.75 to 5.23 ha (see *Table 3.4*). But, including the smallest holdings, the private share of total arable land is 3.7 per cent, of cattle 3.3 per cent, pigs 8.2 per cent, poultry 24.5 per cent, sheep 71.2 per cent, hens 42.5 per cent, horses 43.5 per cent.

Table 3.3

**Private sector (excluding cooperatives) percentage
of each sector's contribution to GNP**
(1991 – preliminary estimates)

Industry	2.7 per cent
Construction	26.5 per cent
Agriculture	12.2 per cent
Retail distribution	23.2 per cent
Commercial road transport	5.9 per cent

In *transport* (1991), the share of the private sector grew especially in lorry transport. We registered about 20,000 entrepreneurs providing these services, of which about 7,000 owners operate full-time.

Table 3.4

Distribution by size of private farms

Area in hectares	Number of farms	Per cent of private land area
2-5	3,778	73.8
5-10	972	19.0
10-30	340	5.2
Over 30	28	1.0
Total	5,118	99.0

In *domestic commerce*, the private sector developed rapidly, thanks to small-scale privatisation and property returned to former owners under restitution claims. In *retailing*, it grew from 7 per cent to 42 per cent by the end of 1991. Under the small-scale privatisation, 2,492 units were sold in auctions, representing about one third of the total. Of the privatised units, about 50 per cent were shops,

10 per cent catering facilities, and about 20 per cent other services. Growth should be at least as fast in 1992.

The big-scale privatisation is planned for 1992. The ownership pattern of big companies in all fields of industry will change significantly; the statistics quoted in this paper will be very different. But one of the major problems in the privatisation process remains the lack of capital. The new owners have very little money with which to modernise and develop their enterprises.

We are at the very beginning of the creation of a competitive environment. To change the structure of our economy will not be easy. To abolish enterprises' monopolistic or dominant positions is exceedingly difficult because, for one thing, the respective ministries are not very helpful. To establish a new structure can be achieved only by opening our markets gradually to foreign products, by changing the production structure of existing enterprises and by creation of new capacities founded by new entrepreneurs. To develop competition in Czechoslovakia will take a long time: that is best shown by the share of private sector in GNP – while in Czechoslovakia it is approximately 8 per cent, in developed economies it is as much as 50-60 per cent. To shorten the transition, we must introduce the necessary legislation and promote the economic development of small and medium-size enterprises. We are fully aware of the fact that only competition – nothing else – can lead to good quality and appropriate prices.

Chapter 4

THE ROLES OF FOREIGN COMPETITION AND OF FINANCIAL INTERMEDIATION IN REVITALISING THE CZECHOSLOVAK ECONOMY

Miroslav Hrnčíř[*]

4.1 Incentive aspects of competition

Market economies based on the driving force of competition have proved much more conducive to economic efficiency than centralised systems relying on macroeconomic planning. The incentive aspects of competition are particularly apparent: every economic agent is motivated and pressed to reduce costs and to improve the quality of products and services, i.e. to move from the points *inside* the attainable transformation curve towards a point *on* the curve. Also, in a dynamic setting, competition is a driving force for technical progress and technological development, i.e. for applying new production techniques and for introducing new products, implying the shift (expansion) of the existing transformation curve.[1] Particularly because of the static and dynamic technological efficiency inherent in decentralised systems driven by competition, the overall efficiency of market economies increasingly outpaced the level reached by the centrally planned economies.

The transition of the former centrally planned economies back to a market-type economy is expected to check the widening of their technological gap with

---

[*] Institute of Economics, Czechoslovak Academy of Sciences, Prague, CSFR.

[1] This line of reasoning has been developed and stressed particularly in Schumpeter's theory of competition as "creative destruction". According to it, the competition which "counts" is "the competition from the new commodity, the new technology, the new sources of supply, the new type of organisation – competition which commands a decisive cost or quality advantage and which strikes not at the margin of the profits and the outputs of the existing firms but at their foundations and their very lives". J. Schumpeter (1964), p. 58.

55

the developed countries, and to initiate a reverse trend of "catching up". Consequently, it may be claimed that – by contrast with the traditional textbook preoccupation with cost price equilibrium – the main *impact of competition in revitalising the reforming countries is associated with its incentives*, with both the "carrot" of prospective profit and the "stick" of failure and bankruptcy.

That has important consequences for the type of competition which should develop in the reforming economies and, accordingly, for the conditions which must be satisfied to make it effective. If the importance attached to the incentive aspect of competition for progress in transition is justified, then the desirable state of affairs does not require endeavours in the direction of "perfect competition", with atomistic markets and market agents. Instead, the decisive factor is the existence of a competitive pressure, be it real or only potential, strong enough to affect the behaviour of firms. Such situations have been called "workable competition", "contestable competition" "creative destruction" or possibly X-efficiency.[2] They can be sustained with a limited number of firms, even with one only, so long as possibilities of feasible entry exist.

Even with rather wide dispersion in the efficiency level of state firms operating under a socialist regime and institutional framework, the empirical evidence suggests that the "standard" firm has worked far below its efficiency frontier and thus much below its "standard" counterpart in the developed market economies.[3] There is therefore ample space for efficiency gains in the course of transition. They may be of a short-run character: to cope with the existing wasteful methods of using inputs and equipment, "organisational slack", overstaffing, outmoded routines. But even more important are dynamic inefficiencies: failure or delay in introduction of new technologies and new products. The crucial issue thus seems

---

[2]   Clark, J.M. (1940), "Toward a concept of workable competition", *American Economic Review*. Baumol, W.J., Panzar, J., Willig, R. (1982), *Contestable markets and the theory of industry structure*, New York, Harcourt, Brace, Jovanovich.
Schumpeter, J. (1966), *Capitalism, Socialism, and Democracy*, London.
Leibenstein, H. (1966), "Allocative Efficiency vs. X-Efficiency", *American Economic Review*.
See also Bienaymé, A., Chapter 1 in the present volume.

[3]   Kolanda, M. and Kubišta, V. (1990), e.g. identified a rather differentiated performance of Czechoslovak manufacturing firms on Western markets.

to be whether, and in what conditions, the incentives and pressures of competition generated under the "imperfect" interim conditions of transition are, or could be, strong enough?

4.2 Controversial issues in restructuring policies

In Czechoslovakia, (write in April 1992) little more than two years have passed since the "Velvet Revolution" of November 1989. Nevertheless, quite a few features of the economy have already changed considerably. Macroeconomic stabilisation measures have been implemented, traditional foreign trade and foreign exchange monopolies have been dissolved and a limited "internal" currency convertibility introduced, parallel with price and foreign trade liberalisation. On the other hand, although a privatisation process has been promoted and a number of institutional and legal acts passed, yet it can be hardly claimed that a regime change on the micro side has so far been accomplished.

Consequently, a *certain asymmetry has been developing between progress in macroeconomic stabilisation and liberalisation measures on the one hand and the microeconomic and institutional dimension on the other*. Given that state of affairs, the outcome of the transition has been rather controversial. The price level was successfully stabilised in the course of 1991 and the balance of payments ended in much better shape than expected; but the results in the real economy, particularly in the level of economic activity, were disappointing – certainly much worse than initial expectations (see *Table 4.1*). Macroeconomic stabilisation and liberalisation achievements, accompanied by high cost in terms of lost output, could hardly be sustained in future because of the lack of corresponding microeconomic foundations. Without parallel and effective changes in the behaviour patterns and values of economic agents, any loosening of restrictive policies or revival of economic activities would probably lead to another destabilisation.

In the light of the first lessons learned from developments in the CSFR, as well as in other reforming countries, the general conclusion must be that, unlike some initial expectations, transition is proving a more complex and lengthy process than reforms in other parts of the world economy, and consequently more costly and demanding than initially expected. The main constraints are evidently the *slowness and unsatisfactory progress in the "restructuring" of economic agents*. Such restructuring represents, however, the very core of transition.

Table 4.1

Czechoslovakia: Basic indicators of macroeconomic development in 1990 and 1991

	1990	1991
Per cent change from previous year		
Net material product	-3.1	-19.5
Gross domestic product	-3.5	-15.9
Gross industrial production	-3.7	-21.2
Construction	-6.6	-30.5
Real wages	-5.6	-24.0
End-of-period figure		
Unemployment ('000)	77	523.7
Unemployment rate (per cent)	1	6.6
Current account balance in convertible currency (US$ bn)	-1.1	+0.3
Gross foreign debt (US$ bn)	-8.1	-9.4
State budget balance (Kcs bn)	+3.5	-18.6

Source: Statistical Bulletin, Federal Statistical Office.

The slow pace of change in institutions and behaviour need cause no surprise, since such changes, unlike stabilisation and liberalisation measures, are long-term issues "by definition". A certain delay between developments in the macro- and micro-dimensions of the transition is therefore inevitable. A more controversial issue is to what extent the strategy adopted, and the policies followed, contributed to this delay or, at least, failed to shorten it significantly. From the example of the CSFR it may be claimed that the importance of deliberate support for microeconomic restructuring, for the entry of new firms, for the constitution of markets and market institutions from the very beginning of the transition process, has not been given due weight or, more precisely, has been recognised only with a considerable delay.

The implied assumptions of the policies in the initial phase of transition in Czechoslovakia seemed to be that:

–   restructuring of economic agents will happen under the impact of macro-economic restriction, provided the restriction is tough enough;

–   the privatisation process could, and should, be quick; consequently, not only clear identification of property rights but also the heritage of the past (the indebtedness of state firms), as well as the problems of their incentives, control and management, will be automatically solved through privatisation.

In accordance with these implied assumptions, some damaging consequences followed.

(a)   The strategy adopted was based on the "conventional wisdom" developed for reforming countries elsewhere in the world, particularly in Latin America: the major aim in the initial phase was seen as macroeconomic stabilisation through aggregate demand restriction (to put the economy on a "sound footing"). For countries with hyperinflation the dominant target and the measure of success should certainly be to stabilise the economy as quickly and as thoroughly as possible; but the dominant challenge and constraint in the CSFR was evidently different: lack of markets, and of market institutions and market agents, and institutional and structural rigidities.

The strategy adopted thus implied, at least to some extent, a misplaced therapy. Too much weight was attached to the macroeconomic dimension[4] and *too much was expected from the curative effects of macroeconomic restrictive policies*.

(b)   Government policies in the microsphere have been concentrated on privatisation, preferring speed before other dimensions. A quick process being assumed, the issues of control and incentive schemes, for state and public firms in the interim period, have evidently been left aside. Consequently, a certain *management and control vacuum developed in the state sector* (agents turned to be without principals).

---

[4]   Portes, R. (1991, p. 7) maintained with reference to the transition in Eastern Europe in general: "The main difference between Eastern Europe and Latin America was the initial absence of markets, hence huge distortions and supply side failure. The Latin American experience and analogy, though instructive, has brought undue emphasis on macroeconomics for Eastern Europe".

There was also *a lack of determination to cope with the heritage of the past*, including in particular allowing inter-enterprise indebtedness, and non-performing loans in the balance-sheets of commercial banks to swell. Government policy again relied almost solely on privatisation, considering other approaches both non-feasible and non-productive.

(c)   *The entry of new small and medium private firms* was initially left to spontaneous development: only later was it recognised that the process must be purposefully supported to overcome initial constraints, particularly in view of the considerable contraction of domestic demand.[5]

(d)   The policies for opening the economy and introducing internal currency convertibility were associated with foreign exchange rate changes (devaluations), while there was hardly any set of *consistent policies for export promotion* (such as tariff instruments, export credits and insurance, promotion of commercial, banking and financial services). Again, the signs of a changing approach toward more pragmatic policies began to be seen only in the second half of 1991 – that is with considerable delay and only after some lessons had been learned.

This asymmetry between progress in macroeconomic stabilisation and liberalisation on the one hand, and microeconomic and institutional measures on the other, could hardly be narrowed, given the strategy adopted and the policies followed.

Confronted with restrictive policies and contracting demand, most firms tried to continue their routine production, eventually cutting down its volume. Reacting to diminishing sales proceeds and lack of liquidity, they channelled their disposable funds primarily to wages,[6] at the cost of investment[7] and maintenance outlays and by delaying payments to suppliers, if not altogether failing to honour

---

[5]   This recognition is reflected particularly in the creation of the "Bohemian and Moravian Guarantee and Development Bank" which started its activities in March 1992 and which provides support to newly established small and medium private firms.

[6]   This provides at least a partial explanation of a seemingly paradoxical phenomenon: along with dramatically increasing insolvency of enterprises, their demand deposits almost doubled in the course of 1991 (from Kcs 108.9 bn at the beginning to Kcs 184.6 bn towards the end of the year).

[7]   In macroeconomic terms, capital formation decreased in 1991 by 83 per cent as against 1990.

financial obligations. Along with traditional expectations of eventually being bailed out by the government, expectations of forthcoming privatisation, and the uncertain prospects (particularly for the existing managements), tended to dampen still further rather than to stimulate the entrepreneurial activities of most state enterprises[8].

The existing evidence thus suggests that the competitive pressures remained rather weak and were, moreover, still failing to push the firms to react in the way desired – i.e. to improve technical and quality standards, to innovate and launch new products and services.

4.3 The role of foreign competition – expectations and reality

Given these constraints in the interim period, could domestic competition be replaced by foreign imports?

Most of the former centrally planned economies are relatively small economies. They inherited from the socialist period institutional rigidities and highly monopolised domestic structures, with the dominant role for the state enterprises. Czechoslovakia was an extreme case in that: its private sector was negligible before 1990, even in agriculture and services; big units overwhelmingly prevailed, while small firms were almost lacking.[9]

Given this initial inheritance, it was understood that the reforming countries of Central-Eastern Europe, unlike, for example, Japan, could not achieve tough enough domestic competition in the first phases of transformation. Consequently, considerable weight was placed in the transition scenarios on the *impact of foreign competition on incentives and discipline.*

To make foreign competition feasible and important, the government moved towards opening the Czechoslovak economy at the very beginning of the transition: foreign trade and foreign exchange were substantially liberalised and

---

[8] Those tendencies, called by some cabinet ministers the "pre-privatisation agony of state firms", are thus the opposite of those in the United Kingdom, where most efficiency gains were actually achieved in the pre-privatisation period.

[9] See Zemplinerová, A. (1989).

internal currency convertibility on current account was introduced at the beginning of 1991.

Without doubt, opening the economy is essential for the success of the entire process of transition. Through direct contacts and confrontation with world market standards, the process of learning, imitation and innovation is promoted. Opening the economy should set in train the competitive régime; by providing incentives for catching up with advanced countries, it should contribute to the revitalising of entrepreneurial behaviour patterns.

However persuasive and unambiguous the above hypotheses may appear, the "revitalising" impact of foreign competition on domestic industries and on domestic management turned out to be rather weak and its implementation controversial, particularly with regard to the optimum timing and scope of foreign competition.[10]

Two types of implied factors seem to make the issue of foreign competition in the reforming countries an open and controversial one:
(i)   heritage of the past, resulting particularly in a rather wide gap between the domestic purchasing power of currency and its external value,
(ii)   lack of capacity and inducement to compete experienced on the side of most domestic firms until now.

The heritage of the past

At present, domestic industries and exporters face a productivity and efficiency gap with their western competitors. The existence of a gap due to lower technical and technological standards is nothing extraordinary; the impact of such situations has been treated in trade theories for a long time. In the specific case of the former centrally planned economies, however, the gap proves to be much wider than is warranted by lower technical standards and inferior quality of products alone. The underlying reasons are institutional and systemic defects, such as the lack of distributional networks, of up-to-date marketing techniques,

---

[10]   In comparing the costs and benefits of the radical opening of the Czechoslovak economy, including introduction of currency convertibility, arguments are presented to demonstrate that those moves were ill-timed, premature and too costly. See Pick, M. (1990).

of efficient banking, insurance and trade services and lack of experience in dealing on world markets.

The institutional and incentive constraints already noted affected adversely the export proceeds for most Czechoslovak products, manufactures in particular.[11] As a result, the gap between the domestic and external purchasing power of Czechoslovak currency progressively widened.[12]

Constraints on domestic competition

The lesson which should be derived from the experience of economies in transition suggests that the expected benefits of foreign competition could hardly be won independently of conditions on the domestic market. Only if there are incentives and inducements to compete in the domestic setting, and if at the same time economic agents possess the capacity to adjust does exposure to foreign competition appear both effective and sustainable.

The disappointing impact of foreign competition in the first phase of transition must therefore be attributed to various constraints derived from inherited conditions, as well as to the policies followed.

The dominant defect of transition so far has been slow or delayed adjustment on the supply side, the pace being still far behind the "standard" in developed market economies.

Under the terms of the market economy, a firm is required to make efforts to comply with the standard code of behaviour, to cover costs from revenue and to honour obligations in due time. Both suppliers and creditors monitor development and issue signals demanding change and adjustment, if there are signs of misconduct and potential failure. Under the rules of the game, the options are

---

[11] Czechoslovakia experienced a declining share of exports on the world markets, coupled with increasing substitution of higher value-added exports to the convertible currency markets by the lower value-added products – raw materials, intermediate products and standard consumer goods. Czechoslovakia thus turned to be a case of "regressive specialisation".

[12] After three devaluations during 1990 the exchange rate of the Czechoslovak koruna (Kcs) was fixed at Kcs 28 per US$. The domestic purchasing power of Kcs was estimated at Kcs 7-8 per US$ at that time, implying a deviation coefficient of four – a rather wide gap for a developed economy.

adjustment or bankruptcy and exit. Cases of non-compliance with market rules thus tend to be special cases, mostly individual and/or temporary.

In reforming countries, unlike market economies, cases of non-adherence to the rules and of not honouring obligations in due time prevail; their share has been increasing and the disease became persistent. The seriousness of the situation is indicated particularly by the vast, and cumulatively increasing, amount of inter-enterprise indebtedness, along with the considerable and inert share of bad, non-performing debt in the balance sheets of commercial banks which inherited their portfolio from the previous "monobank".

Table 4.2

Inter-enterprise indebtedness and obligations not honoured in due time

End of	Inter-enterprise indebtedness (Kcs bn)			Number of firms	
	Total	Primary	Secondary	Total	of which, in debt
June 1989	16.3	–	–	–	–
December 1989	6.6	3.2	3.4	1,522	460
June 1990	14.5	7.8	6.7	4,728	727
September 1990	24.9	12.4	12.5	5,566	1,106
December 1990	47.8	20.0	27.8	4,827	1,651
March 1991	76.7	27.1	49.6	7,388	2,766
June 1991	124.3	35.0	89.3	8,201	3,587
September 1991	147.2	36.0	111.2	9,109	3,960

Source: Financial indicators. Federal Ministry of Finance.

The volume of inter-enterprise indebtedness, including both the "primary" and "secondary" forms[13], has been increasing, with some ups and downs, since the early 1970s. Substantial increases occurred in 1981-1982 and again in 1987,

---

[13]   "Primary" indebtedness represents an overhang of payments in arrears less overdue claims on customers. The "secondary" form represents clients' failure to pay in due time (when the firm's overdue liabilities are less than their overdue receipts).

i.e. when the monetary authorities tried to tighten credit. An unprecedentedly sharp increase developed after August 1990 under the pressure of the restrictive monetary and fiscal policies of the transition stage, and accelerated further during 1991.

At the end of September 1991 3,960 firms (43 per cent of the total of 9,109) were in arrears of debt repayments to other firms (24.5 per cent being primary indebtedness and 75.5 per cent secondary). *Table 4.2* also shows that the recent dramatic increase of enterprise indebtedness was due particularly to its secondary form (clients' failures to meet their obligations to suppliers). Without doubt, such a volume of delays in honouring obligations (representing mostly "induced" trade credits) became a major destabilising factor, obstructing a flexible flow of funds and disseminating a contagious tendency for further neglect of payments discipline. Being, at least to some extent, a product of the restrictive policies followed, the growing inter-enterprise indebtedness in fact undermined the real impact of these policies, swelling the money supply in an uncontrolled and chaotic way.

That phenomenon seems to reflect the crucial differences that still exist between a normal market economy and the present situation in Czechoslovakia. By contrast with market economies, the microeconomic conditions for maintaining a close link between M ("core" money) and the overall money supply are still not sufficiently satisfied.

Neither banks nor suppliers generally took action, including bankruptcy procedures, against defaulting clients, even if there was a valid legal basis. Given the existing circumstances, including lack of loan-loss provisions and rather low ratios of own capital to assets, most commercial banks appeared in fact to depend on the survival of their important clients.[14] Similarly, because of the extent of the payments crisis, many firms could hardly find any non-defaulting clients.[15]

It is the huge extent of payments arrears, high proportion and persistence of insolvency cases, coupled with a wide range of feedbacks, that make the problem qualitatively different from the situation in developed market economies and, consequently, so difficult to tackle.

This state of affairs, softening the impact of potential competition and encouraging economic agents to revert to "traditional" channels, is evidently a major barrier to restructuring. The main underlying reason is the inertia found in a non-standard environment, and the non-standard behaviour of economic agents, by comparison with a market-type economy.

To summarise, foreign competition is certainly indispensable for creating a competitive environment in the transitional economies. However, under present conditions in Czechoslovakia, and given the collapse of traditional Eastern markets for manufactures, and the implied "comparative advantage" of cheap labour,[16] accentuated by the massive devaluations of the koruna in 1990, the pressure of foreign competition tends rather to prolong a trend towards "regressive speciali- sation". It implies a shift to lower value-added products, where price and cost competition dominate. The desirable trend should be, however, the reverse. The negative implications of moving to the lower value-added products include the threat of a brain-drain and of an increasing technological gap in the world

---

14) There is, however, a discernible effort to change the situation, under the guidance of the Central Bank. E.g. the Commercial Bank, the largest in Czechoslovakia, succeeded in increasing its capital/assets ratio from 1.7 per cent in 1990 to 5.8 per cent toward the end of 1991. At the same time it managed to allocate Kcs 5.8 bn for loans-loss provisions. (Source: Commercial Bank, Annual Report 1991.)

15) Along with severely contracting domestic demand the phenomenon of increasing insolvency thus hits even the companies with technically advanced products which have good chances to be competitive under the stabilised conditions. An example is the famous off-road truck manufacturer, Tatra Kopřivnice. Domestic demand for its products decreased by a half and, at the same time, solvent clients represented only about 20 per cent of the current diminished demand.

16) The price of labour in dollars appears extremely low, average wages of a qualified worker amounting to less than $ 200 per month.

economy. By contrast, the successful cases of revitalisation elsewhere have been based on narrowing this gap.

A controversial issue in the discussion appears to be how far the trends described are a realistic reflection of reality (however unfavourable they may appear for a once well-developed economy), or whether they represent a distorted picture because of a number of short-term factors. In the latter case, temporary protection and export promotion measures would be justified. They could contribute to the "revitalisation" of the branches and firms which are potentially viable in the medium run but which need a certain "breathing space" and support for adjustment.

4.4 Financial intermediation and competition

A number of observers stress that progress in developing factor markets, their timely introduction and proper functioning, are of crucial importance for the success of the entire transition.[17] A flexible financial intermediation allows mobility of resources among possible options, channelling them to more productive use both in time and space. Consequently, it is in fact a pre-condition for developing workable competition in the real sphere of the economy. Thus the restructuring of the financial system should not be left to later stages of transition, as is sometimes suggested; on the contrary it should be promoted as soon as possible. The apparent delays in that respect in Czechoslovakia, as well as in some other reforming countries, could thus have negative impacts on both the speed of transition and the costs involved.

The core of any financial system is smoothly functioning commercial banking. This is even more true for economies in transition, at least in the short- and medium-term; and non-bank financial intermediaries and markets for bonds and equities are likely to play an increasing role in the future.

---

[17] A seminal paper by Hinds, M. (1990) is particularly revealing in that respect.

There are many signs that in spite of the considerable legal and institutional changes effected,[18] the banking system in Czechoslovakia is still rather under-developed. While routine banking services are often deficient and tardy, and the range of products and services provided for their clients is broadening only slowly, commercial banks maintain wide borrowing-lending spreads and as a rule achieve more than normal banking profits. This implies that competition inside the banking sphere must be weak, if it exists at all.

The main constraint does not seem to be either the number of operating banks, or the hindrances to new entrants. Since the move to a two-tier banking system in 1989, the number of commercial banks increased almost dramatically; against 7 operating at the beginning of 1990, towards the end of 1991 there were already 41, including joint-venture banks and subsidiaries of foreign banks. The new banking law also allows for branches of foreign banks to be established and gives them the same "national" treatment as domestic banks. Any new entrant into banking is, however, subject to approval by the Central Bank and Ministry of Finance; for dealing in foreign exchange transactions a licence must be obtained. The conditions for entry are transparent enough (minimal capital endowment, technical and institutional preconditions) and should not imply any unnecessary barrier.[19]

It is true that the shares of newly created domestic banks and of foreign banks in both credits and deposits are still rather low, even if increasing (see *Tables 4.3* and *4.4*). The "big" banks are mostly those which inherited their port-folios from the "monobank" system, the only exception so far being Agrobank.

The tables show a trend towards a rather more equal distribution between the big banks of both credits and deposits since the end of 1990. This is partly

---

[18] The introduction of a two-tier system in 1989; new laws on the Central Bank and on Banking entering into force in February 1992 set a legal framework for banking activities comparable with that in advanced market economies.

[19] The capital adequacy requirement for new banks (8 per cent of assets) could, of course, prove a restraint on establishment of new banks, and particularly on development of their activities. It is, however, introduced in accordance with international standards and with BIS recommendations, ensuring confidence and creditworthiness in the banking system.

Table 4.3

Distribution of credits across "big" banks in the CSFR
(per cent of total bank credits)

	31.12.1990	30.6.1991	31.12.1991	29.2.1992
Commercial Bank, Prague	47.8	29.7	26.4	26.5
General Credit Bank, Bratislava	20.1	20.5	14.5	14.7
Investment Bank	14.6	14.5	14.8	15.0
Czechoslovak Trade Bank	5.1	7.9	7.9	7.4
Agrobank	1.6	2.0	2.9	3.1
Czech Savings Bank	6.7	7.4	9.2	9.9
Slovak Savings Bank	3.6	3.3	4.3	4.6
Consolidation Bank	–	12.1	15.7	14.3
Total big banks	99.5	97.4	95.7	95.5
Other banks	0.5	2.6	4.3	4.5

due to the provision of the Competition Protection Act[20] defining monopoly and dominant positions, and reflected in the new Banking Law, under which no bank must hold more than 30 per cent share of credits or deposits. (Although the law provides a three-year interval for compliance, in fact only one bank exceeds this limit – deposits in the Czech Savings Bank.)

The development seems also to confirm that the genuine barriers to competitive behaviour are hardly to be found in existing market shares. In contemporary conditions some "big" banks are evidently needed and desirable, and suggestions to increase competitive pressures by splitting existing big banks would be misplaced.

---

[20] Law No. 63/1991, became effective in February 1991.

Table 4.4

Distribution of deposits across "big" banks in the CSFR
(per cent of total bank deposits)

	31.12.1990	30.6.1991	31.12.1991	29.2.1992
Commercial Bank, Prague	17.5	14.7	17.8	16.9
General Credit Bank, Bratislava	7.9	6.7	8.0	6.8
Investment Bank	8.9	7.4	7.0	8.4
Czechoslovak Trade Bank	2.7	4.7	4.1	3.8
Agrobank	0.4	0.6	0.9	1.0
Czech Savings Bank	42.3	40.8	39.0	38.5
Slovak Savings Bank	20.0	18.6	17.4	16.9
Consolidation Bank	–	3.2	3.2	3.1
Total big banks	99.7	96.7	97.4	95.4
Other banks	0.3	3.3	2.6	4.6

A more serious constraint seems to be a certain inertia in segmenting banking activities, both by function and geographically. Even if the law provides for a universal type of bank, including both commercial and investment activities, traditional financial circuits still dominate the activities of the individual banks: savings banks take care of households and their deposits, commercial banks provide services to firms; and some licensed banks include foreign exchange transactions. The foreign banks have also been developing their activities rather cautiously, restricting themselves mostly to specialised foreign exchange and international services for multinationals and foreign firms, but not moving into retail banking in any substantial way.

A process of de-specialisation and integration of various financial circuits is taking place, at least to some extent: savings banks move into commercial business, while commercial banks develop household deposits. But several obstacles render the process rather slow.

A parallel constraint on competition is territorial fragmentation, between the Czech and Slovak republics, as well as between various regions. Especially the newly created banks have only a limited branch network or none at all. Consequently, outside the main centres, and particularly in some regions, there has been hardly any expansion of choice. At the present stage, the development of a competitive environment in banking is also constrained by technical barriers (e.g. without an inter-bank clearing system working in real time, it is hardly possible to deal in "hot" daily money), as well as by lack of qualified personnel, particularly for foreign exchange transactions.

However important the above barriers really are, the crucial structural constraints on radical change in competitive behaviour lie in the undercapitalisation of the banks, coupled with the inert weight of bad and non-performing loans in their portfolios and with the vast extent of inter-enterprise indebtedness. These are mostly inherited from the past and in fact lock the banks into "traditional" methods, preventing them from acting as real commercial banks.

The options suggested for coping with these weaknesses include: currency reform; cancellation of past loans entirely or partially either by direct recapitalisation of the banks or by a debt-for-equity swap; the spontaneous "solution" of a high inflation rate; or solution by privatisation.

Government policy in Czechoslovakia, ruling out currency reform and erosion of the existing money balances through hyperinflation, and trying also to avoid increasing the state debt, relied on privatisation. Contrary to expectation, however, privatisation proved a long-term process. Under the pressure of growing financial disarray, two interim measures were taken by the authorities to alleviate the situation and to strengthen banks' balance sheets:

(i) In March 1991 a Consolidation Bank was created to take over from the commercial banks a large share of "perpetual credits for inventories". These were hardly credits at all, as only a very low rate of interest and no fixed maturity were set.

(ii) In October 1991 a partial recapitalisation was decided for four big commercial banks which inherited their portfolio from the "monobank system". By a debt-for-equity swap (at the cost of privatised property) an amount of Kcs 50 bn was allocated: Kcs 12 bn directly to the banks and Kcs 38 bn for writing-off the loans of those firms which, after the bail-out, have good prospects for survival and to which the commercial banks would be ready to extend new credits.

4.5 In conclusion

Workable competition, providing incentives to adjust for all economic agents, should become a main driving force in revitalising the former centrally planned economies. In developing such a system of workable competition in the transition period, both foreign competition, and the establishment of effective financial circuits, are expected to play substantial roles. Experience confirms, however, that their impacts cannot be made effective enough, given the inherited environment in the domestic economy.

The crucial factor is a fundamental change in the behaviour pattern of economic agents – a change in their experience, interests and expectations. But these microeconomic changes are feasible only in an adequate macroeconomic setting. It follows that a radical macroeconomic alleviation of the existing financial disarray (inter-enterprise indebtedness, non-performing loans in banks balance sheets) must be effected in parallel with microeconomic and institutional reforms, if the aim of a decisive change of regime is to become a reality.

References

Hinds, M. (1990), "Issues in the Introduction of Market Forces in Eastern European Socialist Economies", *World Bank Seminar Paper*, IIASA, Laxenburg, March.

Kolanda, M., Kubišta, V. (1990), *Costs, performance and behaviour of the Czechoslovak manufacturing enterprises on the world markets in the 1980s*, Institute of Forecasting, Prague.

Pick, M. (1990), *Productivity, purchasing power parity and rate of exchange*, Institute of Forecasting, Prague.

Portes, R. (1991), Introduction to *European Economy*, Special Edition, No. 2.

Schumpeter, J. (1966), *Capitalism, Socialism, and Democracy*, London, p. 58.

Zemplinerová, A. (1989), *Monopoly in centrally planned economy*, Institute of Economics, Prague.

Chapter 5

PRIORITIES OF THE CZECHOSLOVAK ANTI-TRUST OFFICE

Imrich Flassik[*]

5.1 Functions of the Competition Office

The Federal Office for Economic Competition has been established as the central office in the administration of the CSFR for support and protection of competition (by constitutional law No. 296/1990). The activities of the Office have been defined by the Law on competition protection (No. 63/1991), which came into force on 1 March 1991. Today, the office has 70 employees. Of the university-educated staff 50 per cent are lawyers and 50 per cent economists.

The decision-making activity of the office focuses on issues of monopoly or dominant positions, investigation of cartel agreements and approvals of mergers. In the present transition to a market economy, all these activities have great significance, but coping with dominant or monopoly positions is a priority. The reason is that the Czechoslovak economy entered the transition period with a great number of enterprises in monopoly or dominant positions. Inadequate supplies and poor selection of goods and services, at prices available to most citizens, create favourable conditions for enterprises and entrepreneurs to misuse their market positions.

Foreign companies participating in mergers often demand conditions for the establishment of joint ventures that they would never dare to expect in their home countries.They look for certain concessions for the protection of their desired markets, such as customs privileges, taxation relief, etc. The foreign partners in the joint ventures seem surprised by the reaction of the office and by its rights it has, though in their home countries they would not behave in this way.

---

[*] Chairman of the Czechoslovak Federal Competition Office. In Dr. Flassik's absence, the paper was presented to the workshop by Ivan Kalina.

The same applies to the managements of our own companies and even to some economic functionaries. At the same time, as a new institution working under the new conditions, we find it quite complicated to devise proper measures for the necessary and justified strict adherence to the law. But if we demand too severe terms, we may discourage many foreign investors; that would restrict the creation of the competitive environment, affecting particularly the future relaxation of protectionist measures in relation to the EC.

To cope with misuse of a monopoly position we need the support of the disadvantaged entrepreneurs. Their wish to cooperate with us is, for the time being, weak, because strong links between customers and suppliers, or dependence on the central suppliers, still persist. This is the consequence of the weak competitive environment.

Certain phenomena from the previous economic system still exist and the producers take them for granted, though they discriminate against the consumer. There is, for example, the practice of "tied sales". Our consumer is still placed at a disadvantage by insufficient choice of competitive products and services. At present there is no competition for many products. There are still barriers – economic, administrative and legislative – to entry to the market by other entrepreneurs. Our consumer in many cases does not provide enough stimulation for further dynamic development of production. The monopoly producers extort conditions which they would not dare to attempt in conditions of fully functioning competition. The consumer himself, and also producers who lack stimulation for development, pay for this.

For these reasons, discovering misuse of dominant or monopoly positions in the transition period has the highest priority. These issues may be illustrated by the following cases dealt with by our office.

5.2 Case studies in competition control

We see the solution of the present unfavourable situation in our *domestic car industry* as lying first of all in abolishing the 15 per cent (or 10 per cent) import tax and in encouraging competition. The office was absolutely opposed to the 15 per cent import tax. From a competitive point of view, this tax is unwarranted for domestic producers – mainly the producers of personal cars. In many cases, it has removed the only competition that existed in the CSFR. The purposeful

74

support of competition provided by the office could have been considered as the best service that could be offered to customers and distributors. However, the standpoint of the office has not been accepted, because of the disapproval and opposition of the Federal Ministry of Finance. But the office managed to get customs tariffs reduced on the import of new personal cars, which we consider a success.

The office pronounced against the state enterprise *Mototechna* Prague, for the misuse of its dominant position in the market by selling certain products only in sets, although this was not justified either technologically or commercially. It concerned for example padding sets, wheel covers and brake tubes. This kind of activity (tied sales) was forbidden by the office. Thus customers are protected and are not forced to buy products that they do not want.

The office has also forbidden misuse of the dominant position of the *Liquor Distillery in Boškov*, which used to sell the liqueur "Fernet Stock" on condition of buying other kinds of spirits produced by its distillery. Such activity raised distributors' costs for buying the popular Fernet Stock and customers were forced to buy other less favoured and even more expensive liquors. In this case it was necessary to investigate substitutability. We realised by interviewing customers that Fernet Stock is not replaceable by any other kind of spirit from the point of view of the distributor.

Our office acted in the case of the *Skloobal Nemšová* company. By misuse of their dominant position they forced customers to purchase unsuitable goods (bottles that could not be used in time for production) and demanded price changes in spite of valid contracts.

We have forbidden the cartel agreement on prices between *ČSA Prague* and *Slov-air Bratislava*. Those airlines reached an agreement on uniform prices for comparable lines and thus substantially eliminated competitive pricing. At the same time they caused a disservice to consumers by providing services of different quality. On the other hand we approved the cartel agreement between these airlines for unified trade conditions linked with the IATA international regulations. We judged in this case that the agreement does not create a disservice to consumers.

The office approved the *EuroTel Joint Ventures* between SPT Prague, SPT Bratislava and Atlantic West Amsterdam. In both ventures, SPT took advantage of its monopolistic position in concluding the agreements; restrictive clauses restrained other entrepreneurs from entering the relevant market for radio-telephone services and data networks, for periods of 20 and 10 years, which exceeded the terms of the licences. Approval of the agreement was given by the Federal Competition Office but on condition that the parties to the agreement will not act on the clauses just mentioned.

In the investigation of the position of the company *Škoda Mladá Boleslav* in the market for automobile materials, this enterprise notified our office that it was unable to state its market share. Hence the office made its own calculation to determine its jurisdiction and the grounds for approving or disapproving the merger between *Škoda and Volkswagen*. In spite of the merger definition and entrepreneurs' obligations under the Competition Protection Act, and in spite of the explicit direction that entrepreneurs must apply for approval of mergers, Škoda did not ask our office for approval until eight months after the agreement was concluded. Before the agreement was approved, there were many unsupported opinions, and accusations of offences by various public functionaries. But the office insisted on following the principles and procedures established by the law, and it succeeded. At present the office is investigating whether the price rises of 9 per cent from 1 March 1992 should be considered misuse of a dominant position (88 per cent market share in the Czech Republic and 97 per cent in the Slovak Republic).

There were similar problems concerning the merger between *Avia-Liaz* and *Mercedes Benz* now awaiting agreement. Again, the domestic management tried to prevent the office from acquiring the relevant information. Some ministries supported an interpretation of the law that would prevent our office from requesting any important documents from the entrepreneur; and suggested that if we were to request documents, the entrepreneur was free to decide whether or not to release the relevant information.

Publication of the Škoda case in the press caused a major change in the attitudes of most entrepreneurs to our office. Obstructions and never-ending polemics about interpretation of the term "merger" have been fully resolved. On a positive note, we have received many letters of thanks from many consumers.

Concerning the approval of the *EuroTel* merger (SPT Prague, SPT Bratislava, Atlantic West Amsterdam), the Federal Competition Office prepared information for the Government of the CSFR. On that basis, the government charged the services of the Minister of Communications and Telecommunications with preparing a draft on restructuring the monopolistic enterprises concerned. The preconditions for competition in the sphere of telecommunications services will then exist and we hope that the entire sphere of telephone charges will be clarified and that the way will be open for progressive modernisation of telecommunications.

5.3 Conclusion

This paper is a brief introduction to the activities of our office so far completed; more than 45 decisions have been made. Most of them are enforceable by law and demonstrate our efforts to improve the protection of citizens/consumers.

The main feature of first year's performance of the Federal Competition Office is its endeavour to protect the economy against the excessive concentration of economic power in the hands of producers. The fewer the producers supplying the market with certain goods, the greater the danger that they behave to the detriment of consumers. And that is why we intend to support economic transformation by an antimonopoly policy that secures the creation of an active and fully-operational market comprising guaranteed competition and, above all, the strongest possible protection of the consumer.

Chapter 6

PROMOTING COMPETITION IN HUNGARY

Péter Pogácsás[*)]
János Stadler[*)]

We review in this paper two main influences on development of competition in Hungary: change in the macroeconomy; and the new legislation on competition.

6.1 Change in the macroeconomy

By the end of 1991 it became clear that fundamental changes had taken place in most sectors of the Hungarian economy. The shortage economy – which had dominated preceding decades – was over; the profit motive, and, often, the pressure of competition, emerged.

The evolution of competition was determined by external factors, both by economic policy decisions and by the restructuring of economic units. We will present the macroeconomic processes grouped under five heads:

(a) market change
(b) price and import liberalisation
(c) privatisation and capital inflow
(d) economic legislation and deregulation
(e) the state of the market and the laws regulating it.

(a) Market change

In 1990 and 1991, trade among East European countries collapsed. The share of ex-CMEA countries in Hungary's foreign trade fell from 45 per cent in 1988 to about 20 per cent by the end of 1991. Companies earlier producing for Eastern countries tried to sell most of their products on the domestic market but

---

[*)]   Hungarian Competition Office, Budapest.

in quantities, quality, composition and price-level which could not meet current demand patterns.

At the same time domestic demand diminished considerably, retail trade turnover falling in 1991 by 29 per cent.

In such an epoch-marking change-over it necessarily happens that entrepreneurs miscalculate demand for some products, which contributes to the imbalances.

Some of the products accumulated could, however, be shifted to non-CMEA markets; exports to OECD countries increased in 1991 by 31 per cent, which means that Hungarian goods face harder international competition.

(b) Price and import liberalisation

In the early 1970s, for only 20-25 per cent of products were prices determined by the market without state intervention; by the early 1980s, the proportion rose to 45-50 per cent; at present (early 1992) 90 per cent of prices are free.

Price liberalisation was accompanied by serious economic and social tension. This also reflected the effect of other important policy instruments, such as the reduction or elimination of subsidies; the interaction of external and internal market prices, etc. The government has attempted to harmonise import liberalisation, changes in economic equilibrium and price liberalisation,

For a small country like Hungary competition from imports must play a decisive role in breaking down monopolistic and dominant positions. But because the balance of payments was in continuous deficit due to the country's indebtedness, imports could not be liberalised until 1989, when it was carried out in three stages: in the first phase technological and machinery imports, in the second phase raw materials and semi-finished products, and in the third consumer goods.

The degree of import liberalisation can be measured by the percentage of items of industrial production open to imports: 1989: 42, 1990: 66, 1991: 72, 1992: 90.

For some imports of consumer goods a global quota is in force; this increased from $ 200 mn in 1990 to $ 750 mn in 1992 while the number of products falling under the quota is continuously decreasing. In 1973, Hungary joined the GATT and, as a result, import duties were reduced. By 1989 and 1990 the average level of duties was 13 per cent; thus import liberalisation was accompanied by parallel tariff reductions: so that in a relatively short time Hungarian companies confronted keen competition on domestic markets.

The collapse of CMEA trade, the restrictive economic policy including cuts in price subsidies, the decline of demand and increasing import competition radically changed the economic environment for Hungarian companies and plunged many of them into a hopeless situation. Competition is intensified, too, because some energy-intensive metallurgical and building materials flow in from the ex-socialist countries at low prices which continue in these countries as a result of state aids, low energy costs etc.

At the end of 1990, the procedures for dumping and market-protecting measures were revised. A committee was set up which can impose anti-dumping duties or extra duties or import quotas. (For such extra duties the approval of the president of the Competition Office is also necessary.)

(c) Privatisation and capital inflow

The economic reforms, which began as early as 1968, gave Hungarian companies considerable independence, further enlarged in the 1980's. These fundamental changes led to shrinking markets for most companies, many of them running into debt. The way out for the company is to be bought up by a foreign investor well provided with capital and marketing outlets. Political and social changes made private ownership possible and desirable, and coincided with strong economic pressures on the individual companies. This created a certain competition for the inflow of real capital.

To canalise the process, the State Property Agency (SPA) was set up at the beginning of 1990 with the aim of selling state assets by applying several privatisation methods and by trying to resolve the contradiction between quick sales and maximum income. The Agency obtained $ 140 mn in 1990 and $ 500 mn in 1991 from the sale of companies, 85 per cent of the receipts being in hard currency in both years. (In 1990 20 per cent of the income, in 1991 more than half of it, was spent directly on redeeming state debt.)

Hungarian privatisation is based on selling firms at market value. Because of the shortage of domestic capital, foreign investors far surpass Hungarian capitalists. On the basis of two years' experience is appears that foreign capital invested in Hungary went mostly into companies with steady markets, which generally means firms having dominant or monopolistic positions within the country. Fields affected in the first place are infrastructural services, building materials, the paper and food industries and firms well implanted in retail chains promising quick returns.

Although there have also been big investments in other manufacturing branches subject to keen competition, experience shows that if high technology is necessary, Western firms prefer new investments to participation in old companies with obsolete machinery (e.g. the Suzuki, OPEL and FORD automobile manufacturing projects).

Privatisation is a non-recurrent event allowing competition to be promoted, by breaking down market concentration, simultaneously with ownership changes. Sales of huge companies, or of complete branches with high market shares or natural monopolies, made clear the necessity for institutional safeguarding of competition during privatisation. The Guidelines on Property Policy issued in 1990 oblige the State Property Agency to consult the Competition Office when a company with a dominant position (i.e. having more than 30 per cent market share) is to be sold.

By contrast with the mechanism in Poland and Germany, the president of the Hungarian Competition Office only has the right to give his opinion about proposed sales. This is partly because Hungary's domestic market is smaller and imports might result in striking differences between dominant position and market power; but also because competition is only one of the several aspects that the SPA must consider. A situation often arises in which the State Property Agency ought to reject a quick deal promising a favourable price as against a precarious privatisation possibility at an unfavourable price but which would promote competition. In spite of earlier expectations, it became clear in practice that privatisation of a monopolistic or dominant position cannot be prevented on the basis of the merger rules of the Competition Law, since the law applies only if increased market concentration is envisaged. But in most privatisation cases, only the owner changes while the degree of concentration remains unaltered.

By the end of 1991, $ 2.8 bn of working capital flowed into Hungary of which $ 1.4 bn in 1991. Almost 80 per cent of foreign capital was invested in industry.

(d) Economic legislation

The radical political and economic transformation is accompanied by a legislative process without precedent in Hungary, designed to lay foundations for the new system in all fields of society and the economy. Following the reforming efforts of the previous regime, the first serious step was the enactment of the Company Law at the beginning of 1988. In addition to the general state-owned companies and cooperatives covered by earlier legislation, this law introduced classifications and rules for joint-stock companies, limited liability companies, limited and unlimited partnerships, associations and joint ventures. The so-called Transformation Law enacted one year later allowed state-owned companies to become joint-stock, limited companies, etc., and in the course of transformation to seek external capital.

Making use of the opportunities opened by these two Laws, existing small companies reorganised themselves, state-owned companies divided into smaller units and other organisational changes took place. This led to a real entre-preneurial boom in Hungary. The number of economic units with a legal entity grew from 10,800 at the end of 1988 to 13,500 by the end of 1989, to 27,600 by the end of 1990, and to 47,000 by the end of 1991. From 450 in 1989 the number of limited companies increased to almost 40,000 by the end of 1991.

According to a Government decree, by the 31 December 1992 all state-owned companies have to be transformed into a form of economic organisation stipulated by the Company Law.

The Law on Foreign Investments in Hungary (1988) provides full protection and security for investments of foreigners and guarantees that both profits and invested capital can be freely repatriated in the currency of the investor.

The so-called Deregulatory Law (1990) was indispensable: it declared invalid all laws and decrees of the previous system which might block the development of private ownership and the market economy.

A group of bills awaits action by Parliament to harmonise the provisions of laws related to privatisation. Accordingly, one more organisation, the State Trustee Shareholding Company, will be set up to manage assets remaining in state ownership (totally or by majority holding), although some of these properties may be sold in due course, some will remain more or less under state control indefi-nitely.

In 1991, Parliament enacted the Concession Law determining to what state or local authority monopolies the state or the municipality can give concession rights. This law determines only the framework for concession agreements: giving it concrete shape will be the task of branch laws to be framed later.

In 1990 a legal and institutional framework was created for a Stock Exchange and trade in securities. The Hungarian Stock Exchange was then launched – another facet of market economics, and an example of concentrated competition. Unfortunately, high interest rates hinder investment in securities, so that the Stock Exchange could not yet play the important part intended for it in restructuring of capital and in privatisation.

The Law on Banking Institutions (1991) lays down general rules for the share of reserves to be held by banks, methods of qualifying outstanding credits and debts, and ownership conditions for banks; and provides that by 1997 state shares in the crucial Hungarian commercial banks must be reduced to 25 per cent. Liberalisation of competition in banking is however withheld to a certain extent since so much debt accumulated in the past remains on the books.

(e)   The state of the market and the laws regulating it

As already observed, in place of the earlier excess demand, diverse pressures have not only created buyers' markets in most sectors of the economy, but have sometimes created such huge surpluses that suppliers may be forced to take steps which they would not normally consider. At best they may be induced to penetrate export markets, but they could also be led to reduce capacities (mainly in fields like building materials and the food industry) or to ask for market-protecting measures from the authorities.

In this difficult situation many of the state-owned companies use the opportunities provided by the Transformation and Company Laws to found affiliated private companies out of their divisions; the former company centre continues to function as a holding company. Although the number of market actors can be multiplied in this way, the degree of concentration in the branch has not in fact changed.

The government's industrial policy may also affect concentration. In Hungary – as in other East European countries – limitation of the economic role of the state, and the transformation of the institutional structure of individual branches, are realised simultaneously through privatisation. In connection with sales decisions of the State Property Agency, there have been efforts to ensure that before actual privatisations the Ministry of Industry and Commerce should assert the viewpoints of industrial and competition policy.

The Ministry of Industry and Commerce encourages partitioning: factory units, using the provisions of the Transformation Act, can become separate entities while remaining in state ownership. (In 1991 out of 100 such applications, in more than 70 the Ministry approved the state company's proposal to partition its production and sales units.)

A third factor affecting market structure, concentration, and consequently competition, is the proliferation of new enterprises. Though the laws on Private Enterprises etc. were not followed by significant tax reductions, or other reliefs necessary to support new entrepreneurs, there has been a rising trend in the number of small businesses:

Table 6.1

Hungary: Number of economic organisations by size[a]

Number of employees		1989	1990	1991
More than	300	2617	2599	2380
	50-300	3460	4469	5257
	21-50	2387	4129	5907
Less than	20	5105	16465	33550
Total		13569	27662	47094

a) Legal entities with economic activities, whether state-owned or private, excluding individual entrepreneurs.

The number of employees of small and medium-size enterprises, together with "individual entrepreneurs" (300-400 thousand), represents 42 per cent of the total labour force – but their share in exports was less than 10 per cent (1990).

In spite of these facts, the degree of company concentration in Hungary has hardly changed in recent years. The share of the big old companies in production and consumption is still decisive for several reasons:

- In many cases production capacities exceed the size of the Hungarian market. (This will not change if a big company is split up into smaller companies.)
- The steep decline in demand does not necessarily change the companies' market shares;
- In certain industries, privatisation leaves company sizes unchanged.

However, although market shrinkage and increasing competition did not affect the degree of concentration, the market power of the huge companies weakened, and many of them became vulnerable.

At the end of 1990, the Hungarian Parliament, after several years of preparation, passed the Competition Law, to be discussed below. Although the legislators kept in view markets with excess demand, they tried to frame a law which is also effective in a market of oversupply. However, the transition period often puts the administrators of the law in a dilemma.

A Consumer Protection Law is to be expected in the near future. Some of its provisions relating to unfair market activities are also included in the Competition Law. Legislation will certainly accentuate the differences between the interests of individual consumers and the common interest of fair competition.

Many experts think that a Chamber Law is necessary to regulate the self-organising activities of market actors. In advanced economies, rules of proper conduct are to a large extent set and regulated by professional associations and legally organised mutual interest groups.

6.2 Outline of competition law

Preparations to organise a competition office and to draft a Competition Law were initiated in about 1987 and continued for three years until the Law on Prohibition of Unfair Market Practices entered into force on 1 January 1991; the Hungarian Competition Office – the Office for Economic Competition – began to operate at the same time. This well-prepared and well-managed action – so rare today in Central and Eastern Europe – resulted in transforming the Price Office into a real Antitrust body. After more than a full year, experience shows that the Competition Law is an effective instrument, and the performance of the new Competition Office in enforcing the Law has been improving continuously. So the tools of competition policy have been created and can be used to shape the Hungarian market economy.

We will indicate the main characteristics of the Hungarian Competition Law and Competition Office.

The Competition Law:

A general clause (para 3 of the Competition Law) declares that (i) "entrepreneurs are required to respect the freedom and fairness of economic competition", (ii) "it shall be unlawful to engage in unfair economic activity, including in particular, any conduct that offends or jeopardises the legitimate interest of consumers or is contrary to the requirements of fair business practices".

Western observers have criticised this paragraph, because, by defining the aim of the Law, it also extends its scope to certain activities not covered by other paragraphs. Nevertheless, this general clause cannot be waived since the transformation process very often produces abrupt situations which cannot be dealt with by legislation but which can appropriately be treated juridically.

In cases of unfair competition practices such as damage to reputation, abuse of business secrecy, boycotting, appropriation of trade names, speculative withholding of commodities from sale, tying the sale of one commodity to the purchasing of another, and frauds in biddings, tenders, auctions and stock exchange deals, the Competition Office is entitled only to investigate while judgement is reserved for the competent court.

In cases of deceiving the consumer (i.e. false information about products, deceitful description of goods and services concealing failure of the product to meet standards, misleading labelling and publicity) the interested individuals and legal persons can choose between submitting a complaint to the Competition Office or suing the producer/distributor at the Court of Justice.

The Competition Law lays down a general prohibition of agreements restricting or excluding competition (price-fixing, market-sharing, choice limitation, etc. discriminating restrictions or exclusions), but exempts from prosecution agreements which aim at stopping the abuse of a dominant position (i.e. monopoly) or where the concomitant advantages outweigh the disadvantages.

86

According to the Law, favourable prices, improvements in quality, distribution/ delivery terms and technical progress might be claimed as advantages. On the other hand, it should be regarded as disadvantageous if the participants' joint share exceeds 30 per cent of the relevant market.

If the parties to a proposed agreement consider that it might violate the Competition Law by being regarded as a cartel agreement, they may ask the Competition Office for preliminary approval.

Monopolies cannot be prosecuted as such under the Competition Law, since only *abuse* of a dominant position can be unlawful. (The Law sets guide lines for defining possible "dominant positions" and "abuses".) The basic philosophy is that either sellers or buyers can be in a dominant position, if one party is forced to buy from, or sell to, the other party; but the abuse must always be proved.

The Hungarian Competition Office has a supervisory role for mergers and fusions of companies. Preliminary permission of the Office is obligatory if the joint market share of applicants in the previous year exceeds 30 per cent, or if their joint overall turnover in the same period was more than Ft 10 billion ($ 125 mn). Mergers cannot be authorised if they could impair competition, but even mono- polistic positions might be acceptable if economical advantages outweigh disadvantages (e.g. help entry into international trade).

In the light of the antitrust regulations in most industrially developed coun- tries, the acquisition of Hungarian assets by foreign companies in the course of privatisation should be regarded as mergers. According to the Hungarian Competition Law, mergers need the authorisation of the Competition Office only if they increase the degree of concentration; in most cases the foreign company wholly or partly replaces the Hungarian owner (the State), so instead of an official procedure the privatisation depends on the decision of the State Property Agency alone.

The Competition Office:

The Hungarian Office for Economic Competition is an independent state body, answerable exclusively to the Parliament. Its President and two Vice- Presidents are nominated for a six-year term by the President of the Republic, upon recommendations of the Prime Minister. The Office is funded from the State Budget. The Office has full competence to enforce the Competition Law *except* in banking, insurance and the security markets, which are all subject to a separate juridical entity, now being organised.

The Office has three main sections:

The *Board of Experts* is responsible for investigating cases; the expert in charge reports to the *Competition Council*, which acts as a special arbitration court, according to the rules for administrative courts. Hearings are held by a 3-member panel and the decision is enforceable. If violation of the Law is confirmed, the Competition Council may: announce the infringement; prohibit continuation of the illegal practices; assure the injured party that further illegal practices and damages will be blocked; impose fines up to twice the value of profits realised or of damages caused to competitors or consumers.

The third main section is the *Department of Competition Policy*, where theoretical issues are dealt with. If the Office serves as consultant to the government or the Parliament on questions of economic competition, the connected tasks are also carried out by this Department.

The Competition Office may either act on complaints from enterprises (entrepreneurs) or individuals, or may itself take the initiative. The Law sets deadlines: decisions in cartel cases must be made within 45 days, in merger cases in 90 days and in all other cases (the majority) in 60 days. Once the procedure has been started the Competition Office may extend the deadline by 45,180 or 60 days, respectively.

For violations of Chapter I (prohibition of unfair competition, paragraphs 4-10) the Competition Council is entitled to file a suit only at the competent Court of Justice.

If the decision of the Competition Council is not acceptable to any of the parties, they may sue the Competition Office at the competent Court. By the end of 1991, 12 decisions were contested: in three cases the judgements of the first instance Courts of Justice are available (in two the decision was overturned, in one approved).

In 1991, 176 cases were started by the Competition Office of which 71 reached the Competition Council – the real juridical stage. The decisions reached, by type of case, were as follows:

cartel cases:	violations	6,	acquitted	14
abuse of dominant position:	violations	12,	acquitted	15
merger control:	permitted	4,	refused	1
deception of the consumer:	violations	7,	acquitted	0
unfair marketing practices:	violations	6,	acquitted	6

We may now sum up the experience of the first year of operation of the Competition Law.

Because monopolistic positions and routine authoritarian behaviour are the disadvantageous legacies of the past, abuses of dominant positions are still very frequent in the former socialist economies. The rulings of the Competition Office inform the public about bad market habits, but the real remedy is real competition.

In this transformation period, the kind of anti-trust cases familiar in the West, such as cartel agreements, have not been frequent; the novelty of the new market structures created much uncertainty. Cartels are more characteristic of long-established and stable markets. Doubtful agreements may have been concluded before the new laws came into force. However, of the 17 investigations initiated by the Office only three resulted in confirming illegal practices.

Cases of consumer deception and unfair business practices were the most frequent sources of enforceable decisions. The reason is that the new markets create favourable conditions for unfair practices.

Breaches of contract and individuals' claims of injustice – as distinct from the laws promoting competition – are in the first place subject to civil law suits or to general measures for consumer protection. Competition Law could apply if the actions of certain entrepreneurs or industrial organisations indicated tendencies that could jeopardise fair competition to a serious extent; the procedures of the Competition Office should then be brought into play.

We conclude that the development of markets must always be in harmony with competition legislation and jurisdiction. Antitrust bodies like the Hungarian Competition Office must always keep watch over markets and the actors therein.

Chapter 7

CREATING A COMPETITIVE ENVIRONMENT IN RUSSIA

Ruben Yevstigneyev[*]

In Western societies more and more perfect forms and methods of competition have been elaborated; meanwhile the Soviet economy continued to function under all-embracing monopolism, leading towards a grandiose crisis of the socio-economic system.

A peculiarity of monopolistic structures in the USSR, as in all other communist countries, lay in the fact that these structures penetrated the economy both vertically and horizontally. On the one hand, the distribution of the plan targets and investments resulted from the bargains between the Centre and the ministries as well as between the ministries and the enterprises, the low-level units in their turn playing the role of a monopoly in relation to the higher-level ones. On the other hand, the strict attachment of each consuming firm to a supplying firms meant nothing else than converting each of them into a monopolist in relation to the other.

This organisational monopolism was added to a technological one, and their interaction strengthened them both. The technological monopolism is exhibited by a census taken by the State Commission on Statistics in 1989. According to the published data, in each of 209 out of 344 product groups the biggest enterprise produced more than 50 per cent of the total production and in 109 groups this figure exceeded 90 per cent.[1] Monopolistic production in the engineering industry approached 80 per cent of the whole volume (information of the former Gossnab). The Law of the Russian Federation "On Competition and Restriction of Monopolistic Activities in Commodity Markets" (March 1991)

---

[*] Deputy Director, Institute of International Economic and Political Studies, Academy of Sciences, Moscow.

[1] *Pravitelstveny vestnik*, No. 31, July 1991.

declared, in accordance with western standards, that a firm is not "monopolistic" if its share in the market falls below 35 per cent. A lengthy list of "monopolistic" enterprises, producing from 50 to 100 per cent of consumer goods in the Federation, has been published.[2]

At the same time so-called "economic monopoly", which "results from the competition in the market"[3], hardly exists yet in the country, but will inevitably appear in the process of economic reform. This kind of monopoly grows out of competition and assumes that innovation is proceeding.

7.1 The *perestroika* period – a variety of organisational forms

After 1985 the term "competition", after a gradual transition from the notion *sorevnovaniye*, has at last returned to our economic science. "It is becoming more and more evident" according to one recent author "that just a contradiction between monopolism and competition is the crucial point of the present *perestroika* of the economic mechanism. It is exactly this contradiction which leaves on the one side stagnation, parasitism, dictatorship and on the other side dynamic and efficient development of the society"[4].

In conformity with the strategic aim of creating a competitive environment in the USSR, simultaneous implementation of the following changes was announced: first, introduction of the most important market elements (modern tax, credit and price systems, convertibility of rouble etc.); second, creation of alternatives to state forms of business activities (leased firms, joint-stock companies, cooperatives, joint ventures, small enterprises, farms, commercial banks, commodity and stock exchanges). The proportions of different forms of business activity in the former USSR are given in *Table 7.1*.

Employment rose most rapidly in the leased firms and joint-stock companies as well as in different economic associations (concerns, amalgamations): the number employed there increased in 1991 compared to 1990 almost three times and approached 11 million.

---

[2]   *Ekonomika i zhiznj*, No. 24, 1991. Publication by State Commission on Statistics of Russia.

[3]   Yasin, Y., in *Planovoye chozyaistvo*, No. 1, 1990, p. 36.

[4]   Starodubrovskaya, I. (1990), *From Monopolism to Competition*, Moscow, pp. 52-53.

Table 7.1

Structure of employment by form of organisation
(former USSR)

	1990		1991	
	million	%	million	%
Total employment	**138.2**	**100.0**	**135.7**	**100.0**
of which –				
state-owned enterprises and organisations	108.8	78.7	98.9	72.9
enterprises on lease			9.0	6.6
joint-stock companies	} 3.8	2.7 {	1.0	0.7
economic associations				
(concerns, amalgamations)			0.7	0.5
public organisations (funds)	1.8	1.3	1.8	1.3
joint ventures	0.1	0.1	0.2	0.2
collective farmers and cooperative sector	18.8	13.6	17.6	13.0
of which –				
producer and service cooperatives	4.0	2.9	3.2	2.4
private and individual entrepreneurship	4.9	3.6	6.5	4.8
of which –				
farmers	0.1	0.1	0.2	0.2
individual subsidiary enterprises				
(homesteads)	4.6	3.3	4.6	3.4
individual entrepreneurship,				
contracts etc.	0.2	0.2	1.7	1.2

Source: Delovoy mir (Business World), 7 and 9 January 1992.

Leasing in service, retail trade and construction has embraced already more than a quarter of the total volume of production in these sectors. Nevertheless, the potential of this form has not been yet realised in full. The main reasons (not mentioning those which apply to the economy as a whole) are, first, the lack of an efficient mechanism of privatisation of the state property by redemption following leasing and, second, the resistance of ministries and local authorities which assumed the right to lease state property.

The fate of the *cooperatives* turned out to be rather complicated. The number of cooperatives, which came into existence as far back as 1988, i.e. before other non-state forms, increased 5.5 times during that year. High rates of growth continued in 1989 (increase of 115,600). But the next year the increase was only 52,200. And in the first half of 1991 the total number of cooperatives was reduced from 245,000 to 197,000. The number employed in them shrank from 6 to 5 million (partly because of transition to other forms of property, especially to joint-stock companies and the private sector). Why did this happen? Most of the cooperatives – 90 per cent – were established within state-owned enterprises, because otherwise they would lack raw materials and all the necessary facilities. One should keep in mind that the market infrastructure is still only in embryo in this country. But since the earnings of the workers in cooperatives were well above those in the state-owned firms, the doors were opened for converting "money into cash". Thus the cooperatives became a source of a surplus issue of money. That is why the authorities began to restrict the activities of the cooperatives in every way they could.

More than 4,200 *joint ventures* (most of them small, with about 10 billion roubles of fixed capital) were registered in the USSR by July 1991. One third of this capital then belonged to the foreign partners. Almost all the employees were Soviet citizens. The joint ventures are not yet very effective in our country. Suffice it to say that only one-third of them produce anything, and then not more than 0.4 per cent of total industrial output. Virtually, the joint ventures make no contribution to the modernisation of the enterprises and do nothing to promote application of new western technologies in industry. At the same time, the volume of exports by the joint ventures make up 1.4 per cent of total exports (2.1 per cent of imports). In the main, the joint ventures are concerned with the export of a few conventional foreign trade commodities. For instance, in the first half of 1991 the shares of the following commodities in the total exports of the joint ventures were: fish and other marine products – 19.3 per cent; oil and oil-products – 17.3 per cent; timber and paper – 7.1 per cent; ferrous metals – 5.6 per cent; aluminium – 5.1 per cent; raw leather – 3.4 per cent. In exchange they import mainly computers, radioelectronics, cars and other non-conventional items.

One of the most promising forms in our multi-form economy is the *small business*. In 1991 there were 15,900 small firms in industry with 1.2 million employed. They produced 4.2 per cent of total industrial output. In building, the share of small firms was 4.5 per cent; in trade – 0.3 per cent. It is significant that the Russian Union of Small Enterprises became at the beginning of 1992 a co-founder of the Euro-Asian League of small and medium firms, including firms from Russia, five newly independent states of our Commonwealth, as well as from Bulgaria, China, Poland and Czecho-Slovakia.

Potential *farmers* have had a very difficult starting point. First, the local authorities are generally most reluctant to give them convenient plots. Second, it is very difficult for them to get the necessary building materials, machines etc. Third, a serious problem has arisen of defending the farmers from racketeers. Nevertheless, by 1 March 1992 the number of homesteads in Russia came to 75,000, more than one third of them registered in January and February of that year. Each homestead occupies on the average 40 hectares. It is important to note that the process of converting collective and state farms into joint-stock companies, agricultural cooperatives and individual farms has at last started. During the first quarter of 1992 2,200 such enterprises (90 per cent) were re-registered.[5]

The soaring number of *commercial banks* in recent years has become a serious factor creating money and capital markets. In 1991 the number of these banks beat all world records, approaching 2,000 in USSR, including 1,500 on the territory of Russia. I believe this process is inevitable, although the number of commercial banks will shrink before long as a result of bankruptcies and fusions. The relations between the Central Bank and commercial banks are now very complicated. To my mind, both sides are responsible for this situation. The Central Bank of Russia tries by all means to restrict the independence of commercial banks (for example, in giving licences for hard currency operations); and the banks, in their turn, are reluctant in providing credits to producers, showing a preference for various commercial firms which are much more lucrative now.

Creating non-state economic structures is not a smooth process, for at least two reasons.

(a) In their attempts to find a way out of the crisis, the enterprises prefer to use not market, but, on the contrary, non-market measures, both conventional

---

[5]   *Nezavisimaya gazeta*, 10 March 1992.

and new ones. A typical example is given by "Uralmash", one of the largest monopolistic machine-building plants. In the course of transition to the market economy this giant has begun to experience many difficulties; but instead of adapting to them (by dividing into several units, partly leased or privatised) it continues to demand the differential preferences which were normal in recent years for all loss-making firms[6]. Among the new non-market measures the most typical are barter deals, which now also cover relations between the former CMEA countries, and "dollarisation" of trade within Russia and other former republics of the Soviet Union.

(b) The second reason that hindered the creation of non-state economic structures was macro-economic policy. V. Pavlov's "Anti-crisis programme" as well as N. Ryzhkov's "Stabilisation programme" did not in effect attempt to undermine the command model, though both of them used widely market language. Main attention was paid to the development of the basic branches of industry. The structural changes extended only to the conversion processes. The breaking of the cooperative links between enterprises formed as a result of the centrally organised distribution of all products, was seen as a tragedy. It was supposed to enhance prices and, accordingly, introduce a legitimate indexation of revenues (for the most part, administratively). V. Pavlov called it "a regulation of price liberalisation". The law permitted the introduction, step-by-step, of a private sector, but only as a supplement to the state sector, although everyone understands that a private enterprise is the most appropriate way to engage in market relations.

This policy did not hinder radical economic reform, but simply toppled down all the market elements, because the economy, unlike politics, does not tolerate compromises. The idea of "a third way" for the economy, and all other attempts to combine plan and market, lead to deadlock.

The policy of compromises did not allow the country to escape "shock therapy", but, on the contrary, brought it nearer. It was quite clear that any delay was fraught with a rapid rise in "the social price" of the economic reform. The authors of the "500 days" and the so-called Harvard programme, appearing just on the eve of the London meeting "7+1", realised this very well.

---

[6] *Izvestia*, 2 August 1991.

7.2 After August 1991 – slow progress towards privatisation

The Russian government of Yeltsin/Gaydar, found itself a hostage to the policies of the previous Soviet governments. Nevertheless, for the first time during the years of *perestroika*, it has dared to begin a real movement towards the market. The package of macroeconomic measures, the so-called "shock therapy", was unpopular to begin with, but the government had no reasonable alternative.

Public attention was led to focus on the problem of creating a competitive environment from the beginning of 1992. It was evident that the application of financial and monetary methods to overcome a deep economic collapse requires the simultaneous creation of competing economic agents. Their absence, certainly, was an essential factor in the huge price increases, unprecedented in post-communist countries, during the first month of the shock therapy. But their creation always and everywhere lags behind the formation of a market infrastructure. Thus a situation emerged in Russia when the monetary scalpel of a surgeon began to be used for operations when ruder instruments would have been more effective. Indeed, it was hardly possible to rely only on the scalpel in eliminating the budget deficit, slackening the pace of inflation, restraining the slump in production, and taking 90 per cent of the population out of poverty – to do all this while the economy remains heavily monopolised. That is why all efforts were then turned to speeding-up demonopolisation and to commercialisation and privatisation of state assets – that is, to creating economic agents adaptable to market methods.

We might remember that as far back as March 1991, before the USSR was broken up, Russia adopted a law "On Competition and Restriction of Monopolistic Activities in Commodity Markets". (It may be pointed out that this law was adopted exactly a hundred years after the Sherman Act – the first antimonopolistic law in the USA – was enacted). Despite the undoubted merits of the law, it could not come into force for the reasons mentioned above. Besides, because the Union treaty was not yet signed, the conflict between union and republican laws continued, involving the law just referred to and also the "Law on Restriction of Monopolistic Activities in the USSR".

After August 1991 many obstacles were removed from the operation of such Russian laws as those on enterprises and entrepreneurship, on property and the anti-monopolistic law referred to. The Committee for Anti-monopolistic Policy and Encouragement of New Economic Structures started its work at last.

The 4th session of the Supreme Soviet of the Russian Federation (January 1992) decided to put an end in the first place to the state trade monopoly, in which, in Yeltsin's words, "the interests of bureaucratic and criminal monopolies have all combined".[7] Under this decision, the so-called *torgi* (intermediate links between a wholesale base and a retail shop), which have hitherto distributed supplies and dictated prices to the shops, are to be liquidated. A retail shop, like any other enterprise, now has to become an independent juridical person dealing on its own with wholesale organisations and producers. Price rises have to be reduced from 25 per cent to 7-10 per cent, and shops will sell their goods for agreed prices.[8]

Demonopolisation in industry has now been put on the agenda. After the branch ministries were abolished various corporations and associations were established, but did not change the feudal relationships with their firms. On 20 January 1992, the Supreme Soviet adopted the branch and regional pro- grammes of demonopolisation for 1992-1993, envisaging the breaking up of most of the monopolies. Among them are mighty monopolists such as the Agroprom (often called an "AgroGULAG"), which has hitherto controlled the thousands of collective and state farms. Demonopolisation of other branches of the economy is also in preparation.

Control over large monopolistic enterprises was gained by a compulsory register of 1,700 enterprises whose activities exceed the limits of local markets, and many thousands which operated only in regional markets. All these enter- prises must declare any price increases (a tax on monopolistic profits is to be introduced shortly), record the volumes of their production to the State Statistical Committee and be responsible for the quality of their products in accordance with a recently drafted law on the defence of consumers' rights. Thus the Anti- monopolistic Committee will get control over the three main characteristics of

---

[7] *Rossiyskaja gazeta*, 17 January 1992.

[8] Ibid. In addition see the Decree by the President of the Russian Federation "On Free Trade" in *Rossiyskaja gazeta*, 1 January 1992.

monopolism: price, volume and quality. Certainly the elimination of monopolistic prices may not be achieved until the economy outlasts the all-pervasive shortages.

True, there is a danger that an antimonopolistic policy, in the above mentioned sense, could itself encourage the revival of command methods. One can see that the methods most likely to be used by the *apparatchiks* in their own interests still dominate the implementation of this policy. All sorts of restrictions and sanctions, up to forced disintegration of enterprises or forced sale of a part of their assets, can become just an administrative pressure on enterprises. Being cut off from the sphere of entrepreneurship, the struggle against monopolism could become mere camouflage.

Demonopolisation not accompanied by commercialisation (corporativisation) and not followed by privatisation, unfortunately, forces the government to retreat from the guidelines of the reform and to adopt decisions such as a recent decree "On Provisional Measures of special regulation of the business activities of the Monopolistic Enterprises in the first half of 1992 in the basic industrial branches" (27 February 1992), including in particular the establishment of marginal levels of profitability for individual branches. This is why privatisation has become the problem Number One for creating a competitive environment in Russia.

The first privatisation programme was adopted by the President and the Supreme Soviet on 29 December 1991. At the time of writing, it is too early to speak about the essential role of the private sector in the Russian economy. At the end of January 1992, the Government adopted decisions to accelerate the programme; the Presidential Decree was issued on the acceleration of privatisation of state and municipal enterprises, together with a package of rules for privatisation. Since March 1992, the process of giving limited parcels of land to the peasants has started in Russia. The land left is to be sold to anyone who wants to buy it or to lease it with the right to purchase later on. A Memorandum by the Government to the IMF promises to privatise in 1992 50 per cent of enterprises in the building materials industry and wholesale trade, 60 per cent of enterprises in the food industry, agriculture and retail trade, 70 per cent of enterprises in light industry, building, motor transport and repair work.[9]

---

[9] *Nezavisimaya gazeta*, 3 March 1992.

7.3 A sceptical conclusion

I have serious doubts about the possibility of fast privatisation. There are forces in society that overtly object to the market methods of privatisation envisaged in the programme (auctions and other forms of sale). In principle, I agree with the governmental approach, which is, I believe, the only possible way to create genuine owners, i.e. people who along with their interest in property rights are interested in investing their revenue. But in my opinion it is necessary, to avoid corruption of the state officials, to sell the assets through different investment funds, stock exchanges and banks instead of state holdings and so forth as the programme envisages.

Contrary to this approach, the populist idea of giving away the enterprises into the hands of their labour collectives is now being actively pushed. The international experience has not been taken into consideration; as is well known, this experience, especially the Yugoslav, has proved the inefficiency of collective property, which leads to waste of assets, fails to stimulate long-term investments, and hinders labour mobility. It is not surprising that the trade-unions, the Union of Working Collectives, and the leftists should adhere to this approach. But it is funny, indeed, to find it supported by some right radicals (like L. Piyasheva, who, in addition, insists on immediate privatisation – a fact which awakens recollections of bolshevism). Indeed if we try to apply this method people will be afraid that somebody will encroach upon his property (that in essence is not his) and will occupy it. But the real question is whether the management can manage. It is more probable that very soon the workers will sell their shares to real investors and entrepreneurs – or simply go bankrupt and into unemployment. Will this choice be socially more just than the official proposals? I believe not. To my mind, a redistribution of property allowing some to own modern assets and leaving others with obsolete equipment is generally unjust.

The second privatisation programme, as a compromise between the two approaches mentioned above, was adopted in June 1992. In particular, a vouchers system was included in it, but I do not think that one should attach much hope to vouchers, taking into consideration the Czechoslovak experience. (I understand that the enterprises there are reluctant to give away a part of their assets; also foreign investors do not as a rule want to have anything to do with enterprises privatised in that way.)

Nevertheless, the endeavours to supplement the current financial and monetary measures with the long-term programme of privatisation raises hopes of a transformation for the better in the near future. But the key problem now is a more flexible monetary policy preventing a deeper depression.

Chapter 8

PRIVATISATION, MARKET STRUCTURE AND COMPETITION: A PROGRESS REPORT ON CROATIA

Rikard Lang[*]
Dragomir Vojnić[*]

8.1 Background

As in other Eastern European countries, competition is evolving in Croatia in a period of historical change. The existing problems cannot be solved simply through the preservation or increase of competition as in established market economies, but by efforts directed towards creating the fundamental preconditions for the working of competition. This fact determines the content of this progress report on competition in Croatia. It refers therefore to the creation of the preconditions for competition in an economy in the process of transition to a market economy. This process, with its present meaning, started only recently.

The countries of Eastern Europe share many features of the process of transition to market economies and also of the evolution of competition, its nature and role. The interest of economic theory was until now primarily concerned with competition in well-established market economies. The transition towards market economies confronts economic theory with new challenges. Competition was very limited in the "pre-transition" period in ex-socialist countries. The evolution of competition in these countries is directly related to their overall progress in the transition towards market economies.

The fundamentals of the process of transition, and of the role of competition, is basically agreed among economists. Here too appears the present "convergence of scientific judgement" (James M. Buchanan). But differences appear related to the choice and application of available policy alternatives. Thus

---

[*]   Professors at the Institute of Economics, Zagreb University.

discussion concerns not the general attitude towards competition but the proper policies.

An appropriate competition policy is designed under the impact of different factors, such as the existing economic conditions, the effects of various forms of the market structure as a consequence of the character and degree of competition, and the overall objectives of economic policy. Generally, Croatia like other ex-socialist countries is in an early stage of the transition to a market economy and in the revaluation of competition in the functioning of the economy.

Croatia is a small newly formed country, under severe pressure from internal and external shocks in the process of transition. The situation has very specific features. Departure from the pre-transitional economic, political and constitutional systems are occurring simultaneously. A new economic system, heading towards a modern market economy, is in its early phase. The introduction of missing institutions for such a market economy and in this context also for establishing competition, are now being approached. To this must be added the consequences of a savage war. These and other factors, such as the problems of the birth of a nation state, the severance of former economic ties with other republics, the arduous task of the development of international economic relations under changed circumstances, all affect the progress to competition and the choice of proper competition policies.

The economics and politics of transition became a general preoccupation of all the ex-socialist countries of Europe, concerning Croatia as well as the other republics of former Yugoslavia. The Economic Institute of the University of Zagreb has been much engaged, in the course of the past years and decades, at home and abroad, in comparative studies in this field.

This engagement of the Institute on the international scientific level was also achieved through cooperation with institutions in other countries of Europe and the USA. We mention only some of them. Among European Institutions appear

The Vienna Institute for Comparative Economic Studies[1] and the Institute for Research in International Economic and Political Relations of the Academy of Sciences of the former USSR. Among American institutions we particularly mention the Center for Yugoslav-American Studies, Research and Exchanges of the Florida State University, Tallahassee.[2]

After the independence of Croatia and the other Yugoslav republics the Economic Institute of the University in Zagreb continued its intensive scientific activities under the new circumstances. The basic orientation and characteristics of this work are directed towards new insights and challenges in connection with the necessity to apply the economics and politics of transition. Because of this orientation the Institute is particularly engaged, on the initiative of the Government of the Republic of Croatia, in activities connected with elaboration of the concept and strategy of development of Croatia. The starting point of this activity is awareness that the basic strategic and development problems of independent Croatia must be solved on the basis of the economics and politics of transition.

The goal of the first phase of such a concept and strategy of development is transformation of the economy and society of Croatia in accordance with a model of civil (perhaps it is more appropriate to say market) democracy.

The economy and policy of transition in this phase of development is especially important within four complexes: the market, property, political organisation and the macroeconomic environment. These complexes are interdependent, which means that only through their simultaneous pluralisation can the urgently

---

[1]   In view of earlier events in the ex-socialist countries, we would especially emphasise the role and place of The Vienna Institute for Comparative Economic Studies; which deserves much credit for the continuous activity, through many years, of the International Workshop on East-West European Economic Interaction (since 1990 the International Workshop on European Economic Interaction and Integration). The International Steering Committee made a good decision when it decided that its XIII session should take place in Tübingen under the title "Economics and Politics of Transition".

[2]   The last annual conference of this Center, which took place in November 1991, marked the thirtieth anniversary of its continuous activities. It was then agreed, because of the events in Yugoslavia, that the Center will function in future as an International Center for comparative studies. Simultaneously there was formed a new Center for Croatian-American Studies, Research and Exchanges of the State University of Florida, Tallahassee.

needed process of democratisation of the economy and society be achieved and a way found out of the deep and many-sided crisis. The synthetic expression of this crisis appeared through many years as low economic efficiency. The other side of the medal is the fact that the degree of political democracy is not satisfactory.

Efficiency and markets

Economic efficiency, as well as the quality of development, are inadequate and can be quantitatively measured; the data are presented in *Tables 8.1, 8.2* and *8.3*. The comparative data for Yugoslavia, Croatia and Slovenia (*Table 8.1*) are based on the Harrod-Domar macroeconomic models.[3]

Tables 8.2 and *8.3* are derived from the analysis of the quality of economic growth generated by the Cobb-Douglas production function. We do not intend to consider the different analytical aspects which this table offers, and indicate only general conclusions. One is the conclusion that the economic development of former Yugoslavia as well as of Croatia has been in the long term achieved through very intensive investment and a relatively unfavourable efficiency of investments.[4]

Another general conclusion is the relatively unsatisfactory quality of economic growth, measured by the share of technological progress (assuming that the residual in the production function basically represents technical progress), as is shown by great differences in the contributions to technological progress between Croatia and some countries with market democracies (*Table 8.3*). There exists no doubt that the unsatisfactory economic efficiency of investments and the unsatisfactory quality of economic growth were decisively determined by the

---

[3]   In fact, the two models are very similar as regards the construction and starting points (Harrod, R.F. (1939), "An Essay in Dynamic Theory", *Economic Journal*, June; Domar, E.D. (1957), *Essays in the Theory of Economic Growth*, Oxford University Press, New York).

[4]   This low efficiency of investments can be demonstrated by calculating that if economic efficiency during the period 1960-1980 were equal to some countries with similar structural characteristics (Greece, Turkey, Spain and Portugal) Yugoslavia in 1980 could have reached twice as great a gross national product. For more detailed information see Bajt, Aleksander (1988), *The Self-Management Form of Social Ownership*, Globus, Zagreb, pp. 13-21.

Table 8.1

Rates of gross investments, capital coefficients and rates of growth of the economy, 1953-1989

1972 prices

	YUGOSLAVIA			CROATIA			SLOVENIA		
	Gross invest-ment % GDP	Capital coefficient (1):(3)	Growth of GDP % p.a.	Gross invest-ment % GDP	Capital coefficient (1):(3)	Growth of GDP % p.a.	Gross invest-ment % GDP	Capital coefficient (1):(3)	Growth of GDP % p.a.
	(1)	(2)	(3)	(1)	(2)	(3)	(1)	(2)	(3)
1953-55	20.7	1.9	10.7	16.9	1.3	12.6	21.7	2.0	10.7
1953-60	19.3	2.2	8.9	16.7	1.9	9.0	16.9	1.9	9.1
1956-60	18.6	2.4	7.8	16.6	2.4	6.9	14.8	1.8	8.1
1961-65	19.7	2.9	6.8	18.0	2.7	6.6	16.1	2.3	7.0
1961-70	20.4	3.2	6.3	18.8	3.0	6.3	16.4	2.4	6.9
1966-70	20.9	3.6	5.8	19.3	3.2	6.0	16.6	2.4	6.8
1971-75	20.9	3.5	5.9	18.3	3.5	5.3	20.8	3.1	6.8
1976-80	24.0	4.3	5.6	23.0	4.2	5.5	21.8	4.0	5.5
1981-89	16.3	32.7	0.5	15.7	157.2	0.1	14.9	149.2	0.1
1953-89	19.5	3.7	5.2	18.2	3.6	5.0	17.6	3.3	5.4
1953-80	21.5	3.2	6.8	19.3	2.8	6.8	19.3	2.7	7.1
1953-75	20.4	2.9	7.1	18.2	2.6	7.0	18.1	2.4	7.6
1953-65	19.5	2.4	8.1	17.4	2.1	8.1	16.5	2.0	8.3
1956-70	20.0	2.9	6.8	18.3	2.8	6.5	16.0	2.2	7.3
1961-75	20.6	3.3	6.2	18.5	3.1	6.0	18.3	2.7	6.8
1961-80	21.9	3.7	6.0	20.2	3.5	5.8	19.6	3.0	6.5
1971-80	22.7	4.0	5.7	21.2	3.9	5.4	21.4	3.5	6.1
1976-89	18.9	8.2	2.3	18.2	9.1	2.0	17.2	8.6	2.0
1966-89	19.5	5.1	3.8	18.3	5.2	3.5	17.7	4.4	4.0
1956-89	19.5	4.1	4.8	18.2	4.1	4.4	17.5	3.5	5.0

Source: Statistical yearbook, SZS, Belgrade, 1991; Institute of Economics, Zagreb, Center for economic informatics and statistics.

entire macroeconomic environment. The basic characteristics of this environment were reflected in the very limited role of the market, consisting only of the markets for goods and services, whereas the institutions and instruments of labour and capital markets were completely absent. These limitations of the market, especially the weakness of competition, are still very prominent as consequences of the high

Table 8.2

Contribution of factors to economic growth
in Yugoslavia and Croatia
% of GDP growth

	Labour	Capital	"Technical progress"
Yugoslavia			
1965-1974	23.4	42.2	34.4
1965-1987	57.8	20.0	22.2
1975-1987	93.5	23.4	-16.9
1980-1987	244.4	66.7	-211.1
Croatia			
1965-1974	18.1	36.9	44.9
1965-1987	44.6	40.6	14.8
1975-1987	83.1	43.0	-26.1
1980-1987	287.5	150.0	-337.5

Source: Puljić, Ante (1991), "Comparative analysis of economic growth, the growth of the productivity of labour and technological progress", in: *Actual Problems of the Economy and Economic Policy in Croatia*, Volume 2, Institute of Economics, Zagreb, pp. 93-107.

concentration of supply and the existence of monopolies and oligopolies. One essential stage in the economics and politics of transition concerns the development of institutions and mechanisms of the labour and capital markets; another is the essential change of the market structure by reducing concentration of supply and increasing competition. So far the necessary steps have been taken in Croatia to create the necessary legal framework. However, little has been achieved in practice to create the institutions and mechanisms.

The characteristic of the macroeconomic environment which leads to unfavourable performance is the system of social ownership – which can probably be better described as "non-ownership". Pluralisation and privatisation of ownership are essential for the increase of economic efficiency as well as for the development of entrepreneurship, competition and competitiveness. This trans-

Table 8.3

**Contribution of factors to economic growth
in 1960-1985, selected countries**
% of GDP growth

	Labour	Capital	"Technical progress"
France	-5	27	78
Germany	-10	23	87
Japan	5	36	59
United Kingdom	-5	27	78
USA	27	23	50
Croatia	37	37	26

Source: World Development Report 1991 (1991), Oxford University Press, p. 45. The estimates for the Republic of Croatia were prepared by Ante Puljić in the Institute of Economics, Zagreb.

formation of ownership towards privatisation must be achieved simultaneously with changes of the market structure reducing the concentration of supply.

From many aspects, linked with changes of the market structure, privatisation is decisive, and we shall focus attention on it in the next section. It is hardly necessary to stress that the monopoly sphere of (social) ownership affected also the formation of monopolies and oligopolies in the areas of the market and in the distribution of political power. The consequences have been weak economic efficiency and poor competitiveness. The political monism is a related feature. No less important is the fact that the monetary system and policy, based on the "soft budget constraint" and the corresponding fiscal policy, customs policy and protection, contributed to unfavourable economic efficiency and weak competitiveness. In these circumstances the emphasis of the concept and strategy of development has been on import-substitution and the export of surpluses – characteristic of a closed economy.

Thus, the goal of this phase of development of Croatia, in the coming years, is to apply a concept and strategy of development based on the economy and policy of transition; this implies applying the model of an open economy with the emphasis on domestic and international competition and exports. The key issue in beginning the implementation relates to the complex of privatisation and changing the market structure away from the concentration of supply.

8.2 Privatisation and transition

The central question for the transition in all ex-socialist countries is the pluralisation of ownership towards privatisation. Theoretical insights and the very limited and brief practice show that privatisation is essential for developing the institutions and instruments of the markets for labour and capital and also for the general democratisation of the economy and society. Privatisation is of special and decisive importance for the development of market structures which render possible competition as well as the market allocation of investments and capital.

However, in spite of its decisive importance, the process of privatisation in ex-socialist countries started hesitatingly and has resulted in many dilemmas and vacillations in seeking the ways and means most suitable for the given conditions. In the summer of 1991, there took place in the Hoover Institution, Stanford University, a great international conference on the Economic Transition in Central and Eastern Europe. The participants were politicians and scientists from all the European ex-socialist countries. All agreed that privatisation has a decisive role in the whole transition. This was particularly emphasised by the American economists and Nobel laureates (Milton Friedman, George Stigler, Kenneth Arrow, Jeffrey Sachs and George Schultz). All agreed, too, that privatisation would best be implemented through the sale of shares to domestic and foreign buyers. In this manner, two crucial problems would be solved: improvement of the quality of management and increase of profitability and overall economic efficiency.

This second problem concerns the additional investment which is absolutely needed for the structural changes, the structural adjustment to market conditions and for development itself. Although it was generally agreed that the sale of shares is optimal for achieving privatisation, most participants also emphasised the great limitations in practice; against the huge supply of enterprises for sale in the ex-socialist countries, there appears only a very limited and modest demand. A small number of especially attractive profitable enterprises in different ex-socialist countries will certainly be (or have already been) sold. They are, however, only marginal; in macroeconomic terms, net financial surpluses do not exist either in Europe or in the USA.

A way out of this situation is the application of an open strategy which envisages the use of other methods, besides the sale of shares, such as the distribution of shares and vouchers to workers and citizens on the basis of specific criteria.[5]

Although it was widely agreed that without an open strategy it will be impossible to carry through privatisation (within an acceptable time), yet differences of attitudes appear about the method of distributing shares and vouchers. Most scientists accepted without hesitation the absolute necessity of distributing part of the capital through shares and vouchers. Most politicians manifested much more reserve about the free distribution of shares and vouchers. Nevertheless, all agreed that part of the capital would be distributed to workers and citizens in the course of 1992 if a general standstill in privatisation should occur. It is interesting that the strongest supporters of free distribution of part of the capital were the American Nobel laureates, especially Milton Friedman. He presented a series of politico-economic theses which in the course of the discussion on the transformation of ownership in Croatia were also proposed by the present authors.

Among the interesting theses of practical importance are those which stress the unique historical sequence: pluralism and domination of private ownership represented in our civilisation basic brakes and, so to say, the mortal enemy of any monopoly and monism. That applies equally to the market (because without private ownership there can be no competition) and to the distribution of political power. The new democratic authorities (and governments) in all ex-socialist countries found themselves in a completely new and unknown situation in the history of our civilisation.

These new democratic governments must, by their own volition and political decision, consciously create through privatisation the enemy to any monopoly and monism including their own. That is not only a new historical phenomenon but also a great challenge.

---

[5]   This proposal was presented by *Vojnić* in his paper "Some Issues on the Economics and Politics of Transition in Croatia and Yugoslavia". All papers from this conference, which took place in Stanford from 8-10 May 1991, are mimeographed and are to be found in the Hoover Institution, Stanford University.

Pluralisation and privatisation of ownership have slowed down in Croatia not only as a consequence of the dilemmas and hesitations, but also because of the war and its ravages. Without going deeper into the effects of war on privatisation in Croatia (and other former Yugoslav republics) we must consider some differences from other relevant countries.

These differences refer especially to the initial character of ownership – social ownership in former Yugoslavia. The process began in other ex-socialist countries from state ownership. These initial differences, by their very nature, impose great differences on the methodology of ownership pluralisation and reprivatisation. The ex-socialist countries where the existing concept is state ownership cannot escape the more or less direct administrative role and function of the state.

Croatia and the rest of former Yugoslavia must start from the existing dominant concept of social ownership. Apart from the well-known weaknesses of this concept manifest in the past decades, one can argue that it would be an error to implement the pluralisation of ownership in former Yugoslavia in the same way as in ex-socialist countries dominated by state ownership.

Despite its known defects, from the aspect of reform and democratic change social ownership has some advantages by comparison with state ownership.[6]

These advantages (even in an environment with all the defects of integral self-management) appear in the somewhat different behaviour of all economic subjects under conditions of decentralised decision making, and despite the very defective market environment which did not admit the market formation of factor prices. The advantages were also expressed in the slightly greater economic efficiency of the use of assets in social ownership (by comparison with state ownership) and in the consciousness of the workers that they are some kind of

---

[6] This advantage, of course, does not appear as a consequence of social ownership as such. As is well known, it can be defined more adequately as non-ownership instead of ownership which (as is the case with state ownership) has its titular owner. The advantage appears nevertheless because social ownership developed in a kind of market ambiance and (at least partly) decentralised management by workers who through the years developed a feeling of quasi owners.

owners or, perhaps more accurately, quasi owners.[7] These advantages (without regard to all the criticisms rightly uttered regarding social ownership) must be considered in defining the approach to transformation of ownership towards dominant privatisation and strengthening the sector of public ownership.

Transformation methods and progress

In spring 1991 the Croatian parliament passed the law on the transformation of state enterprises.[8] In the public discussion accompanying the preparation of this law, a group of collaborators of the Institute of Economics of the University of Zagreb prepared the study "Privatisation in the Policy of Economic Development".[9] The basic message of this study is that privatisation should be implemented by an open strategy, i.e. by sale (with or without premia) as well as by free distribution combined with possible mixed methods. In Croatia, additional possibilities exist for the sale of capital against the so-called "old foreign currency" savings of citizens which are now blocked as a consequence of war and other circumstances. The basic message of this study is that stagnation of privatisation would be the worst solution from the economic, political and social aspects.

The accounting net value of the capital of Croatia (according to the balance sheet of 31 December 1990) amounted to approximately US$ 27 bn, of which 20 per cent consists of the capital of important public enterprises in such areas as oil, railways and electrical energy. In the optimal (or better to say ideal) interpretation of the law, the sale of capital on the free market would leave unsold approximately 70 per cent of the entire capital. Domestic purchasing power could not be seriously relied upon in the course of the next few years. This means that the largest part of the capital would either remain under the control of the state, or its price would fall so much that the resuit would be (as Jeffrey Sachs and

---

[7] A somewhat broader consideration of these and related sets of problems can be found in the study of Josip Županov (1990), "Self-management Socialism: the End of a Utopia", in: *Socialism in Reform. Experience and Problems of the Yugoslav Economic Reform*, Institute of Economics, Zagreb (in Croatian).

[8] The Law on the transformation of social enterprises, *Narodne novine*, No. 19, Zagreb, 1991.

[9] Zdunić, S., Baletić, Z., and Bendeković, J. (eds.) (1991), *Privatisation in the Policy of Economic Development*, Institute of Economics, Zagreb.

Milton Friedman warned) a kind of bargain sale (not to say plunder) of national wealth. However, it must be emphasised that such a result could be achieved only if all creditors (domestic and foreign) were to transform their claims into shares.

Even then, theoretically, US$ 6 bn of capital could be transformed on the basis of internal (domestic) transactions and about US$ 25 bn by foreign transactions through the transformation of foreign debts into shares of domestic enterprises. The unreality of such a transaction (also on the domestic level) can be illustrated by the fact that at the end of 1990 the total money assets on the accounts of legal persons in Croatia amounted to approximately US$ 4.5 bn. The attempt to promote such a transaction would undoubtedly lead to a general monetary collapse.[10]

The events of 1991 created new limitations. The sudden decline of production and the standard of living (as a consequence of war and war ravages as well as from loss of markets) has almost halved the already low prewar level of the purchasing power of the population. Besides that, it has to be realised that the population would give priority in the use of its modest purchasing power to the acquisition of homes. All owners (about 400 thousand) of homes in social ownership have the right (under favourable conditions) to purchase them, according to new laws. All in all, the limitations of privatisation in Croatia through the sale of shares are very great. In fact about 100 enterprises, out of about 3,000 enterprises in state ownership, have so far (May 1992) been privatised.[11]

The existing law provided that all enterprises must be privatised by 30 June 1992. Subsequently all decisions regarding the transformation of ownership for all remaining enterprises falls to the Agency of the Republic of Croatia for Restructuring and Development. One can assume (without regard to the actual form of transformation) that after this reform about 95 per cent of enterprises

---

[10] More detailed information can be got from the study of Dr. Vojnić, with Željko Rohatinski, under the title *Economics and Politics of Transition – Problems of Privatization*, Institute of Economics, Zagreb, 1992.

[11] In these circumstances it is important that the right to privatise in Croatia is best implemented on the basis of free entry, through a great number of new small enterprises, shops and firms. About 1,500 such enterprises (more accurately business units) have so far been opened.

would be (directly or indirectly) under the influence of the state. It is generally felt that this would be undesirable because state ownership, by comparison with social ownership, is a backward step. On this basis, neither profitability nor overall economic efficiency could be increased. This is the reason for new (scientific and political) initiatives for the acceleration of privatisation. Two institutions of Zagreb University – the Institute for International Relations and Development and the Institute of Economics – organised a conference on "The Renewal and the Economic Transition in Croatia", which emphasised the urgent need for political initiative and decisions to forward privatisation. On the method of privatisation, the model of an open strategy was supported with special insistence upon the distribution of shares and vouchers.[12]

From these discussions two proposals emerged, one of which was submitted to the parliament of Croatia. According to this proposal two thirds of the capital of the Croatian economy of about (the estimated lower limit of) DM 45 bn would be distributed (through vouchers) to all citizens in accordance with definite criteria. All citizens entitled to the distribution would be divided into three groups. Those employed or formerly employed in the economy would get DM 10 thousand each. The employed, formerly employed (and unemployed) in the state and public sector, about 400 thousand, would each get about DM 7 thousand. These two groups would get a discount of 20 per cent, plus one per cent for each year of employment. In the third group are all other citizens of Croatia of over 18 years, with at least 5 years residence. The remaining one third of the capital (about DM 15 bn) would remain on the capital market for domestic and foreign buyers. This proposal, which includes the existing Croatian fund for development and the Agency for Restructuring and Development, could be implemented by changes in only two articles of the existing law on the transformation of public enterprises.

The second proposal is not yet in public discussion and has not so far been submitted to Parliament. Under this proposal, the procedure for acceleration of privatisation is divided into three phases. The first ends on 30 June 1992, i.e. the term foreseen by law for the free implementation of privatisation. In the second phase, priority would be given to the purchase of shares to citizens with (at

---

[12] Lang, Rikard, and Vojnić, Dragomir (1992), *The Concept and Strategy of Development of Croatia in the Light of the Economics and Politics of Transition*, Institute of Economics, Zagreb.

present blocked) foreign currency savings accounts. In the third phase the rest of the social capital would be grouped into several holdings and one share of each holding distributed to every citizen.

Granted the needed political support, both proposals require detailed elaboration. But although we are anxious to have most detailed study of each proposal and of its consequences, we must be aware that great uncertainties about privatisation will still remain. Personally, we hold that there are not, and cannot be, good solutions. The proposed models of privatisation (although containing elements of economic and social logic and fairness) cannot be realised without great problems. The consequent problems are economic, social, moral and legal. From the very first, social problems, especially in Croatia as a consequence of war and economic decline, will have to be relieved. Later, problems of social differentiation and great social differences will emerge. These problems are inescapable and must be solved through the economic, social and tax policy of the social state. In underlining all these issues we do not dispute the need for a fair privatisation, we merely emphasise that we are conscious of the great and difficult economic and social problems which we have to face.

8.3 Market structure and competition[13)]

Market reforms in the former Yugoslavia were started in the early 1950s. However, in spite of attempts made in the great socio-economic reform of 1965, and in the long-term programme of economic stabilisation of 1983, clearly oriented to the market economy, the function of the market was limited and defective. The lack of institutions and instruments for the labour and capital market rendered impossible the market allocation of the factors of production, especially for the market allocation of the accumulation of capital and investments. Consequently a market structure was formed which did not meet the preconditions of a market economy. As is well known, the market structure of a developed market economy has a whole range of characteristics. From the aspect of competition, two are especially important: One is the great dispersion of enterprises by size implying

---

[13)] We thank Izak Drutter for allowing us to use his study, not yet published, for the Institute of Economics, Zagreb, under the title "Market Concentration and Competition in Yugoslavia and Croatia in the Process of Transition".

Table 8.4

Yugoslavia: Change in the concentration of supply
1963 to 1984

Concentration of supply[a]		Product groups		Economic organisations		Employed	
		1963	1984	1963	1984	1963	1984
	%	Number		Number		Thousands	
Very high	100	25	20	72	56	69	28
High	75-99	29	27	269	218	214	84
Medium	50-74	23	34	408	533	206	185
Low	25-49	22	50	992	2057	383	598
Very low	to 24	4	24	498	2991	161	805
Total		103	155	2239	5855	1033	1700
		per cent		per cent		per cent	
Very high	100	24.3	12.9	3.2	1.0	6.6	1.6
High	79-99	28.2	17.4	12.0	3.7	20.7	5.0
Medium	50-74	22.3	21.9	18.2	9.1	20.0	10.4
Low	25-49	21.4	32.3	44.3	35.1	37.1	35.2
Very low	to 24	3.9	15.5	22.3	51.1	15.6	47.0
Total		100.0	100.0	100.0	100.0	100.0	100.0

a) Percentage share of 4 largest organisations in total output of group. Data relate to industry and mining.

Source: Drutter, Izak (1992), *Market Concentration and Competition in Yugoslavia and Croatia in the Process of Transition*, Institute of Economics, Zagreb.

Data for 1963: Drutter, Izak (1965), "Market aspects of concentration", *Economic Studies*, Institute of Economics, Zagreb, No. 3, pp. 5-51. Data for 1984: balance sheets processed in the Institute of Economics, Zagreb, Center for economic informatics and statistics.

the importance of small and medium enterprises. The second – the other side of the medal – is the relative dispersion of sources of supply. In former Yugoslavia, the market structure had several characteristics of a centrally-planned economy, with a dominant role for large enterprises and great systems. From theory and practice it is known that such conditions hinder competition because the concentration of supply is relatively important. (See *Table 8.4*.)

The concentration ratio is the percentage share of the four largest organisations in the total income of each product group, defined by a sixteen-digit code. Although not sufficiently homogenous, the subgroupings are the narrowest for which data are available for calculating the concentration ratios.

The analysis at market concentration in industry and mining for 1984 (*Table 8.4*) shows remarkably high concentration of supply, even if the subgroupings are too broad for homogeneity of products.

In 1984, 20 out of 155 groupings had each not more than 4 organisations and their share of the income of the grouping amounts to 100 per cent. Such groupings are defined as being very concentrated. In another 27 groupings the concentration ratio is higher than 75 per cent – a high rate of concentration.

The distribution of groupings indicates that the concentration of supply as a whole is indeed very high. In 81 of the 155 groupings, more than half, the concentration is more than 50 per cent. At this level of concentration, the control mechanisms are already set in motion in some countries. In 47 groupings the concentration ratio even surpassed 75 per cent. At this level, the question arises of a dominant position on the market.

Most groupings consists of a small number of organisations. In 81 groupings, where the concentration ratio surpasses 50 per cent, only 807 organisations appear, of which 92 groupings have less than 10 organisations each, and only 4 groupings contain less than 20 organisations each.

Between 1959 and 1984 there was a significant reduction in the general level of market concentration. The share of product groupings with a low concentration ratio increased, and the share with higher ratios diminished. The degree of concentration remains high however by comparison with market economies. It is also higher than appears from comparison of the indicators, because the size of market groupings is much broader for Yugoslavia. All findings indicate that in Yugoslavia oligopolistic markets predominate.

Besides the high rate of concentration, competition has been restricted also by other factors, such as the closed communal and republican economies, the social contracts and compacts about everything, and even the absence of market mobility limiting competition between factors of production.

Separation increases concentration

The creation of new states on the territory of former Yugoslavia intensifies the problems of insufficient market competition. By achieving independence the internal markets of the individual former republics were considerably diminished, as was the number of enterprises in the individual market groupings. The so-called "parallel capacities", which the republics built up in their efforts to round off their republican economies (competing to a certain extent within the former Yugoslavia), will become monopolies in the independent republics. The firms from different republics which formerly cooperated must either enter into new relations with their previous partners or lose their traditional markets or sources of supply. It is not clear what kind of relations will be established between the independent republics, but it is certain that the conflicts and the war devastations have already split the Yugoslav market and isolated its individual parts.

The influence of this separation on market structures can be shown by the example of Croatia. By separating the 1984 data for enterprises with headquarters in Croatia, and using the same method of analysis as for Yugoslavia (*Table 8.4*), we can display indicators of market concentration in Croatia in 1984 (see *Table 8.5*).

The data for Croatia include 138 groupings as compared with 155 in the data for Yugoslavia. The difference of 17 groupings appears because in 14 groups there are no enterprises with headquarters in Croatia, and in three the enterprises declared that they had no income.

About 46 per cent of the groups in Croatia, against 13 per cent in Yugoslavia, fall in the category of very high concentration; for high concentration, the proportions are 22 per cent against 17 per cent. Correspondingly at medium and low degrees of concentration, the proportions are lower in Croatia. The considerably higher degree of concentration indicates how in Croatia, formerly the second largest republic and producing more than one quarter of the social product of former Yugoslavia, market concentration has been increased by separation. In the smaller republics this increase is even greater. The number of groupings dominated by a very small number of enterprises is greater in Croatia while the number with a large number of enterprises is less.

Table 8.5

Croatia: Frequency distribution of 138 product groups
by degree of the concentration of supply 1984

The degree of concentration of supply	%	Product groups number	%	Enter-prises number	%	Overall income mn din	%	Employed number	%
Very high	100	63	45.65	145	9.38	529766	28.06	50923	12.94
High	75-99	31	22.46	218	14.10	281704	14.92	58659	14.79
Medium	50-74	22	15.94	326	21.09	434523	23.01	71166	17.94
Low	25-49	19	13.77	698	45.15	562262	29.78	173494	43.74
Very low	to 24	3	2.17	159	10.28	90033	4.24	42366	10.68
Total		138	100.00	1546	100.00	1888188	100.00	396608	100.00

Source: Drutter, Izak (1992), *Market Concentration and Competition in Yugoslavia and Croatia in the Process of Transition*, Institute of Economics, Zagreb.

Although in Yugoslavia as a whole there appeared 6 groupings with one enterprise each, in Croatia there were 17. In Yugoslavia there were 2 groupings with 2 enterprises each, in Croatia 23. The number of groupings with a relatively large number of enterprises is different: in Yugoslavia 14 groupings had more than 100 organisations, in Croatia there were no such groupings. Yugoslavia had 36 groupings with more than 50 organisations, Croatia only 3.

From 1984 to 1992, the unfavourable market structure could not improve enough to alleviate the position. On the contrary, the war must have brought about a further deterioration because of the devastation, the interruption of transport and communications, the breakdown of financial flows, the blockade etc. The war also results in strengthening the role of the state in the process of transition, which again, unfavourably affects the strengthening of competition.

The problems of market structure and competition, which appear in all ex-socialist countries, are especially marked in the countries created by the division of Yugoslavia, most notably in Croatia, exposed to the greatest war devastation.

The general conditions for the development of competition will be affected by the whole body of systemic changes and by an economic policy establishing a favourable institutional framework for market behaviour, making possible the transformation of social or state enterprises into private and public ones, promoting the liberation and stimulation of private initiative, implementing market mechanisms for the free mobility of goods, labour and capital, introducing conditions for integration into international exchanges, attracting foreign investments, stimulating the establishment of new enterprises and creating a series of other general conditions for the development of competition.

In addition it is necessary to act with special measures for separate sectors. In some activities (such as retail trade, catering, small crafts, small industries, transport, building, agriculture, services, and other activities which do not require large investments and whose optimal size is small in relation to their markets), quite a fast expansion of the number of enterprises could occur and thus strengthen competition without special incentives. Nevertheless, here too, because of the lack of assets, insufficient training and a poor experience of security and stability, the establishment and support of the business activities of the small enterprises calls for adequate tax, financial, educational and other measures.

In activities which are natural monopolies, such as some infrastructural activities, particular management regimes are required to insure their efficient management in accordance with the needs of the users.

In a considerable part of industry and mining, transport and other activities, especially in small countries, it is impossible to establish sufficiently competitive conditions within the limits of the domestic market, because it is too small in relation to the optimal size of these enterprises. They need therefore to be integrated into European and broader markets. In the countries of the former Yugoslavia, the problem will be the formation of new forms of (international) cooperation allowing, without regard to political ties, the greatest possible freedom of mobility of goods, labour and capital as well as the continuity of business, cooperative and other ties established for many years.

Joining the integration processes within the European Community offers these countries not only great opportunities for more efficient competition by broadening their markets, but also numerous other advantages on condition of accepting the standards and criteria of the EC. This includes also integration into European and world financial markets, the support of international financial institutions as well as attractions for foreign investment. Without them even in the

119

least capital-intensive sectors it is not possible to establish numerous new enterprises as a consequence of the lack of domestic capital.

Besides the incentives for competition, it is necessary, as in developed countries with market economies, to introduce and carry out a policy of restricting monopolies and monopolisation as well as all other procedures which have as a consequence the restriction of competition.

8.4 The present stage and prospects of development of Croatia

The economy and society of Croatia have in 1991 suffered from great war ravages and borne huge war damages. According to latest estimates the total war damages amount to over US$ 18 bn (see *Table 8.6*). As a result, great problems have appeared in production and employment accompanied by a marked decline of the standard of living and the purchasing power of the population.

The greatest problems are in the social sphere, especially because over 300 thousand citizens of Croatia have had to leave their homes. The housing stock suffered great war devastation so that many of the exiled will have no home to return to. The economic recovery of Croatia will require several years (see *Table 8.7* for some projections).

The great decline in the social product in 1992, according to our estimates, is the consequence almost equally of war damage and the loss of markets in former Yugoslav republics and other ex-socialist countries.

The economy and society confront heavy problems to be solved in the coming years. Recovery must be achieved simultaneously with the economics and politics of transition.

Table 8.6

War damages in Croatia
(mid-December 1991)
in US$ million

Sectors	Direct damages	Indirect damages	Total	Structure in % total=100	economic sectors=100
Industry	1600	900	2500	13.4	18.9
Agriculture and foodstuffs	780	520	1300	6.9	9.8
Forestry and wood industry	630	330	960	5.1	7.3
Water supply	150	140	300	1.6	2.3
Transport and communications	1500	500	2000	10.7	15.2
Trade	10	870	880	4.7	6.7
Catering and tourism	230	1480	1710	9.1	13.0
Communal and construction	3550	–	3550	19.0	26.9
Total economic sectors	8460	4740	13200	70.6	100.0
					total social=100
Social welfare	50	900	950	5.1	17.2
Education, culture	2500	–	2500	13.4	45.4
and sport	620	190	810	4.3	14.7
State budget and other	100	1150	1250	6.7	22.7
Total social activities	3270	2240	5510	29.4	100.0
Total	11730	6980	18710	100.0	

Source: Estimates from the relevant departments of the Government of Croatia.

Table 8.7

Croatia: final use of the social product
dinar billion, prices of 1990

	1990	1991	1992	1993	1994	1995	1996	2000
Social product (GDP)	228	179	165	185	202	218	223	291
Personal consumption	138	121	115	120	126	132	137	172
State material expenses	27	35	42	42	44	45	46	52
Gross investments in fixed assets	36	21	25	37	45	48	52	65
Growth of stocks	12	-4	0	4	4	4	5	6
Export of goods and services	117	80	88	115	132	156	169	221
Import of goods and services	-112	-102	-108	-134	-149	-168	-176	-224
Balance of goods and services	5	-22	-20	-19	-16	-11	-7	-3
Net exchanges with other regions; Net differences, rate of exchange; errors and omissions	10	27	3	0	0	0	0	0
Available assets for consumption								
Personal consumption	138	121	115	120	126	132	137	172
Material expenses of the state	27	35	42	42	44	45	46	52
Saving	8	-10	-6	7	15	23	30	42
Domestic consumption and available assets	173	146	151	169	185	200	214	266
Net domestic social product	206	158	149	167	181	196	210	262
Transfers to the population from abroad, net	-9	-5	5	6	6	7	8	9
Income of foreign capital, net	-3	-4	-3	-3	-3	-3	-4	-6
Transfer with other regions, net	-21	-2	0	0	0	0	0	0
Financing and capital								
Investment in fixed assets	36	21	25	37	45	48	52	65
Growth of stocks	12	-4	0	4	4	4	5	6
Loans to other regions, net differences in size, errors etc.	-11	24	3	0	0	0	0	0
Gross accumulation and financing	37	42	28	41	49	53	56	70
Depreciation	22	21	17	19	20	22	23	29
Saving	8	-10	-6	7	15	23	30	42
Inflow of foreign capital, net	7	30	18	16	13	7	3	-1

Source: Concept and strategy of development of Croatia, Institute of Economics, Zagreb, 1992.

In this adversity there are, however, some advantages: as a consequence of restoration and privatisation the changes of the economic structure will be achieved more easily. The development of the labour and capital markets, which will accompany privatisation, will certainly tend to improve the market structure and competitiveness. However, it will not be possible to achieve all this without much help and support from international financial institutions and friendly, especially neighbouring, countries. If all proceeds relatively well, we expect only in the course of 1996 to achieve the same level of production (and GDP) as we had before the war.

8.5 For a conclusion

The economic and political transition in Croatia (as in most ex-socialist countries) has only begun. Croatia had some advantages from a somewhat greater role of the market (although limited to the market for goods and services) as well as from a system of social ownership linked to a wider sense of management and quasi-ownership than elsewhere. These advantages have not so far been used. The economy and society of Croatia suffered huge war damages (estimated at US$ 18 bn).

The social product of Croatia in 1992 will be almost 40 per cent smaller than prewar. This reduction is caused equally by war ravages and the loss of markets. With a consistent implementation of the economics and politics of transition, on the basis of privatisation and structural change of markets and production, the prewar level of the social product could be regained but only in the course of 1996.

That is possible, but only with the universal support and aid of international financial organisations and of friendly, especially neighbouring, countries.

COMMENTS ON PART II:

András Inotai[*)]

In discussing competition policies, one must consider the economic environment for introducing more competition and deregulation. The East European
countries followed different paths: Poland and, partly, Czechoslovakia rapidly
dismantling trade barriers, and Hungary following a more gradualistic approach.
In the end, after a relatively short period, both Poland and Czechoslovakia had
to introduce temporary measures to restrict imports (higher tariffs and import
surcharge).

Trade liberalisation policies should be designed after taking account of some
basic characteristics of the transforming economies. First, although to differing
extents, these economies have had little preparation for fierce competition.
Second, most of the traditional actors (large enterprises and Foreign Trade
Organisations), some of which would be able to compete, have been dissolved,
disintegrated or are struggling with serious financial and institutional problems.
Third, internal demand is rapidly declining. This in itself leads to decreasing
market shares. However, it is the collapse of the CMEA market which makes this
shrinking process particularly dramatic. Fourth, an increasing slice of the shrinking
domestic market is being conquered by foreign companies as a result of import
liberalisation and growing foreign direct investment in the host countries.

Small- and medium-size companies, which are apparently mushrooming in
East European economies, have to compete in this environment. In contrast to
the traditional Western development of competitive national firms, they have to
work under very different international economic conditions. As they mostly have
not had a learning period to prepare themselves for international competition, and
since national protection is neither politically and legally feasible nor financially
viable (budget deficits, indebtedness), they have to face international competition
from the beginning. In these circumstances, improved market access is fundamental to their development, as well as to the prospects for economic and political

---

[*)] Director, Institute for World Economics, Budapest.

stabilisation in the region. As their entrepreneurs are supposed to represent the most dynamic portion of society, their failure – not necessarily for lack of competitiveness and experience, but because of market entry barriers – will have important and negative secondary impacts on overall economic development and political structure.

Two additional factors adversely affecting competitiveness have to be mentioned. First, the collapse of the CMEA has hit not only exports to this area, but also price competitiveness of exports to convertible currency markets for firms exporting to both markets, and for which economies of scale were an important factor of general competitiveness. In a number of Hungarian companies with the largest dependence on both Eastern and Western markets, sharply declining exports to the ex-CMEA led to serious underutilisation of capacities, raised unit costs, and saw productivity fall. In sum, economies of scale advantages were destroyed in exports to the West. Second, frequently hidden competitive advantages cannot be adequately used because of the underdevelopment of infrastructure. Similarly, institutional demonopolisation is hindered by the lack of adequate infrastructure. In consequence, a successful competition policy should not be confined to trade liberalisation, privatisation and better conditions for foreign direct investment. It must also integrate supporting measures in favour of small- and medium-sized firms, far-reaching infrastructural development and active economic diplomacy into its set of policy instruments.

The question has been raised about the international competitiveness of East European countries with special reference to the German market. Surprisingly, Hungary and Poland after 1989, and Czechoslovakia after 1990, could substantially increase their exports to the OECD area. The growth rate of their exports surpassed by far the growth rate of total imports of the OECD and of most of the individual OECD member countries. No fundamental research has been carried out on the underlying reasons for this export boom. Therefore it is very difficult to assess the sustainability of this export drive, and to identify those economic policy issues that are needed to maintain or even expand market shares in the OECD.

German import demand played the most important role in dynamising exports of East European countries. While all these countries were able to increase their exports to Germany faster than total German import demand (which

125

itself exhibited the fastest growth within the OECD), this growth was confined to the former West German market. The collapse of the former East Germany, one of the major export markets for Czechoslovakia, and an important partner for Hungary and Poland, led to dramatically falling exports to the East German states. However, West German import expansion more than compensated for this loss in the aggregate. But it certainly could not provide adequate compensation for all individual firms, since exports to the former East and West Germany were substantially different in commodity composition.

David G. Mayes

Establishing case law for competition agencies

Although the legal frameworks set out in these papers for the new competition and antitrust agencies indicate the way they will behave, their initial actions – both in the way they undertake investigations and the way they frame judgements – will be crucial in establishing their authority and a pattern for competitive behaviour. The initial judgements need to cover a wide range of illustrative cases, establishing core principles and the grounds on which judgements are made so that market players can know what to expect. If priorities make this possible, it helps credibility and may avoid borderline cases which the agency may lose in the early days. Later, the agency itself will want to clear up these border issues but from a position of strength.

A similar approach should cover the agencies' approach to investigation. The aim is to try to achieve compliance without the need for investigation, still less for prosecution. The agency needs to establish a reputation under which co-operation is rewarded and destruction heavily penalised (both by fines in particular cases and by threats of close surveillance and "own initiative" investigations in the future). A reputation for fairness and efficiency will help reinforce this. Again the method of working in the early cases will be crucial. Examples of quickly abandoned investigations and clear favourable judgements for compliant defendants will also help. However, the reputation also needs to extend to those who bring potential actions to the attention of the agency. A willingness to listen and encourage relevant cases needs to be matched by deterrence of trivial

126

actions. In particular there needs to be a distinction between infringements of trading standards, civil disputes and anti-competitive cases.

One of the most difficult problems comes from overlaps and conflicts between different policy agencies. Conflict between industrial and trade policy is an obvious example. Ideally an approach where rules are clearly objective and "transparent" will make life easiest. Again, inter-agency disputes which give confusing signals are to be avoided.

An example from New Zealand

There is a tendency to look for instructive examples from the developing world but these are not particularly relevant as the East European countries are already heavily industrialised if with a distorted structure. An alternative is to look to the most controlled of the OECD countries, New Zealand, and to its very rapid process of liberalisation since 1984. New Zealand illustrates the problems of speed and sequencing (it has a further problem of geographical peripherality which does not affect much of Europe). The example is extensively explored in Bollard and Mayes (1991).

The following issues are worth highlighting.

(a)   At an early stage, New Zealand liberalised foreign exchange and floated the dollar; this led to revaluation and to high real and nominal exchange rates. Although the ensuing deflation helped bring down inflation to very low levels, the process was extended by at least a year by a switch from direct to indirect taxation which caused an inflationary "blip".

(b)   Stabilisation policies were quite successful; most subsidies to industry (and agriculture) were rapidly abolished, quantitative restrictions on trade were removed and tariffs reduced quickly towards more normal OECD levels. A few key industries were exempted (cars, clothing, steel, for example) and had industry plans which involved the reduction of protection over a five-year period. The shock to the system was considerable: agricultural land prices halved and many areas of inefficient small-scale industrial production were effectively eliminated. However, the structured nature of the change prevented any drastic overall slump and the picture was one of recession rather than depression.

(c)   The macroeconomic reforms were matched by an extensive range of microeconomic reforms, opening the country up to the full rigour of international

127

competition. A Commerce Act set up a Commerce Commission with investigative and judicial powers. A dramatic change in behaviour has taken place in a country formerly characterised by price controls and detailed regulations, generating a "climate of enterprise" and a number of successful new "niche producers" as well as concentration by larger producers. In such a small and isolated country a large number of monopolies is to be expected.

(d)   Reform extended to the public sector where a wide range of organisations were turned into state-owned enterprises (SOEs), and given commercial criteria (including a rate of return on capital) but ownership remained firmly in the public sector, with the relevant minister. Unfortunately, overall budgetary difficulties (from the combination of high interest rates and depressed tax revenue) pushed the government (Labour, or socialist) into privatising in order to raise revenue. Both domestic and foreign participation were encouraged, although there was considerable reluctance to permit strategic industries falling under foreign control. However, that is now accepted and both the steelworks and the airline now have foreign ownership. Some SOEs remain, showing that ownership and commercial operation can be distinguished.

(e)   New Zealand had one other benefit, namely closer economic relations with Australia, which is an extensive form of integration, going much further than free trade. This stimulated exports and competition at a time of general deflation and meant that new markets were readily found for many suppliers. Although there has been no dramatic growth, the New Zealand economy is now (1992) expanding again but the process of transformation has taken nearly eight years. A favourable outcome to the GATT Round could stimulate that recovery.

I think all these five lessons have parallels for East European companies, not least from the aspect of opportunities in each other's markets.

Reference:

Bollard, A. and Mayes, D.G. (1991), *Corporatisation and Privatisation in New Zealand* (forthcoming in T. Clark (ed.), proceedings of conference on International Privatisation at University of St. Andrews).

Alain Bienaymé

The process of privatisation, like the promotion of competition, is more a means than an end in itself. Both offer in most cases powerful incentives for economic efficiency. But the implementation of privatisation ought to fit the realities of each industry in each country. Thus grass-roots capitalism in small business activities is open to the burgeoning of private initiatives. By contrast, the state keeps some responsibilities in helping big companies in heavy industries to find the good mix of capital for large-scale operations; some kind of stability is needed in order to conceive and to implement long-term investment projects.

As French and Italian experiences seem to show, the public ownership of big corporations is a cloth which can cover very different realities. After the first government of Pierre Mauroy had largely extended the public sector, through nationalisation of large international French companies in 1982, the successor government made it quite clear (in 1984) that the executive officers of the public companies would be reappointed and rewarded on showing their capacity to restore the profitability of their businesses. The signal was widely understood, and in a few years a large part of the public manufacturing sector got out of the red.

Public control can be exerted directly through public ownership of the relevant industrial firms. But it can be also exerted indirectly through the publicly owned banks which hold equity and are the natural partners of the manufacturing sector. Here again, the role of the state may be very ambiguous if the instructions given to the banks and other financial intermediaries remain unclear. For example, these public financial organisations may adopt a large array of investment strategies in the manufacturing sector: they may aim at high yields and frequently switch their asset portfolios; or they may invest heavily in the equity of a few selected companies in order to exert a permanent and active control. Or they may opt for a few companies and stay at arm's length just in order to restrain operating costs.

The privatisation of a monopoly in a small- or medium-size national economy should be associated with breaking the monopoly when cost functions indicate clearly that efficiency will not be impaired. The best solution then is to reduce and finally eliminate the tariff protection and public subsidies. The commitment of the state to extend free trade is thus of paramount importance to make these companies more efficient.

The state should concentrate its own responsibilities on monetary stabilisation with free convertibility of currency, and on modernising those parts of the infrastructure which are most helpful for market expansion: e.g. communication and telecommunication networks, education in technology and management.

János Gács[*]

I agree almost wholly with the paper by *Pogácsás* and *Stadler* on competition in Hungary (Ch. 6) except for the authors' opinion that it was impossible to begin trade liberalisation before 1989. My studies of policies and of intensity of competition demonstrate that liberalisation of trade in Eastern Europe in 1989-1991 was badly prepared and accomplished in a rush. In the early phase it produced no major tensions, but in 1991 and thereafter the emergence of protectionist pressures may be leading to a reversal of the liberalisation process. Also experience in Hungary shows that neither excess supply, nor privatisation of state enterprises have led to a more responsive, more competitive behaviour of the firms in any deterministic way.

Flassik (Ch. 5) dealt with some problems of the Anti-trust Office in Czechoslovakia, including the difficulties of securing cooperation from firms that suffer from monopolistic practices and even from government agencies.

I feed that in addition to the Marshallian (Walrasian) type of competition, the Schumpeterian approach should also be considered, i.e. the need for restructuring and innovation. While the importance of import liberalisation and the change in market structure is usually accepted, little attention is paid to the structural incentives for economic agents and the conditions of entry and exit. Under the notion of structural incentives, such problems as the impact of workers' councils, the ability of banks to exert financial discipline, the lack of real owners and the still existing features of soft budget practices, should be analysed.

---

[*] International Institute for Applied Systems Analysis (IIASA), Laxenburg, Austria.

PART III – VIEWS FROM THE WEST

Chapter 9

COMPETITION POLICIES: THEIR ROLE IN FORMING A MARKET ECONOMY

Guy Charrier[*]

Policies on competition are among the main instruments used in modern economies. All the "Western", industrialised states have a number of instruments at their disposal, of which they make considerable use. Most economic experts agree that countries undergoing a transition toward a market economy should set up an institutional and legal framework, first of all in order to promote competitive relations – at least, to begin with, a competitive psychology – among economic operators. In fact, this is basically what is under way in the new economic democracies of Central and Eastern Europe.

Of course measures intended to foster competitive policies are only part of a whole. It is useful to review them, if only to take stock of the effort required in the area of competition, and to link them with other necessary measures. To simplify this presentation, which cannot be exhaustive, let us say that two main types of measures are needed: those that respond to the preconditions without

---

[*]   Rapporteur permanent, Conseil de la Concurrence, France.

which a market economy would have no meaning, and those which are an indispensable accompaniment to any coherent reform.

First of all, a free market system is based on individual initiative and efforts by each operator to maximise profits through contracts under private law entered into with other operators. For this system to replace state economic planning, the status of private property and the conditions governing contracts must be spelled out. It is clear that access to the market by the largest possible number of operators cannot take place unless the right to free enterprise is proclaimed loud and clear, i.e., by a company law which sets up rules for creating companies and for going bankrupt (efficiency requiring that an unsuccessful operator leave the market so that resources can be allocated elsewhere).

To sum up, the principle of freedom of trade and industry must be promoted. More generally, it is advisable to reach as quickly as possible a consensus for setting up a state governed by the rule of law, as well as the specific rules of the game, in order to create a real economic and social area based on solidarity.

Secondly, a whole series of measures to accompany the transition to a market economy must be implemented. These are mainly the adoption of a market price system based on free prices, wage control, the creation of a statistical apparatus, and of a money market which brings together the supply and demand for capital, a free exchange rate, and convertible currencies; this set of measures requires a system of social protection to attenuate, if not eliminate, the consequences of the unavoidable exclusions which result when the cards are redealt (minimum wage, unemployment compensation ...).

In an article which appeared in several newspapers in various capitals of Eastern and Central Europe entitled "A Monnet Plan for the East", the former French Planning Minister, M. Stoleru, made an inventory of the measures to be taken; he suggested that they should be adopted in stages, given the complexity of fitting together the various elements which in the end relate to the same concerns as what we are here calling competition policy, i.e., adapting to the world market in order to better satisfy the citizen consumer.

The role of competition policy having now been placed in context, we will review the specific objectives of competition in the play of the market and will spell out the means which are generally useful and even necessary in implementing a competition policy.

132

9.1 The objectives of a competition policy

Ideas on the goals of a competition policy are evolving; the successive changes in approaches to competition which took place in France since the Second World War are worth mentioning in this respect. They are of particular interest in three areas: inflation, the organisation of the marketing system, the elaboration of industrial policy.

(a) Changing approaches

For a long time, competition policy had three main objectives:

- consumer protection, to allow the freest and broadest choice as part of a concern which was both economic and social;
- fighting inflation, competition being presented as the necessary counter-weight to free prices and as a decisive tool for overcoming the structural causes of inflation;
- giving national companies the means to compete internationally, i.e., accepting their behaviour on the domestic market as the most effective means for strengthening them and giving them the best chances abroad.

The presentation that has been made over the last few years in France, and which happens to be similar in other ways to that generally made by officials in other countries (for example when the OECD asks the question), is quite different, the accent being on behaviour vis-à-vis market structures. This of course does not mean that previously emphasised concerns have been abandoned, but the fact that the centre of gravity has changed is indicative of a different concept. The turning point came when new legislation was passed, i.e., the ordinance of 1 December 1986 on "freedom of prices and competition".

The goals of competition law flow from the concept according to which, in a competitive system, individual pursuit of profit by producers leads them on the one hand spontaneously to use production factors in as efficient a way as possible, and on the other, to increase the supply of goods whose quality/price ratio will best satisfy consumers.

The price hierarchy is an exact reflection of that of the goods' minimal production costs (i.e., the cost of the resources strictly necessary to produce them, taking into account existing technology).

From this point on, events tend to interact:
- the less efficient companies are destined to close down,
- or else they go into a different field of activity, choosing the ones with the best opportunities;
- the most efficient companies take over the markets.

But companies fearing the verdict of the market and the obligations it entails may be tempted to protect themselves:
- for example by opposing an increased supply of goods (whose production costs are low and which satisfy consumers),
- by maintaining artificially high prices,
- or by raising barriers to the entry of new players into promising markets.

In these circumstances, there is a considerable risk that companies will get together, or that certain companies will abuse the dominant position they have acquired on the market. This results in higher costs for consumers, since in the end, it leads to higher prices or lower quality, and finally, probably to lower quantities.

Government should intervene to avoid these undesirable consequences. It should act both on the structures and on behaviour, by applying rules which are relevant but strict. From this point of view, there are three main lines of conduct which the authorities in charge of regulating competition should follow.

First of all, they should take into account market dynamics and their evolution over time. So realities should not be frozen as they appear at any given time. Market analysis in terms of competition makes it indispensable to take the time factor into account. In examining concerted and abusive practices, such as dominant positions and mergers, the authorities must draw conclusions in terms of their repercussions on competition, not only at the time they occur, but also in the future, by evaluating the consequences for economic progress (for example by examining the likelihood of the emergence or blockage of new technologies and products). This type of analysis, mainly on a case by case basis, tends to sweep aside dogmatic concepts of competition law – either laissez faire in the sense that any intervention is contrary to the natural laws of the market and therefore damaging, or systematic intervention on the basis of preestablished rules.

A second principle flows from the first: that of the subsidiarity of competition rules: the principle is freedom; regulation and intervention are exceptions. Competition law punishes anti-competitive abuses, but it cannot put into question a given company's situation on the market *a priori*, claiming it could hinder the free functioning of the market, since everything depends on effective or potential market behaviour. (For example, a dominant position is not reprehensible in and of itself, whatever the market share of the company may be; only if this position is abused should action be taken.)

Thirdly, there is one pitfall to be avoided; competition law is not intended to protect competitors. It would be contrary to market fluidity and free enterprise to set up or reestablish an equilibrium that in fact would turn out to be a prolongation of the *status quo*. The purpose of a competition policy is not artificially to support uncompetitive companies in difficulty, or to act as an insurance against poor market positioning. Operators are responsible for their strategies, and reap the benefits or the losses; market punishment of risks should be understood as a precondition for economic efficiency.

However, these principles do not exclude government and the judiciary from playing an important regulatory and punitive role when there are abuses, or from arbitrating other values which necessarily interfere with economic policy in a complex world; this comes under the heading of the moralisation of economic relations, and takes into account the unacceptable social costs of certain structural adjustments, and the maintenance of activities which are in the public interest, which either function independently of market rules or are doomed in the name of profitability.

There are examples in the relationship between competition policy and the fight against inflation, or "industrial policy".

(b) Competition policy and price policy

Within the context of old concepts, in particular those implemented in France starting in 1945, economic policy was in large part based on price controls. At that time it was believed that competition policy could complement a policy of administered prices; but it was given a secondary role, especially in terms of structures.

Later, it was recognised that competition could play an additional role in some cases, as a substitute for price controls in areas of activity not covered by regulatory measures, taxes or blockages; here competition acted to compress price levels.

It was only at the third stage that competition was considered independently from its effect on price levels, as an instrument of economic efficiency that affected structures. According to this last concept, the competitive process can lead to an allocation of resources of interest to the community, since that will force suppliers to be as efficient as possible, and therefore keep costs as low as possible (or achieve the best cost/quality ratio); yet there does not seem to be a direct relationship between the intensity of competition and the maintenance of prices at a level considered non-inflationary.

Inflation is not a question of price levels, but of their variation over a certain period. The price of a product may be higher where there is a monopoly than in a competitive situation, but there is no indication it will rise faster. Taking action against monopolies can be justified, but not within the framework of a conjunctural price policy.

A competition policy is therefore recognised more for its action on market mechanisms than as acting directly on price levels, even if, in the end, the pressure it exerts has a beneficial effect on the behaviour of operators in determining the prices of their products.

This has two consequences:

- Competition policy can be considered independently of price considerations, as a tool which can help improve market adjustments. As such, it is necessary.
- Competition policy does not necessarily make government action on prices superfluous (one is even tempted to say that it makes such action all the more necessary, since competition normally does not play this role); but this action should only be taken under exceptional circumstances, those in which there is no market adjustment, for example in a transition situation from a planned economy to one which is subject to market forces, in sectors being privatised, or in crisis periods.

Thus, as has happened with some legislation, the French regulations which followed the 1 December 1986 decree reverse the principle; they make producers free to set prices while leaving open the possibility for the government to intervene in certain specific circumstances, via temporary measures, when the market fails to play its normal regulatory role and when competition is inefficient or impracticable. For example, during the last five years, the French government has regulated prices in sectors where price competition was judged to be limited, due either to a monopoly situation (transport, school lunch rooms, motorway tolls, towing in ocean ports, electricity, gas, various activities in the overseas departments, prices in retirement homes), or due to long-term supply difficulties (as for certain products in the Island of Saint Pierre et Miquelon), or when specific legislation exists (taxis, highway tow services).

It would seem obvious that, even after converting to a free market system, countries that have lived under price controls will have to set prices in situations such as those mentioned above. It is better to have an instrument at hand which has a proper framework, than be forced to improvise.

(c) The role of distribution in the emergence of market mechanisms

Observation of economic development in certain countries, especially in France where the phenomenon is particularly remarkable, owes much to the emergence and use of the power of *distributors*. Highly interesting lessons can be learned by countries in transition toward market economies. And government can encourage this evolution in order to protect competitive conditions.

Since demand – from final consumers – conditions and spurs supply – the producers – the role of intermediaries, i.e., distributors, is capital. No one knows and appreciates the prospects of consumer arbitration better than a distributor who can thus help producers take into account potential choices.

In other words, producer strategies will be all the better adapted to consumer needs if the distribution chain is efficient in making known those needs and imposing them. The evolution of this triangular relationship, influenced by public policy, is full of ups and downs, some of which will be mentioned here.

Increased consumption ("the consumer society") opened the way to new types of marketing, which competed mainly by lowering prices and then by delivering services. The dynamism of distributors, coupled with increased stock turnover, enabled them to sell at low prices, putting new products within reach of mass consumers.

A series of phenomena was then released: since mass distribution weighed on prices, and thus on the level of inflation, it was encouraged by government through protective measures which outlawed fixed resale prices and refusals to sell which could be attempted by producers in response to what appeared as price cutting. But also, under pressure from small shop keepers, regulations forbid loss sales and unjustified discrimination; then, in order to counter giant super-market, "commercial urban planning" was closely controlled by requiring authorisations for shops above a certain surface. In reality, under cover of an equilibrating policy and in order to foster transparency for fair competition, government intervened in the market functioning process, in contradiction with the principles of free enterprise.

However, the general evolution, which in the long run fostered greater efficiency, continued. A three-pronged movement was visible. Big chains, which could not enlarge their stores, turned to outside growth, first through concentration, then by creating national chains, buying-groups and even super buying-groups which serviced several groups; consumers demanded ever lower prices to compensate for slower growth following the two oil crises and were aided by emerging consumer power; meanwhile producers adopted a more aggressive marketing stance in order to meet demand and the power of distributors.

In the end, the power of national chain stores and their demand for low wholesale prices, on the one hand, and producer resistance on the other, as well as the need for producers to adapt their productivity, intensified competition.

An over-energetic intervention by government to deprive the protagonists of their arms by forbidding their use – the arms of one side being the demand for conditions which could eventually be discriminatory, while loss-selling, fixed resale prices and refusal to sell were those of the other side – could in fact be considered anti-economic. For this reason, the new French legislation – except for loss-selling and fixed resale prices (on which the debate continues) – depenalised these acts, and now provides no punishment except when there is abuse, according to the rules on concerted practices and dominant positions (under the jurisdiction of the Competition Council) or based on civil responsibility (under the legal system).

We should add that small businesses have not necessarily been excluded – at least merchants who adapted by underscoring the services they could offer better than supermarkets, i.e., by being close to the consumer (bigger stores exist mainly in the suburbs), or by product demonstrations and service. Others have joined as franchises, or responded to the need to organise distribution arising from producer actions (exclusive or selective distribution).

This has had several consequences:

- increased demand, transmitted by distributors, pushed producers to adapt their marketing strategy, develop new products and improve productivity;
- large distributors, too, developed image and communication strategies and ended up selecting brand products, and playing brands off one against another to obtain the best conditions;
- small businesses tended to develop a new service policy;
- globally, consumers benefited from distributors' and producers' efforts.

From this approach, it appears that diminishing or making better use of constraints fosters competition and thereby the satisfaction of the final consumer. But this is not incompatible with – it even renders indispensable – government intervention, not only to punish abuses under competition law, but also to adopt different types of measures intended to make adjustments economically and socially bearable (by reducing exit costs for non-performers through social measures), and by reducing entry costs to increase the number of actors (through a policy of attractive business leases). Also, vigilance with respect to the legal and physical protection of consumers should be proportionate to the pressures upon them, which are all the stronger the fiercer the competition.

(d) Competition policy and industrial policy

How can a society mobilise its production factors most efficiently, thus bringing citizens the highest revenues and maximum satisfaction? This is of course the main question all governments face, all the more so in countries where market economies are forming. While there is no question of a centralised administration dictating every choice, it is just as unreasonable to deny the need for overall vision and action.

Without going too deeply into the well-known discussion on the conflict between competition and industrial policy, both at the national and Community level, some remarks are in order to limit the debate and to draw the lessons for countries in transition.

"Industrial policy" in fact has two facets: government intervention on the overall environment, and tactical actions on a case by case basis.

The first facet is concerned with the conditions under which economic activity is exercised and with influencing productive structures by defining the regulatory framework, by financing training and research, etc.; in these matters interference does not seem detrimental to competition, so long as subsidies do not distort it, in particular at the Community level in the EC countries – a matter to which the Commission in Brussels pays special attention. In addition, but this is another debate within a European context, the question is whether there should be a shift towards promoting a European industrial policy which would go beyond the main projects of general European interest such as Esprit (applied research in information technology), Race (telecommunications), Brite (new technologies for traditional industries), Bap, Eclair (biotechnologies), Flair (nutrition), Media (audiovisual), etc. In fact, precautions have been taken in defining these main orientations of industrial policy so that they are "in conformity with the laws of the market and do not imply any sort of government dirigism".

The second facet is more delicate, since the question is whether government should intervene directly in companies to orient their strategies and activities for purposes supposedly in the general public interest. Notwithstanding liberal doctrine, this type of support and restructuring, initiated by government, remains considerable and can come into conflict with national competition law (and Community law).

The main declared purpose of competition policy can sometimes be sorely tried; but the fact that an independent authority has the decision-making power is a sure guarantee. Also, the area of competency of competition law, which specifically covers the activity of public entities (in terms of their industrial and marketing activities), is another safeguard.

To conclude this point, it seems useful to draw a line between overall interventions defined by broad orientations (resulting from flexible planning), and support measures taken on a case by case basis. The former, which can lead to subsidies being determined according to priorities that in the medium term increase competition, either by increasing the number of suppliers, or by improving their market potential, are compatible with, and most certainly necessary, in setting up a market economy. We would emphasise once again at this point

140

that competition is only one way of achieving economic efficiency; if efficiency is achieved by other ways which accelerate the process via adequate intervention, there is not only no contradiction but a synergy is created. On the other hand, interventions of the second kind, which maintain artificially obsolete industries, can have short-term negative consequences.

9.2 The instruments of competition policy

The new economic democracies of Central and Eastern Europe have already set up institutional and regulatory frameworks which include anti-monopoly measures. So, even if it were possible, it would not be appropriate to suggest an ideal system. But we can modestly underline the fact that no system, however well constructed, is permanent or beyond improvement. This is shown by the many amendments, and even basic changes (such as the ones being planned in Sweden or in Great Britain), that are constantly being made in all the countries which have long had such systems.

The purpose is to show the main lines around which competition policy is shaped, as well as its institutional framework and rules.

(a) A proper institutional framework

From a very general point of view, the observation of economic systems shows that structures determine operator strategies, and strategies make performance possible. This defines the various roles and their limits.

For controlling strategies, the role of government is necessarily limited; the contrary would entail a bureaucratising effect and hamper initiatives by private enterprise. This control is not normally part of government's duties, except in terms of overall orientations (which is certainly not negligible).

On the other hand, government – in the broadest sense, i.e., the executive and the judiciary – must control performance, that is certain forms of behaviour such as concerted practices, abuse of dominant positions, and individual restrictive practices based on a lack of transparency in transactions.

Also, "countervailing powers" should be organised to foster economic democracy, through debate, exchanges of views and training of economic operators as well as government officials; decision-making powers and consultations should be set up at all levels. Links between government and consumers are necessary; chambers of commerce, producers' and shopkeepers' organisations, as well as consumers, are useful as counterweights to government power.

Specifically, several organisational modes are viable; but observation of existing systems reveals certain similarities, even though there may be national particularities. The most obvious of these is the fact that a government agency that oversees competition, whether from an administrative or judiciary point of view, is relatively independent of the government itself. Even when the two functions, the elaboration of competition policy and the implementation of rules, come under the authority of one entity (the *Bundeskartellamt* in Germany), this entity retains its independence, even if the responsible Minister has discretionary powers. This independence is all the greater when the two functions just mentioned are clearly distinguishable; this is the case in France and in Spain where there is an office in charge of competition policy that answers to the executive, and an independent Council (or court).

The fact that independence is emphasised, is not only a functional advantage; it indicates a will to give operators guarantees, subject to the rules governing competition. Legislative amendments always tend to reinforce this aspect. Undermining competition is considered a serious offence and penalties are often heavy. Thus, within the framework of a State governed by law, procedural guarantees must be built in. The right to defend oneself, access to one's file, confidentiality concerning business dealings, the possibility of making one's observations known, are among the basic principles over which the Court of Justice of the European Community is very watchful, as are government and national jurisdictions.

A last point concerns the advantage of linking jurisdictions of common law, both civil and penal, to competition oversight. Without wishing to "export" the French system, which is organised in this manner, as are other national systems, it is useful to have an operational division of functions in order to uncover, on the one hand, anti-competitive practices which hinder the market – and which concern specialised government officials in charge of competition – and, on the other, restrictive practices which bring into play contractual relations between two companies; the latter answer to the common law contracts court, or when necessary to the criminal courts.

142

Thus in the French system, for example, the complementarity of powers and competencies is organised around three poles: common law jurisdictions, government, and specialised independent authorities.

(b) Effective juridical rules

We should first like to observe that no definition of the concept of competition is generally included in law, nor is any other element relating to the economic justification of this notion. French executive decrees are no different. It is true that such considerations belong more to the preamble of a law than to its substantial provisions. However, it is useful to emphasise the main lines.

In France, the texts of decisions by the Competition Council or of decrees by jurisdictions give us some indications. In addition, the Competition Council, in its annual reports, has explained the economic role of the competitive process, as well as the conditions under which it can take place.

The Council recalled that a competitive situation is characterised mainly by three principles, which are enunciated in a similar presentation by the Luxembourg Court of Justice (in particular the ruling in re Suiker Unie): market actors must have independent decision-making powers; they must be uncertain as to the intentions of other economic operators, and they must not adopt exclusionary strategies which limit or forbid the entry into the market of potential competitors.

These are the principles that guide officials in charge of competition in their daily efforts to protect the market in terms both of behaviour and structures.

(i) On the principle of forbidding concerted practices

Most national laws include the general principle of outlawing, with exemptions, a list of practices which could be considered as agreements hampering competition, drawn up in similar language; several EC countries use the wording of Article 85 of the Rome Treaty. There are however procedural differences (on notification, for example).

There is every reason to believe that the recently elected governments of Central and Eastern Europe will in the near future be confronted with the same

143

practices as those which have so often been criticised, in particular by the French Competition Council or the EC Commission, some of which have been the subject of spectacular debates. Some such practices are described hereafter as examples:

– Horizontal agreements, for example agreements among companies to fix prices through price lists, recommendations, trade association price lists, exchanges of information, agreements to share out public or private markets, consultations for excluding a company from the market. In this respect the Council has specified the limits of the role of professional organisations; their usefulness, far from being up for question as indicated above, should be encouraged as economic links in the countries of Eastern Europe, on condition that their acts do not lead to restrictions of competition. This can happen when they publicise recommended prices, or organise information exchanges or boycotts, or when they take over their members' role in conducting commercial negotiations. Without infringing the rules of competition, their functions include providing information on price trends and costs of raw materials, technical information on manufacturing techniques and on those involved in providing services.

– Vertical agreements deriving from contracts between a producer and his distributors, in particular within the framework of selective or exclusive distribution contracts: In the area of vertical restraints, the Council had occasion to refine its jurisprudence by deciding that a supplier's sales conditions are not a unilateral act, but constitute agreements between the supplier and his entire sales network (and are therefore subject to competition rules). Continuing in this direction, it examined these conditions according to the same validity criteria as selective distribution contracts which, by discounts, can act as mechanisms of selection in the same ways as those used by this type of distribution. The Council also considered that a producer may grant qualitative discounts to those of his distributors who offer services which are appreciated by consumers and which contribute to his brand image, this being a practice that intensified competition between brands on the same market.

– Joint companies: The creation of joint companies or "joint ventures" can come under the heading prohibiting agreements or constitute a concentration operation (cf infra); but while the creation of a joint production company made up of several companies on the same market does not in itself constitute an anti-competitive practice (as would probably be the case for a joint distribution company), companies that join together may not use this joint structure to implement concerted practices which could limit the free play of competition.

– Agreements between companies belonging to the same group: In connection with public contracts, the Council does not consider it contrary to the competition rules for companies having legal or financial ties to renounce their commercial autonomy and get together to set up and transmit, even separately, proposals in response to calls for bids, as long as they so inform the prime contractor and the master of works when submitting their bids.

(ii) *Prohibiting the abuse of dominant positions*

The question of knowing whether to penalise dominant positions or only their abuse is central. An interventionist concept leads to casting doubt on any company which is in a dominant position, and which, through this position, is likely to hinder competition; this seems reprehensible to the extent that it tends to give credence to the idea of an ideal state of competition and of a market situation that has to be kept stable, contrary to the fluctuating nature of the market. It is normal that a company should try to dominate, to reach and maintain the "tranquil life of the monopoly" which consumers bestow upon it through their choice when they consider that its products or services are the best. Hence the systematic condemnation of companies that go beyond a certain threshold market share – always difficult to define in advance – does not necessarily foster economic efficiency.

In establishing provisions relating to abuse of dominant positions, the Competition Council takes a pragmatic approach. It defines markets by determining the products that can be considered as belonging to each market, according to their substitutability; their degree of substitutability is evaluated according to several elements, including the characteristics of the products themselves, the technical conditions for their use, their utilisation and delivery costs, and the strategy adopted by suppliers in marketing them. The same is true when defining a dominant position; the Council enquires whether the company is able to escape from the pressure of competition, and to what extent its supremacy can be threatened by new actors on the market; it also examines market shares and whether the company in question belongs to a group.

The Competition Council has also dealt with a second group of situations of dominance where economic dependence was alleged by a distributor against a producer or an importer. It ruled that this type of situation should be assessed by taking into account the four criteria that have to be fulfilled: the fame of the producer's brand; the importance, on the one hand, of his share in the market being considered, and on the other, of the seller's turnover, and finally the difficulties for the distributor in obtaining equivalent products.

(c)   Controlling concentrations

It is clear that to maintain a competitive economy, it is important to intervene in structures and behaviour patterns, when privatisation, restructuring of sectors in which there are monopolies, or mergers occur.

It should be observed that legal provisions generally establish rules spelling out the principles and methods for controlling concentrations; such rules closely resemble that resulting from the EC regulation adopted at the end of 1989 and applied in September 1990, or those applied in Germany or in France, even if there are important differences (for example in the distribution or competencies between the authorities in charge of competition and the government). A choice must be made between two solutions: either the power of decision resides with the executive (for example in France) or with an "independent" authority (in Germany and Italy). The first solution enables the government to adopt measures that take into consideration not only the competitive situation and the economic progress which results, but also other preoccupations mentioned above (social for example), which can be useful in certain vulnerable sectors or economies. This division of roles does not exclude modification by setting up bridges between the two: if power is invested in an independent authority or office, a right of veto can be granted to the executive (for example, in Germany, as a last resort, the Minister of the Economy can authorise activities which the *Bundeskartellamt* has forbidden); on the other hand, when the decision is to be taken by the French Minister, a preliminary opinion may be requested from the competition authorities.

Analysis of practices used in controlling concentrations in France shows that while French government interest is currently increasing, for a long time it was at a low level. Of course, it is not enough to count the number of cases submitted to the Competition Council (which is not obligatory for authorising operations), in order to evaluate this interest. Before forbidding anything (and this should be preceded by an opinion from the Competition Council), the Minister and his services can start negotiations inviting the companies concerned to improve their project in order better to preserve competitive conditions. But, for information, in the five years from 1987 to 1991, the number of operations was approximately 600-800 depending on the year (notification was not mandatory, and only about twenty operations a year were notified to the Minister by companies); fourteen matters were referred to the Competition Council by the Minister during this period.

When a matter is referred to the Council, it has to answer the following essential questions: does the operation indeed constitute a concentration, according to the definition given and the thresholds required? is the concentration likely to hinder competition? and if the answers are yes, does an economic justification make it possible to conclude that the operation will make a sufficient contribution to economic progress to compensate the negative effects on competition? The decree requires the Minister to answer the same questions, but he must also examine the operations in terms of their contribution to economic and "social" progress.

The main point in controlling mergers is certainly the need to examine operations in terms of the economic progress that will flow from them; to project into the future, to speculate on economic efficiency and not to reason in terms of market shares acquired.

9.3 In conclusion

The evolution of competition and price policies, executed or contemplated, both in developed countries and in countries in transition, demonstrate the convergence among the reforms in progress. The obvious trend is less regulation of economic activities and thus increased room for the play of the market and of competition mechanisms.

The scope of this orientation, regarded as inevitable, is sufficiently wide to enable each country to find its own way.

There is no model. The experience accumulated in certain countries cannot all be transposed. This is clear.

Yet this type of policy does correspond to certain common principles, which can be summed up as follows:

– Competition is not an end in itself. It is a tool, serving objectives which should be recognised.

– The invisible hand of the great classical economists cannot do everything. Government retains an important role. Competition means on the one hand encouraging effective market strategies (commercial and economic policies in general), and on the other hand, preventing restrictions on transactions by operators on the market; this means that government has a crucial role to play: pedagogical, dissuasive and corrective.

– Legislation is no doubt necessary, but is not everything. The fact that there is a law does not mean that problems will be solved. Inversely there are highly industrialised countries with successful economic performance which passed laws only recently (until October 1990, Italy had none); they also did not have a real competition policy.

In the final analysis, competition is an instrument of the market economy, which itself is only a means; in this respect one can but agree with the "Summer Meditations" of President Václav Havel (*Editions de l'Aube*, 1991):

> "For me, a market economy represents the obvious, just as the air I breathe; is it not a form of economic activity that has proved its worth and been confirmed by centuries (or rather millennia) of existence, and which corresponds to human nature? Notwithstanding this evidence, for me it is not, and cannot be, an ideology. And even less the meaning of life. I find it rather ridiculous, and also quite dangerous, that for a certain number of people (...), the market economy should become a cult object, a body of dogmas implacably defended and venerated as if they were superior to what this economy is meant to serve, that is, life itself."

Chapter 10

JAPAN'S POST-WAR INDUSTRIAL POLICY (1945-1970) AS A MODEL FOR EAST EUROPEAN COUNTRIES

Nobuko Inagawa[*]

10.1 Introduction

Recent developments in Eastern Europe leave many open questions about the possible development paths and strategies of these countries. Japanese experience after the Second World War (WWII) and Japanese industrial policies adopted from 1945 to 1970, may be relevant to the policy makers in East European countries.[1] This study aims at evaluating those Japanese experiences that could be useful in principle and are probably adaptable to East European countries.

In answering this question one has to clarify whether, and to what extent, explicit or implicit policies of Japan have contributed to its success. If there is evidence that Japanese strategies and industrial policy instruments seem to have been systematically responsible, at least in part, for the growth record, there arise further questions: if this success has been possible under specific national circumstances, can it be expected to be transferable to another country, or to a different international environment?

To throw light on these questions and to draw lessons for useful economic strategy advice for East European countries, I discuss:

- what is industrial policy? (Chapter 10.2),
- the history of Japanese industrial policy (Chapter 10.3),

---

[*] Special researcher at the Federal Institute for Soviet and International Studies, Cologne, FRG. This paper was presented under the name of Nobuko Maeda (Mrs. Inagawa's maiden name) at the workshop.

[1] Including the former Soviet Union.

- what can Japanese industrial policy offer to East Europe? (Chapter 10.4),
- Conclusion (Chapter 10.5).

Japan's economic growth after WWII can be attributed to macroeconomic policy, expanding world trade, historical background, and industrial policy. Industrial policy might have contributed positively, negatively or not at all to Japan's development; it is an important question.

10.2 What is industrial policy?

I define industrial policy as a policy of technical change, leading to change in industrial structure – the key factor in economic growth. To investigate how the Japanese economic development took place from the structural point of view, one cannot ignore industrial policy and the role it played. I will look into what Japanese industrial policy actually was, its effects, and how the industrial structure reacted. Japanese economic management is neither market mechanism alone nor central planning. It operates through the close connection between government and industry in consensual decisions. Government intervention has been practised mainly for intermediate goods; final demand industry had to remain market oriented. Competitive power in the final demand industries has been so great that it forced the intermediate goods industries to be competitive in spite of government intervention. Competition is viewed as a tool, probably the most important tool, of industrial policy. At the same time it is realised that the costs of competition are also to be controlled.[2]

Industrial policy incorporates all measures that will improve the economy's supply potential: anything that will improve growth, productivity and competitiveness. The main issue is whether policies should be *general*, leaving the structural readjustments needed at the industry level to free market forces, or whether *industry specific* policies are required. When the market mechanism is at the development stage, industry specific policies are needed; but when market mechanisms prevail: general policies are enough. In order to reach the stage

---

[2]   One must not forget the cost of implementing market mechanism. This is true for East European countries implementing economic reform. Success lies in insistence by policy makers that competition will eventually be introduced.

where market mechanism prevails in the economy, one needs industry specific policies. I will review the period 1945-1970 when Japan was in the developing stage. The discussion is restricted to policies that focus directly on the supply side, that is, on shifting production functions and the composition of factor inputs.

Industrial policy is not a new idea; it exists in all countries. But what distinguishes Japan is very strong and close cooperation of people, enterprises, and government in pursuing industrial policy. Proponents of an industrial policy claim that economic growth hinges on performance in the dynamic sectors of the economy and that comparative advantage must be "created" in the current international competitive environment. Opponents deny the need for government intervention. They argue that resources will naturally find their way into the most profitable and socially desirable uses.

Classical and neoclassical economics showed the superiority of free trade, assuming constant returns to scale, perfect competition, and absence of externalities. But in reality increasing returns to scale are central to the explanation of long-run growth. Perfect competition does not exist and externalities do exist. Therefore, in order to help industries become more competitive in the developing stage, government should intervene to create dynamic comparative advantage. Government should influence the incentives in the private sector, thereby establishing the basis for economic growth.

One reason for the effectiveness of industrial policies in Japan is the fact, according to Okuno-Fujiwara (1988), that the committees organised by the government to build and implement industrial policies also provided opportunities for information exchange. Members of these committees, including bankers and managers from different industries as well as government officials, exchanged their information about new technologies and/or potential demand in domestic as well as foreign markets. With the help of such exchanges, they became capable of more consistent and coordinated decisions, with government plans providing a focus. If such an informational exchange promoted economic growth and/or strategic promotion of industries, it worked as a mechanism of coordination. The key factor behind the possibility of coordination lies in the fact that some industries are interdependent and oligopolistic.

151

10.3 History of Japanese industrial policy

The motors driving economic development are capital accumulation and human resource accumulation. This is true for both socialism and capitalism. Japan after World War II took the path of market mechanisms with the help of government policies.

The industrial policy after WWII can be divided into three phases.

(a) Early Post-war Period (1945-1949): 1945; economic democratisation; reconstruction and stabilisation.

(b) The start of rapid growth (1950-1954): Industrial policy aimed at developing industries (according to Komiya et al. (1984)) which met two conditions:

    (i) industries which Western countries already possessed and that Japan could also build up by protecting and "fostering";

    (ii) industries of a certain size and interesting to the public (for example, iron and steel, shipbuilding, machine industry in general, heavy electrical equipment, and chemicals). Later the automobile industry, petrochemicals, and others were added.

(c) Fast-growth era (1955-1970): improvement of industrial structure; building heavy and chemical industry; internationalisation and organisation of the industrial structure.

It must be said first that the pre-war and war-time economy concealed in embryo a variety of elements leading into the post-war economy. To a great extent, the system created during the war was inherited as the post-war economic system; the industries expanded during the war became the major post-war industries. War-time technology was reborn in the post-war export industries; and the post-war national lifestyle too originated in changes that began during the years of conflict.

The legacy of war

The state of the Japanese economy at the end of WWII was as follows.

– Three million dead; material losses yen 64.3 billion;

– Production capacity: the chemical and heavy industries had more plant and equipment capacity during the war than before, bringing reductions in light industry capacity, especially in textiles;

–   Engineers and workers acquired their technologies in war factories which reconverted (machine gun factories turned to making sewing machines; optical weapons factories turned to cameras and binoculars);

–   The spread of subcontracting was also a war-time phenomenon; large firms in the military industries which had produced everything on their own, including parts, to facilitate production increases, developed as an emergency measure a system of subcontracting parts etc. to small and medium-sized firms. This is the origin of the long-term post-war relationships;

–   A system of financial institutions to finance munitions companies was established, so contrived that other financial institutions, as well as the Bank of Japan and the government, backed the authorised institutions. In the post-war reconstruction these relationships reappear and become entrenched in the form of the powerful financial groupings known as "financial keiretsu";

–   The strong administrative leadership which the Ministry of International Trade and Industry (MITI) came to exercise over industry can also be traced to the controls exercised by the war-time Commerce and Industry and Munitions Ministries;

–   In 1942 the Nationwide Financial Control Association was established, centred on the Bank of Japan; this set the stage for such direct controls as "window guidance" in the post-war economy. It was during war-time controls that the guidance relationship was established between firms and the bureaucracy, and between private banks and the Bank of Japan;

–   The origin of post-war labour-management relations can also be found in the war period. In every firm, "Patriotic-industrial associations" (Sangyo Hokoku Kai) were organised with the participation of both labour and management. The Trade Union Law, the Labour Standards Law, and the Labour Relations Adjustment Law were enacted. Later, the war-time industrial associations were able to convert themselves into company unions;

–   The seniority wage system and the lifetime employment system arose from the implementation of wage controls in 1940-1941;

–   Legislation in 1938-41 providing for health and accident insurance became the cornerstone for the post-war social security system;

– The basis of the post-war land reform was also laid during the war in the form of rice price controls, together with at subsidies to some producers for increases in output.

One can see that the post-war social and economic system, technologies, lifestyles and customs took shape during the war and were passed on from the war years.

10.3.a Early post-war period (1945-1949), the reconstruction era

In 1945, there were 10 million unemployed. Agriculture occupied a labour force of 18 million, 4 million more than pre-war, thus modifying the unemployment problem but a problem of low-income underemployed persisted long afterwards. Though half of the Japanese work force were in agriculture, the food supply was insufficient. Capital accumulation and industrial resources were also inadequate. So the main aim was to build up industrialisation through export increases, for which promotion of capital accumulation and development of human resources were necessary. According to the "Economic Recovery Planning, Second Draft" (May 1949), the future level of the economy and living standards depended on exports and this depended on government intervention with cooperation of the population.

Inflation was 85 per cent per year, for the consumer price index, in 1946-1951. An Emergency Financial Measures Order, invoked in 1946, attempted to check inflation by calling for the deposit of all cash in financial institutions, ordering the issue of new currency, implementing a new yen conversion which authorised each household to draw up to yen 500 per month in living expenses, and levying a property tax. But the real solution was not found until the implementation of the Dodge Plan in 1949 (see below).

Japan had five important economic reforms to undertake to get the market mechanism functioning. These reforms will next be described.

(i)   The breakup of the Zaibatsu:

The dissolution of the Zaibatsu was intended to break up the holding companies and to sell their share capital to the public. Of the 443 million shares held in Japan in 1946, 167 million were held by the Zaibatsu companies. By 1951, the Zaibatsu holdings were reduced to only 2 million.

154

Table 10.1

Concentration ratios by industry 1937-1962
(per cent)

	1937		1950		1962	
	Top 3 firms	Top 10 firms	Top 3 firms	Top 10 firms	Top 3 firms	Top 10 firms
Pig iron	97.8	–	88.7	93.0	27.7	38.4
Ferro-alloys	51.2	60.0	48.8	81.2	34.6	69.3
Hot rolled steel	56.2	81.3	49.6	77.1	49.8	78.9
Galvanised iron sheet	19.9	85.5	32.8	70.3	37.6	73.6
Electric-furnace steel	74.9	100.0	73.4	100.0	65.3	100.0
Aluminium	91.8	100.0	100.0	–	100.0	–
Bearings	100.0	–	76.3	95.4	68.7	92.6
Steel ships	67.5	96.7	39.1	94.1	37.7	75.5
Ammonium sulphate	60.6	93.5	41.2	87.3	32.7	78.2
Super phosphate of lime	46.6	80.6	47.3	89.7	32.0	72.5
Caustic soda	55.1	86.5	33.8	71.1	23.5	59.8
Synthetic dyes	56.3	70.1	75.2	92.7	64.8	88.8
Sheet celluloid	77.7	91.2	69.2	89.2	80.6	95.0
Rayon filament	36.5	76.1	70.8	100.0	60.5	100.0
Cotton yarn	33.9	59.1	35.1	88.1	16.6	48.2
Cotton textiles	16.5	30.6	18.6	44.2	6.6	17.2
Pulp	65.2	85.3	39.5	73.0	30.5	60.6
Paper	83.1	99.3	57.0	80.3	39.9	65.9
Soy sauce	20.1	28.2	16.7	23.7	25.3	30.3
Cement	40.1	78.5	55.9	91.3	47.1	82.0
Coal	35.4	60.6	35.9	59.6	31.0	55.8
Foreign trade[a]	35.1	51.7	13.0	30.5	24.8	50.5
Banking	25.8	61.1	21.8	59.6	19.9	54.5
Marine transport	29.8	46.8	18.1	33.1	22.8	56.6
Life insurance	41.4	81.6	47.2	83.7	43.5	85.1
Warehousing	37.8	61.4	25.2	37.4	20.6	31.2

a) Pre-war figures for foreign trade are averages for the years 1937-1943, while post-war figures shown are for 1951 and 1957 instead of for 1950 and 1962.

Source: From Fair Trade Commission, *Nihon no Sangyō Shūchū* (Japan's Industrial Concentration), Data Table 1. Percentages of output held by largest 3, and 10, firms.

Zaibatsu leaders, including members of the founding families, were purged and were prohibited from further activity in the financial world.

(ii)   The Anti-Monopoly Law of 1947 (relaxed in 1949 and in 1953 and stiffened again in 1977) established a basic principle for the post-war Japanese economy. By other legislation in 1947, 18 companies were split up; Nippon Steel, for example, was broken up into Yahata Steel and Fuji Steel; and Mitsui Mining was separated into two parts. (See *Table 10.1*, concentration ratios by industry.)

This set the stage for the fierce competition characteristic of post-war industry in Japan. The expansion of plant and equipment and the technological advances made under the pressure of competition produced economic growth. The anti-monopoly policies exerted great influence over the post-war economy. Intense competition appeared in all industries, particularly the chemical and heavy industries; in steel and automobiles a few oligopolistic firms competed; in textiles a large number of firms were active.

(iii)   Land reform: All the land of absentee landlords, and all but one cho (1.25 cho equal 1 ha) of the property of landlords resident in the rural villages, was to be bought by the government for redistribution to the existing tenant farmers. The government role as intermediary in the buying and selling of land was one feature retained from the Ministry's first draft. The result of the land reform shows that the proportion of total agricultural land area worked by tenant farmers was reduced from nearly 50 to about 10 per cent.

This led to rapid increases in the productive capacity of rice-growing land and introduction of rice-growing technology, bringing higher incomes and an expansion of domestic markets.

(iv)   The Priority Production System (Keisha Seisan Houshiki): In 1946, war-time indemnities were suspended. So business and financial institutions needed a system that would supply both material and financial assistance. Government established the Reconstruction Bank, issuing bonds accepted by the Bank of Japan, and founded the Priority Production System. This aimed at industrial rehabilitation through the levers of crude oil and steel production, then through coal, the primary energy source at the time: imported crude oil would be injected into the steel industry; then the increased steel production would be invested in the coal industry; increased coal production would be reinvested in the steel industry and so on.

156

Once steel and coal production had been raised to a certain level, the increased coal production could then be gradually channelled into other basic sectors to produce overall industrial recovery. To achieve this, Reconstruction Bank funds were invested in the coal industry on a top priority basis, labour was recruited on a large scale, and food and subsistence commodities were rationed as much as possible.

This system brought an expansion of the Reconstruction Bank's funds, accelerating inflation; there also existed black markets. To eliminate the black market economy, to conquer inflation, and to revive production were the tasks confronting the Japanese government in 1947. But the nation had to wait for the Dodge Plan to see the stabilisation of inflation.

(v)   The Dodge Plan: In 1949, a broad programme was developed under the guidance of Detroit Bank president Joseph Dodge. He believed in the free market economy, completely rejecting government intervention and held that capital accumulation and the rehabilitation of industry could be made possible only by the efforts of the people themselves. The three basic policies were:
–   balanced budget
–   suspension of new loans from the Reconstruction Bank
–   the reduction and abolition of subsidies;
and the country must be exposed to international competition, by setting a single exchange rate, 1 $ = 360 yen (at that time, the yen was overvalued).

This was a full-scale deflationary policy, pushing many firms into bankruptcy. Dodge, insisting strongly on the three basic policies, however allowed the Japanese government to take the following measures to cope with problems accruing from deflationary policies. The Ministry of Finance (MOF) and the Bank of Japan (BOJ) put into effect the "Tight Money Neutralising Measure" that would channel the fiscal surplus back into private hands. With the reestablishment of the links between firms and financial institutions which had existed since the wartime era, and the rise of the financial keiretsu, there appeared the "over loan phenomenon" whereby increases in commercial bank lending exceeded increases in deposits; together with the attendant strengthening of BOJ control over city banks, the special characteristics of the post-war economy took shape. The tools were: special tax measures, the provision of government finance (Japan Export-Import and Development Bank loans), and interest rate subsidies for shipping

157

along with the allocation of foreign exchange and the regulation of technology imports.

10.3.b Start of rapid growth (1950-1954)

At the beginning of the 1950s, the industrial protecting and "fostering" policy was begun.

(i) Protection policy and "fostering" policy

Based on tariff and non-tariff barriers, protective measures and various "fostering" policies were introduced to promote dynamic comparative advantage and to pursue economies of scale; capital-intensity; and employment-absorbing industrialisation. These became the main pillars of industrial policy after WWII. Three main policies were introduced. First, the Exchange Control Law 1949, and the Foreign Capital Law 1950; second, recovery of tariff autonomy and implementation of the "new tariff system"; third, implementation of various measures for fostering industries.

Protection policy

Under the Exchange Control Law, exporters and importers required approval from the MITI for both import and export.

Under the Foreign Capital Law, capital transactions between Japan and a foreign country needed permission from the competent department. The practical application followed in the "Import Trade Control Law" for import and the "Foreign Capital Council" for capital transacations. Which goods could be imported and which capital transactions be permitted depended on the industrial policy concept. These two laws are important in Japanese industrial policy after WWII.

Recovery of tariff autonomy and implementation of the New Tariff System allowed protection through the tariff barrier. But since tariff barriers have their limits as protective measures, Japan depended on non-tariff barriers for import control under the "Import Trade Control Law", which controlled imports through foreign exchange quotas. Japan had to take such a measure for balance of payments deficits amounting to US$ 4.1 billion (1945-1953).

158

Because European small cars could pay a 40 per cent tariff, and yet remain cheaper than the Japanese car, MITI decided to protect and foster the car industry, which could stimulate development of the machinery and other sectors. The government announced the "Policy on Car Parts Industry" (October 1952), which allowed technology cooperation with foreign firms but did not permit inflow of foreign capital.[3]

"Fostering" policy

An "Industrial Rationalisation Council" was established (December 1949) and "Japan's Industrial Rationalisation Measures" was issued (February 1951). This was during recovery from the Dodge deflation and when accumulation of capital was slowly increasing. Also the Korean War, in 1950, was a stimulus to recovery.

Three important Industrial Rationalisation Measures were proposed.
−   Proposals connected with changes in the tax system:

(1) reduction of import tax and fixed capital tax on machinery useful for modernisation;

(2) promoting modernisation by implementing short-term special depreciation system for machinery in industries promoting industrialisation;

(3) corporate tax exempted from various accumulated funds for rationalisation and modernisation.

These tax preferences, aiming at heavy industrialisation, can be called a "Priority Tax Exemption System".
−   Proposals connected with application of government funds:

(1) distribution of "counterpart fund" mainly to industrial fund;

(2) the Ministry of Finance's deposit department's working capital should be available for industry rationalisation;

(3) the Development Bank started lending long-term for equipment.

---

[3]   Japan first removed import controls in 1960; liberalisation of direct investment became completely liberalised only in 1973.

– Other proposals to increase public activity:
  (1) investing capital in main industries by readjusting government funds;
  (2) promoting capital accumulation by the tax system;
  (3) establishment of the external economy by fiscal policy.

To pursue these policies, a number of steps were taken. The Japan Export Import Bank (April 1952) was established with 100 per cent government funds, mainly for long-term capital export loans. The Japan Development Bank (April 1951) aimed at supplementing normal financial institutions by supplying long-term funds to promote industrial development. To implement the "Priority Tax Cut", separate taxation for income from interest was introduced to increase savings for capital accumulation. Under the "Industry Rationalisation Promoting Law", the following industries were to benefit: iron and steel, non-ferrous metals, oil and coal, chemicals, automobiles, construction machinery, electric communication machinery, heavy chemicals.

These "fostering" policies promoted investment. In the 1950s Japan's investment rate was not especially high compared with European countries.[4] The reason why Japan during this time could reach a high growth rate is the low capital coefficient (investment rate/growth rate) (see *Table 10.2*). How could Japan increase the investment rate so enormously thereafter, making the main driving force of fast economic growth? Here lies the significance of the industrial policy. The fostering measures have all been investment-promoting in industries. At the same time, the fostering policies measures caused "over competition". When one remembers the many protection measures taken by Japan, one can say that in no country were competition-limiting forces stronger; but in spite of this Japan built up an "over competitive" market structure. One knows that a competitive market is the most necessary condition in pursuing economic growth.

What were the reasons for the emergence of such a competitive market economy in spite of the protection measures? The answer lies in the fostering policies, especially "priority financing" and "priority tax exemption" through governmental funds. These funds include the fiscal fund from taxation and investment and loan funds from postal savings, social security funds, post office

---

[4] Tsuruta (1982) page 64 shows an international comparison of growth rate, capital coefficient, investment rate from 1951 to 1975.

Table 10.2

Growth rate, capital coefficient, investment rate
(1951-1975)

Period		1951-1955	1955-1960	1960-1965	1965-1970	1970-1975
Growth rate		7.6	8.5	9.8	11.2	5.1
Capital coefficient	A	2.2	2.5	2.9	2.9	6.7
	B	1.0	1.3	1.5	1.5	3.2
Investment rate	A	16.7	21.2	28.2	32.6	34.6
	B	8.0	11.2	14.9	17.8	18.6

Capital coefficient = investment as % GDP/growth rate per annum.

A: total fixed capital formation.
B: private firms: capital investment.

life insurance, and industry investment special accounts. Government funds are supplied to governmental finance organisations such as the Japan Development Bank and a small- and medium-sized enterprise finance corporation; various public corporations such as the Japan Road corporation, the Japan housing corporation; the national railway corporation, the national telecommunication corporation; government-based businesses such as national hospitals, postal business; local governments.

The sectors to which these funds were allocated are shown in *Table 10.3*. The most important thing is that 75 per cent of the national funds were allocated to sectors indirectly and directly connected with industrial activities, such as agriculture, fisheries, energy, commerce, transport equipment, telecommunication. Welfare and environment sectors were neglected. This fund allocation had three important economic effects. It increased industry's liquidity and promoted equipment's modernisation. In the early 1950s 40-60 per cent of expenditure on equipment depended on government funds (iron and steel, chemicals, machinery, coal, shipping); in late 1950s and early 1960s dependency decreased, but one cannot ignore the positive role of the government funds in the fast economic growth of Japan (see *Table 10.4*). Secondly, there was the pump-priming, or indirect effect, of government funds. Thirdly, the Japan Development Bank's lending rate was lower than that of commercial financial institutions.

Table 10.3

Fiscal investment and treasury investment and loan according to the economic functional classification
(Unit: Yen 10 billion, per cent)

Period	1954-1957		1958-1961		1962-1965	
Total	25,291	(100.0)	50,727	(100.0)	107,176	(100.0)
Agriculture and fishing	4,292	(17.0)	8,855	(17.5)	15,788	(14.7)
Energy	3,915	(15.5)	5,105	(10.1)	5,808	(5.4)
Industry	2,506	(9.9)	7,131	(14.1)	15,176	(14.2)
of which:						
Large-size	951	(3.8)	2,696	(5.3)	6,796	(6.3)
Small- and medium-sized	1,555	(6.1)	4,435	(8.8)	8,379	(7.8)
Transport	5,749	(22.7)	12,792	(25.2)	33,788	(31.5)
of which:						
Facilities	1,915	(7.6)	5,659	(11.2)	16,571	(15.5)
Equipment	3,834	(15.1)	7,133	(14.1)	17,217	(16.1)
Telecommunications	2,471	(9.8)	5,188	(10.2)	11,374	(10.6)
Welfare	2,253	(8.9)	4,807	(9.5)	10,999	(10.3)
Environment	134	(0.5)	831	(1.6)	2,569	(2.4)
Others	492	(1.9)	1,125	(2.2)	1,951	(1.8)
Local self-governing bodies	3,479	(13.8)	4,893	(9.6)	9,723	(9.1)

The fact that the "priority tax exemption" system had been implemented jointly with the "priority financial" system was the reason why the Japanese economy under protectionism could see high investment among firms, and an emerging competitive market structure, bringing fast economic growth with heavy industrialisation.

Table 10.4

Dependence of industries on government funds
(percentage of equipment expenditure financed by government funds)

Period	more than 60 per cent	40-60 per cent	30-40 per cent	15-30 per cent	less than 15 per cent
1952	agriculture (70)	gas (59) electric power (50) textile (46) fishery (40)	total industry (34) chemical (35) machinery (33) iron (32) coal (33)	chemical (21) transportation (19)	
1959	agriculture (79)	water transportation (41)	coal (37) chemical (34) electric power (31) water transportation (25)	total industry (22) manufacturing industry (15) food (29) textile (18) other manufacturing ind. (21) transportation (16)	chemical (12) machinery (14) iron (6) gas (13)
1965	coal (67) fishery (64) agriculture (69)		chemical (31) electric power (32) transportation (29)	total industry (19) food (20) textile (19) other manufacturing ind. (19) fishery (21)	manufacturing (12) chemicals (12) machinery (11) iron (3)

Source: based on Tsuruta (1982), p. 73.

10.3.c The growth economy (1955-1970)

In the 1960s the growth rate averaged 10 per cent a year and plant and equipment investment grew by 22 per cent (1951-1973). Aggressive behaviour by firms produced a positive capital coefficient, showing that "investment generates investment".

Japanese economic management is neither the Western market mechanism nor the centrally planned economy. It operates through the close connection between the government and industry in consensual decision-making. Stressing this close connection between the government and industry, I will look at how Japanese industrial policy was actually executed, its effect, and how the industrial structure was created. Japanese economic development has been based on pursuing economic prosperity through export promotion. I will summarise the industrial policies applied in this period.

First, the Tariff Council set out principles for a differentiated structure of import duties:

– the tariff should be kept low on primary commodities and increase with the degree of processing;
– a low tariff on production goods and in general a high one for consumer goods;
– a low tariff on goods not made in Japan or on goods in scarce supply where there is no possibility of increasing supply; the tariff should be high on goods produced in Japan which could become competitive with foreign goods;
– for those industries expected to develop (especially with new entrants), a high tariff on the products and a low one on the inputs;
– for those industries now stagnating but with a possibility of stabilising employment, a high tariff on the product and a low one on the inputs;
– for those industries already developed (export industries), a low tariff both on the product and on the inputs;
– a low tariff on necessities and on educational, cultural, and hygienic goods, and a high one on luxuries.

These tariffs, together with non-tariff barriers, build up a complete system of protection for the fostering of industry, so strong that all industries became self-supporting and acquired export capacity.

164

By 1968, the balance of payments came into surplus, so that policies to expand production became unneccesary. It can be said that Japan's development after WWII took off by about 1968. This is why I limit this paper to the period between 1945 and 1970.

Next I would like to explain the system of close connections between the government and industry in decision-making. Parliament (the Diet) played almost no role in setting industrial policy. Groups whose influence was substantial in the formulation of industrial policy on the government side were as follows:

(i)   Genkyoku

For each industry there exists an official genkyoku, responsible for each industry's policy. This system is similar to the organisation of the industrial bureaucracy in former socialist countries, not to be found in other Western countries. MITI is the single most important genkyoku ministry within the Japanese government. In 1970, among its nine bureaus, five acted as genkyoku: for heavy industries, chemical industries, textile and light industries, coal and mining and the public utilities. Internally a bureau is subdivided into product divisions and then into sections. It should be noted that even within manufacturing, MITI was not the only genkyoku ministry.

Each genkyoku was responsible for drawing up policy relating to its industry or industries. First, the genkyoku bureaus and sections of MITI were responsible for drawing up and implementing various industry laws: the Petroleum Industry Law (1962), the Machine Industries Law (1956), and the Electronics Industry Law (1957). Second, the genkyoku drew up proposals for making available special tax provisions for a given industry; changing tariff rates; measures to free imports; and measures to permit direct investment of foreign firms. Third, in terms of transactions between foreign and domestic firms, each genkyoku was responsible, prior to the liberalisation of capital transactions, for approving patent and technology agreements and joint ventures. Each genkyoku was also the authority for issuing licences for industries such as petroleum refining, shipbuilding, and electric utilities, where new capacity was regulated. Fourth, the genkyoku section or bureau, or sometimes the ministerial level, had a deciding voice in the allocation of the funds of the Japan Development Bank and of other government financial institutions.

Proposals drawn up by the genkyoku bureau or section were first considered and coordinated with other policies at the ministerial level. They were then passed to the Ministry of Finance (MOF). The MOF bureaus had overall responsibility within the government for coordinating policy, while legal details would be overseen by the Cabinet Legislation Bureau. However, the MOF at cabinet level would not change what had been decided on, or formally requested, by another ministry. Finally the Fair Trade Commission, which was responsible for antitrust policy, was another prominent agency in the formation of industrial policy. Its existence was largely ignored in the 1950s, but throughout the 1960s its relative status within the bureaucracy was increasing, although slowly.

(ii) Industrial associations

As counterparts to each of the various genkyoku, major industry associations were founded, such as the Japan Iron and Steel Federation, the Japan Automobile Manufacturers Association, the Shipbuilders Association of Japan and numerous minor associations. The main purpose of the associations was to work with the genkyoku to see that the government adopted policies favourable to the major firms. Immediately after WWII, the genkyoku was proposing the policies and tried to pull the industry into line; later on the industries expressed their own interests, so that the genkyoku took on more of a mediating role between the various interests. The industry associations became, rather, friendly gatherings for exchanging information with others in the industry.

Shingikai (Policy Councils)

These are consultative bodies whose deliberations are referred to in the process of policy formation, and whose members, nominated by the MITI, consist of industry leaders, Zaikai (financial circles) members, and former bureaucrats, with a very small number of scholars, journalists, and others. The Industrial Structure Council advised on industrial policy in general, and there were also councils for machinery, petroleum extraction, coal mining, electronic data processing, aircraft, and energy. Proposals that have been negotiated in these councils to reflect vested interests can be implemented relatively smoothly. In this sense the Shingikai process is an explicitly democratic development in post-war Japanese government.

10.4 What can Japanese industrial policy offer to East European countries?

Similarities and dissimilarities can be found between the situation and prospects of East European countries and the circumstances and policies of Japan (in 1945-1970). Some are specific to Japan. Others are more general and seem relevant to the current problems of East Europe.

Similarities: a.   unsatisfied consumer demand,

                    b.   need for export push,

                    c.   need for catching up in technology.

Dissimilarities: d.   ownership structure: Zaibatsu; land reform,

                    e.   banking system,

                    f.   convertibility of currencies,

                    g.   the present world trade situation.

a)   *Unsatisfied consumer demand:*

Both Japan after WWII and Eastern Europe had to satisfy huge demand from consumers calling for massive increases in production. One important point is that the aid from Western countries can be of immediate ameliorative use e.g. for buying food, but that in the longer run builds up demand but not productive capacity. So it is necessary to restructure the economy. Here, Japan's example of restructuring the production system by industrial policy can be useful.

b)   *Need for an export push:*

Japan, scarce in natural resources but with a highly educated population, concentrated on capital-intensive industry, instead of concentrating on labour-intensive industry, as traditional theory might advise. With an export push policy for capital-intensive industry, the advantages of scale would work and thereby increase the import of more natural resources. Some East European countries, also poor in natural resources but with a highly educated human capital, have a similar situation.

For fast economic growth certain conditions are necessary. For Japan we may distinguish two: (i) external circumstances advantageous to Japan; and (ii) domestic forces (population, resources, and technology).

(i)   Under the Bretton Woods system, Japan held a fixed exchange rate (1 $ = 360 yen) for many years. At the same time, low world commodity prices (during most of the 1950s and 1960s) were advantageous to industrial nations and were expected to continue indefinitely.

(ii)   Two contrasting conditions of growth must be reconciled: full employment, and the promotion of high productivity sectors which can absorb only a limited volume of employment. How could overpopulated Japan succeed in fulfilling both conditions? The delicate balance was in fact achieved. The main strategy consisted of the concentration of industrial growth on capital goods and capital-intensive technologies with economies of scale and good prospects for export; this would allow for expanding inputs and employment in labour-intensive consumer goods industries. So long as cheap natural resources can be imported, this strategic balance should permit continuous growth. (See Ozaki (1978), p. 13.) But imbalances in resources and in external transactions emerged in later years.

c)   *Need for catching-up in technology:*

Japan developed its own R&D after WWII with the help of foreign techno-logy, yet without affiliates of foreign firms producing and exporting only their products. Japan did its own research and investment and produced the exports. Japan, like other Asian NICs, succeeded by exporting products of "mobile Schumpeter industries"[5].

---

5)   Industries where the development of new products is in general concentrated in specific research departments with an autonomous scientific and technical research staff. Hence a geographical separation of R&D and production is technically feasible without substantial losses. If quality requirements in production are relatively minor it may be profitable to carry out R&D activities in an industrial headquarter country and to shift the production of new goods to foreign affiliates in low-wage regions. These industries may be called "mobile Schumpeter industries". On the other hand "immobile Schumpeter industries" are those where the successful development of new products depends on intense personal contacts between scientists, engineers and production workers, where it is virtually impossible to draw an institutional borderline between research and production departments of individual enterprises. It is unlikely

d)   Ownership structure

Japan, after World War II, was moving towards dissolution of the *Zaibatsu* and implementation of the Dodge Plan, aiming to become an economy of privatised ownership and free competition. The Zaibatsu programme and the Land Reform are among the most important features of the transformation of ownership structures initiated by the Occupation, and have distinct relevance for the economic reforms in Eastern Europe.

Dissolution of Zaibatsu

The Japanese economy was peculiar in that about ten families, called Zaibatsu[6] – Mitsui, Yasuda, Sumitomo, Mitsubishi and others – controlled about 75 per cent of industrial, financial and commercial activities until the end of WWII. The liquidation of Zaibatsu securities and properties had to be carried out (in a period of about two years) in accordance with the direction of General MacArthur, the supreme Commander for the Allied Powers (SCAP). It was to be carried out under the supervision of SCAP but to be implemented by Japanese Government officials.

The following plan was proposed by SCAP for the firms of Mitsui, Yasuda Sumitomo, and Mitsubishi, referred to as "Holding Companies":

– The Holding Companies must transfer to the Allied Control Commission all securities owned by them and all other evidence of ownership or control of any interest in any other enterprise.

---

that such industries will shift production of high tech goods to low-wage countries because an international transfer of their technology would require the transfer of a substantial part of their employees.

6)

Zaibatsu include any private enterprise conducted for profit, or combination of such enterprises, which, by reason of relative size in any line or its cumulative power in many lines, restricts competition or impairs the opportunity for others to engage in business independently, in any important segment of business; and any individual, familiy, allied group, or juridical person owning or controlling such an enterprise or combination. Total assets of this private enterprise should be regarded as excessive when those of the concern and its subsidiaries and affiliates are greater in the aggregate than Yen 2 billion, according to the US Mission to Japan after WWII.

– The Holding Companies must cease to exercise direction or control of all financial, industrial, commercial enterprises whose securities they own.

– The directors and auditors of the Holding Companies must resign all offices held by them in the Holding Companies and take no part in the management or policies of these companies.

– All members of the Mitsui and certain other families must immediately resign all offices held by them in any financial, commercial, or industrial enterprises and cease to exercise any influence in the management or policies of these companies.

Although the Imperial Japanese Government was directed to proceed with the liquidation of the properties of these companies, there were problems in finding persons unconnected with the Zaibatsu and in a position to take over the properties. Possible purchasers were cooperative organisations, executives and employees of Zaibatsu companies, persons wishing to go into business for themselves, persons driven from ownership by government policy during the war, groups of organised workers, and, in the case of certain public utility enterprises, the state itself.

General MacArthur in 1948 made a conscientious effort to explain and summarise the economic aims of the Occupation.[7] He said that his personal policies were dedicated to setting up a democratic capitalistic society in Japan that will be able to stand on its own feet after the Occupation. He feared that if Japanese monopolies were not broken, there would be a socialist state of some kind. He said that he had no intention to sell Zaibatsu securities regardless of value to selected purchasers, such as labour unions; the sale should be stretched over a period so as to realise fair values.

Land reform

The unsatisfactory state of Japanese agriculture before the reforms can be traced to two fundamental causes: natural limitations and handicaps, and government discrimination against agriculture in favour of industry and trade.

---

[7]   See *Showa Zaisei-shi* (History of Financial System of Showa Period), page 396.

170

–   intense overcrowding of land: almost half the farm households in Japan cultivate less than 0.6 ha (1½ acres) each;

–   widespread tenancy under conditions highly unfavourable to tenants. More than 75 per cent of the farmers in Japan were either partially or totally tenants, paying rentals amounting to half or more of their annual crops;

–   a heavy burden of farm indebtedness combined with high rates of interest on farm loans;

–   government fiscal policies discriminating against agriculture in favour of industry and trade;

–   authoritative government control over farmers and farm organisations without regard for farmers' interests. Arbitrary crop quotas established by control associations often restricting the farmer in cultivation of crops for his own needs or economic advancement;

–   widely fluctuating prices for rice and silk, which comprise 65 per cent of the total value of farm production;

–   a declining income from sericulture;

–   the high price of fertilisers;

–   exploitation of farmers by middlemen in marketing crops.

Actual operations of the Japanese land reform programme began about January 1947. By 31 March 1949, land transferred from landlords to tenants had completely reorganised the pattern of land ownership and of landlord/tenant relations. The amount of land operated by tenants fell from 46 per cent to about 12 per cent of the total cultivated area. Absentee landlords as a class completely disappeared. Owners, only 36 per cent of the total number of cultivators at the beginning of the programme, increased to 70 per cent. This is the end of the feudal land tenancy system of Japan which existed since the Meiji Restoration in 1868. The Allied Forces believed that successful rehabilitation of Japan's economy and introduction of democratic principles on a broad scale required a complete transformation of the existing system of farm tenancy.

The Land Reform Law required almost all agricultural land in Japan owned by non-cultivating landlords to be purchased at fixed prices by the government and sold to tenants. Terms of sale were fixed so that all tenants would be able to purchase land. The principal authority over land was vested in agricultural land commissions – bodies democratically elected by farmers and land owners. Land commissions had final responsibility over selection of land to be purchased, prices and terms of sale, and supervised rights to use all agricultural land.

e) Banking system

The success of privatisation (i.e. ownership by private persons) depends on the development of capital market institutions and on the availability of foreign or domestic private capital. Transition must be rapid to be effective. Oskar Lange (1936) stressed competition rather than private ownership for attaining efficient resource allocation. However, many reformers in East European countries have preferred the view of Von Mises (1951) – that private ownership of capital is a necessary component of a market system. So both private ownership and competition are the essential conditions for a market economy.

In East European countries the monitoring and take-over function should be exercised by the commercial banking system along Japanese lines rather than through share markets. The Japanese commercial banking system provides long-term loans to the non-bank sectors, mainly the corporations, at regulated interest rates lower than market rates.

f) Convertibility of currencies

Convertibility liberalises the domestic economy by importing competitive pressures and a rational price structure. To delay convertibility favours economically irrational and distorting half-way solutions, like favouring exporters by permitting them to retain some part of their foreign currency revenues. Pegging the exchange rate serves as a nominal anchor and by giving relatively stable prices it will speed up the process of arriving at a rational price structure. The question is: at what level and for how long?

In Japan the rate was fixed at 1 $=360 yen (overvalued for that time) so that there should be competitive pressure among the domestic firms, bringing sufficient influence of the world price structure on domestic relative prices. However, in the case of East European countries, account must be taken of the low quality of output and lack of market orientation. The authorities must seek to avoid speculation against an overvalued rate which could threaten the entire economic reform programme, threatening the credibility of price liberalisation, trade liberalisation and convertibility itself.

Since there is no time to lose, East European countries should simply take over the relevant legislation from a representative West European country adapting its own laws to those of the Community (e.g. Austria). Naturally environmental and social legislation must be built independently, but western competition policy should be adopted as was done by Japan. The European Community should also cooperate by technical assistance in drafting and implementing the law.

g)   The world trade environment

How were protectionist measures, private efficiency, and innovation made compatible to each other in Japan? This is important for explaining the success of Japanese economic development after WWII. The answer is: fierce competition between private firms in a protected domestic market.

Japanese firms' strategy was to increase the market share as quickly as possible, instead of pursuing short-term profit-maximising. Increasing market share is motivated by private firms' commitment to job security for the employees under the life-time employment system as well as by the desire to form continuous relationships with banks and customers.

An increased market share can be gained by cutting the price by larger scale of output and by improving product quality through experience in production. Cumulative experience is reinforced in Japanese firms by life-time employment and seniority wage payments. Increased output can recuperate investment by creating the virtuous circle of falling prices and rising demand.

Further, Japan could minimise the adjustment cost associated with structural changes (shifting resources from unprofitable to profitable sectors). First, because firms have commitments to employment security, but not to the specific jobs of individual workers, which enables workers to shift between different occupations (after retraining). Secondly, firms tend to diversify production activities beyond their original fields whenever those original activities become less promising. (In contrast, US and European firms diversify mainly through mergers and acquisitions). Firms transfer both labour and capital from their declining sectors to new activities, sometimes by establishing subsidiary firms mainly financed by the parent company. This system can make access to funds for new risky investment relatively easy compared with venture capital in the stock market. This diversification policy of private companies stimulates competition in new markets by introducing many large firms into new production areas. Low interest rates, assisted by high household savings, have also contributed to ease the finance of adjustment, entry into new activities, and the creation of new business. Government-sponsored rationalisation cartels attempted to ease the adjustment burden on declining industries. These government actions were rather quickly phased out and have not retarded the adjustment process.

The Japanese government could pursue its aims very efficiently because of consensus among the people of a homogeneous society. Firms played a leading role in implementing the policies. Though firms competed so fiercely with each other, yet within each firm stock holders, managers, and employees cooperated to enlarge their market share; the profit being distributed equally among the members increasing their feeling of "togetherness" in the firm.

Japanese people (firms, workers, and consumers) have covered part of the government's cost of market economy policies through cooperation within firms. In general the stress on social equality and on a fair distribution system have been rooted in Japan by this corporate feeling (an exception being land ownership). However, this type of market mechanism would conflict with the European or American type of market mechanism in the world of today. Now that Japan has become one of the big economic powers in the world, she cannot prosper alone.

10.5 Conclusion

In conclusion let me suggest what East European countries can find relevant in Japanese experience, especially in Japan's development in 1945-70. It is first necessary to introduce the free entry of firms: if a new firm enters, old firms must lower wages, thereby increasing the number of firms instead of just enlarging one firm. Also it is necessary to have a banking system like that of Japan, lending funds to firms instead of financing by the stock market.

To execute industrial policy the following conditions are necessary:
a)   the beneficial effect of the market mechanism must be felt soon by the population, building up a middle class;

b) in view of the lack of managers, effective management education is needed;
c) industrial policy should aim at building vertical relationships in the economy (from production to consumption); because East European industries have often been horizontal monopolies;
d) the machine building industries supplying capital goods must be the centre for technology transfer and need restructuring;
e) small and medium-sized firms would be a driving force but so should the privatised managements of the former state enterprises which dominated many industries.

In order to build up vertical structures, infrastructures – the distribution system, the telecommunication system, the monetary and credit system – are essential. Japan can help with knowledge and funds to build these up, especially in the chemical-related and machine building industries. Small- and medium-sized finance institutions are needed. In telecommunications also, Japan should support immediate needs for installing telephone systems, by finance and technology transfers. It is also important to build up research networks where information is assembled.

Development of the market economy in East European countries should proceed fast, since it depends on "learning by doing": A measure of "shock therapy" is necessary but not everything can immediately be left to the free market, The greatest difference between the East European countries now and Japan in 1945-1970 is that the Japanese democratic reform (notably Zaibatsu dissolution, land reform, and the Dodge Plan) was wholly imposed by the US Occupation Mission, not initiated by the Japanese people themselves. By contrast, the East European countries had to suffer more than forty years after WWII before achieving democracy on their own.

In spite of this great difference, East European countries can learn from the methods adopted by the US Occupation Mission in Japan after WWII and also from the ways which Japan followed on with the help of industrial policy so that the market economy could function as soon as possible after the war.

Bibliography

Adam, F., Ichimura, S. (1983), "Industrial policy in Japan", in Adams, F.G., Klein, L.R. (1983), *Industrial policies for growth and competitiveness,* Lexington Books.

Behrman, J.N., *Industrial policies: International restructuring and transnationals,* chapter 2, "Japanese policy".

Bletschacher, G., Klodt, H. (1991), "Braucht Europa eine neue Industriepolitik?", *Kiel Discussion Papers* 177, Institut für Weltwirtschaft Kiel, December.

– (1991), "Ansätze Strategischer Handels- und Industriepolitik: Ein Überblick", *Kiel Working Papers* No. 487, Institut für Weltwirtschaft Kiel.

Calvo, G., Frenkel, J. (1991), "From centrally planned to market economy", *IMF staff paper,* Vol. 38, No. 2 (June).

Dornbusch, R., "Priorities of economic reform in Eastern Europe and Soviet Union", Centre for Economic Policy Research (CEPR) ,*Occasional Paper* No. 5.

Ehrlich, E. (1984), *Japan, a case of catching-up,* Akadémiai Kiadó, Budapest.

Finance Ministry (1984), *Showa Zaisei Shi* (History of public finance of Showa period), series 1 to 20 (Toyo Keizai).

Fink, G. (1991), "A Western investor's view on investment projects in the East", paper presented at the OECD workshop on enterprise finance in Central and Eastern European countries, Paris, 27-29 May.

Grossman, G.N. (1989), "Explaining Japan's innovation and trade: A model of quality competition and dynamic comparative advantage", *Working paper* No. 3193, National Bureau of Economic Research, Inc., New York.

– and Helpman, E. (1991), "Endogenous product cycles", *The Economic Journal,* September, pp. 1214-1229.

Hartel, H. and others (1987), *Neue Industriepolitik oder Stärkung der Marktkräfte? Strukturpolitische Konzeptionen im internationalen Vergleich,* Spezialuntersuchung 1 im Rahmen der HWWA-Struktur-berichterstattung, Verlag Weltarchiv GmbH., Hamburg.

Hughes, G., Hare, P. (1991), "Competitiveness and industrial restructuring in Czechoslovakia, Hungary and Poland", *European Economy,* Commission of the EC, Special edition No. 2.

Junz, H. (1991), Integration of Eastern Europe into the world trading system, Papers and proceedings, *The American Economic Review,* May.

Klodt, H. (1991), "Comparative advantage and prospective-structural adjustment in Eastern Europe", *Kiel Working Papers* No. 477, Institut für Weltwirtschaft Kiel.

Komiya, R., Okuno, M., Suzumura, K. (1984), *Industrial policy of Japan,* University of Tokyo Press.

Kosai, Y. (1981), *The era of high growth* (Nihon Hyoron Sha).

Krueger, Anne O., Orsmond, D. (1990), "Impact of government on growth and trade", *Working paper* No. 3545, National Bureau of Economic Research, New York.

Landesmann, M., Nesporova, A., Szekely, I. (1991), Industrial restructuring and the reorientation of trade in Czechoslovakia, *European Economy*, Commission of the EC, Special edition No. 2.

Marer, P. (1990), "Pitfalls in transferring market-economy experiences to the European economies in transition", paper presented at the Conference on the Transition to a Market Economy in Central and Eastern Europe, co-sponsored by the World Bank, Paris, 28-30 November.

Nakamura, T. (1981), *The Post-war Japanese economy – Its development and structure*, University of Tokyo Press.

Okuno, M., Fujiwara (1988), "Interdependence of industries, coordination failure and strategic promotion of an industry", *Journal of International Economics* 25, pp. 25-43.

Organisation for Economic Co-operation and Development (OECD) (1974), *The industrial policy of Japan*.

Ozaki, I. (1978), "Industrial structure of Japan" (extraction from *Regional Development News*, series 88 to 112).

Romer, P. (1986), "Increasing returns and long-run growth", *Journal of Political Economy*, Vol. 94, No. 5.

– (1990), "Endogenous technological change", *Journal of Political Economy*, Vol. 38, No. 5.

Ryokaku, Y. (1986), *Theory of industrial policy* (Nihon Keizai shinbun sha).

Sabashi (1968), "Industrial policy of Japan", in *Industrial policy theory*.

Schmieding, H. (1991), "External protection for the emerging market economies – the case for financial liberalisation instead of import barriers in Eastern Europe", *Kiel Working Papers* No. 498, Institut für Weltwirtschaft Kiel, October.

Siebert, H. (1991), "Die Integration Osteuropas in die Weltwirtschaft", *Kiel Working Papers* No. 491, Institut für Weltwirtschaft Kiel, October.

Sato, R., Ramachandran, R., Tsutsui, S. (1991), "Incomplete appropriability of R&D and the role of strategies and cultural factors in international trade: A Japanese case", *Working paper* No. 3797, National Bureau of Economic Research, New York.

Tsuruta, T. (1982), *Industrial policy of Japan after World War II* (Nihon Keizai shinbun sha).

Venables, A., Smith, A. (1986), "Trade and industrial policy under imperfect competition", *Economic Policy*, October.

Williamson, J. (1991), *The economic opening of Eastern Europe*, Institute for International Economics, May.

Yoshitomi, M. (1991), "New trends of oligopolistic competition in the globalisation of high-tech industries: interactions among trade, investment and government", in *Strategic industries in a global economy: policy issues for the 1990s*, OECD.

177

– (1990), "How is the post-war economic development in Japan relevant to Central and Eastern Europe", paper presented at Conference on the Transition to a Market Economy in Central and Eastern Europe, Paris, 28-30 November.

Chapter 11

COMPETITION POLICY: AN AUSTRIAN VIEWPOINT

Helmut Kramer[*]

In a very lucid sentence the late Austrian statesman Karl Renner once stated: "For both the bourgeois and the economist, the term Central Europe means cartels instead of competition". And a contemporary Austrian economic policy adviser, J. Farnleitner, meant the same when he wrote "the *meaning* of competition policy in Austria has always been protecting *from* competition rather than protecting competition".

Such pointed statements illustrate to some extent the traditional background of the Austrian debate on competition policy and more recent considerations on that issue have to be seen against it. But it can be shown that the evidence justifies a more balanced view.

Long-term reinforcement of competition on domestic markets

Austria's economic policy ever since the war pursued the aim of opening her economy and integrating it into the open competitive world economy. This task has been monitored by organisations such as the former OEEC, OECD, GATT and EFTA and in practice most thoroughly by the EC, though Austria is not yet a member of it. And it has been approached
- by unilateral as well as bi- and multilateral liberalisation of the foreign trade regime,
- by tariff cuts within the GATT as well as in the EFTA and EC-association frameworks,
- by the step-wise liberalisation of capital movements (arriving, in 1991, at the complete convertibility of the currency),

---

[*] Professor; Director, Austrian Institute of Economic Research, Vienna.

–   by the adaptation, in the early 1970s, of the turnover tax to the value added tax system (abolishing offsetting taxation of imports and, partly unjustified, tax refunds on exports), and

–   last, but not least, by the adoption of a hard currency approach after the end of the Bretton Woods system; that system originally imposed rather high standards for stability and costs on parts of the Austrian economy. But as entrepreneurs, trade union leaders and policy-makers (especially those responsible for prices and incomes policies) gained experience with that kind of *de facto* externally determined (Deutschmark) standard (practically speaking, in tying unilaterally the Austrian Schilling to the Deutschmark) they increased their innovation efforts and learnt to clear the hurdles.

It can thus be seen that the reinforcement of competition by such macro-economic instruments (as distinguished from the narrower institutional sense of competition laws) has been used as a central economic policy instrument in Austria. In this sense it would be unjust to speak of Austrian economic policy as "competition avoiding".

The combined outcome of all these strategic and long-term development lines was a steadily rising intensity of competition, high rates of productivity increases and, therefore, better competitiveness *in parts* of the Austrian economy. The more or less unsolved problem is that the efficacity of these instruments could not be extended to all sectors of the economy with the same impact.

Protected niches

There remain many activities that could not wholly be opened to internal or external competition by the use of macro-economic strategies.

This sheltered sector derives from different historical origins. Many are very old, very well-established in public opinion and very resistant to specific measures. There should be mentioned:

–   the whole body of agricultural policies, as well as

–   some state monopolies,

–   the traditional (in fact competition-restricting) rules for the activities of free professions,

–   most instruments of the housing policy developed in the shortage situation after the wars and never abolished,

- the permissiveness in practice of Austrian cartel legislation and
- the inclination of the bureaucracy to act in the interest of domestic producers of all kinds, even to the detriment of the interests of domestic consumers, of domestic manufacturers buying the inputs concerned, and of competing producers. Sometimes such mechanisms are declared to be "in the well-understood interest" of consumers (consumer protection against obscure suppliers). The economic policy-makers, as well as the professional representatives and bureaucrats, believe themselves to be responsible for the economic well-being of the existing (domestic) enterprises and capacities in question.

A more recent and new source of protection has been the effects of the liberalisation. Where the efficiency of an enterprise finding itself increasingly exposed to competition seemed insufficient, many types of measures have been developed for at least provisional protection from adverse consequences. The complement to increasing liberalisation of the external framework was an increasing degree of subsidisation under a great variety of titles.

Macro-economic consequences of the two-sector model

This "dual approach" towards openness and competition had a number of macro-economic consequences. One was a continuously high degree of employment. The sheltered sector seemed able to absorb the redundancies of the exposed sector. For quite a long time full employment – without, more or less, any qualifications – has been seen as the priority goal of economic policy making in Austria. No responsible politician would have had the courage to stress that this may be leading to inadequate domestic profits and other incomes. The longer this policy continued, however, the more its costs seemed to damage both income levels and the government budgets.

Two pieces of macro-economic evidence may be given. The Austrian GDP per capita in the early 1990s can be measured as some 10 to 15 per cent above the EC average at current prices and official exchange rates! But measured by purchasing power parities it only reaches this average. This observation can be interpreted as an expression of a lack of competition in the domestic markets.

This lack of competition allows sheltered producers to pass cost increases into domestic prices without too much risk of punishment by the market. Typically, unit labour costs developments in Austria run parallel with those of main foreign competitors in the manufacturing sector: but in the rest of the economy these costs have risen much faster. It seems that this dualism is more pronounced in Austria than in Sweden, Norway or Switzerland. The author showed this in an earlier study (Kramer, EFTA 1991) by comparisons with other EFTA countries: The conclusion was:

"*An international comparison of labour cost increases in the manufacturing sector and in the rest of the economy in the 1980s shows that, except for Finland, no EFTA country exhibits such a striking difference in labour cost developments between the two sectors. What alarms us even more is the fact that the shift in the inter-sectoral terms-of-trade seems to have been more pronounced in the 1980s than in the 1970s even though the Austrian economy was more open in the 1980s.(One partial explanation may be that the heavy industries lost their state subsidies in the 1980s and were therefore forced to lay off a considerable part of the labour force, and, in doing so, increased their productivity extraordinarily.)*"

Table 11.1

Sectoral development of unit-labour costs in the 1980s
Indices 1988 (1980=100)

	(1) Total Economy – national currencies –	(2) Manufacturing	(3) Differences (2):(1)	(4) Total economy US$
Austria	131.3	112.9	86.0	137.7
Finland	175.2	143.8	82.1	143.8
Sweden	164.2	151.9	92.5	113.3
Norway	173.7	168.9	97.2	131.6
Switzerland	138.1	139.3	100.8	158.2
Iceland	1,418.0			158.2

Data: *OECD Historical Statistics*, Table 9.10, Paris 1990. *OECD Economic Outlook* 47, Paris, June 1990.

Source: H. Kramer, in EFTA, 1991, p. 34.

This already illustrates how the opening of markets in the 1980s affected the (overwhelmingly nationalised) industries which, up to 1985, clearly enjoyed an above average subsidy proportion.

It is unnecessary to mention that imperfect competition influences the distribution of incomes and of fringe benefits over the economy.

Policy conclusions

Very often restrictions on competition are originally not only socially justified but even economically well-based. But they exhibit a tendency to petrify and to turn into instruments for the pursuit of partial interests. In a situation of scarcities of all kinds and of absence or at least of insufficient social security networks, many types of restrictions were introduced with the broad support of the population. But this same population often became, step by step, the prisoner of the system generated. And it turns out to be a very hard political job to free society from rent seeking that is no longer justified.

The removal of sources of imperfect competition on the domestic market is in the first instance the job of national competition polices. But, as happened in Austria, behind most shelters there developed over time very strong vested interests, strong both in political influence and in economic power. And governments refrained, for some obvious political considerations, to tackle these vested interests directly and effectively, because many of their clients form the core of the political clientele of government-forming parties, if not on the federal level, then on that of the provincial. Therefore some politicians pin their hopes on external support for a solution: so far as international rules of competition must be implemented and controlled, the political price for the abolition of such institutional mechanisms can be kept down. Putting the blame on "Brussels", or on "Geneva", seems a safer way of reaching a more balanced competitive landscape.

In the Austrian application for EC membership in 1989, this consideration was not an explicit reason for either the government's or the parliament's decision. But the debate on how to overcome traditional protective shelters, no longer justified economically, was one of the strongest arguments behind the application.

References

Farnleitner, J. (1986), "Dynamisierung der Rahmenbedingungen als wirtschaftspolitisches Gebot", *Wirtschaftspolitische Blätter*, 33 (3).

Kramer, H. (1989), "Wachstums-, Struktur- und Wettbewerbspolitik", in: Abele, H., Nowotny, E., Schleicher, St., Winckler, G. (eds.), *Handbuch der österreichischen Wirtschaftspolitik*, 3rd ed., Vienna.

– (1991), "Imperfections in European Economic Integration", in: EFTA (ed.), *EFTA Countries in a Changing Europe*, Geneva, July.

OECD Economic Surveys 1989/90 (1990), *Austria*, Paris.

Chapter 12

Carlo Boffito[*]
Alberto Martinelli[**]

ITALIAN STATE-OWNED ENTERPRISES:
SOME LESSONS FOR TRANSITION ECONOMIES

The public sector could play an important role in transition economies in three major ways:
(a) restructuring the productive system,
(b) supporting market mechanisms and breaking of monopoly positions,
(c) reducing unemployment and controlling social tensions.

These goals must be pursued in an international and domestic context with two basic features:
(a) an open economy with strong competitive pressures and deep international economic integration,
(b) a "democracy in the making" with many parties and movements, complex government coalitions and potentially overloaded governments.

Given these goals and the specific context of transition, what lessons can be drawn from the Italian experience of state-owned enterprises? In order to answer this question, we have to analyse the specific features of Italian state-owned enterprises and their evolution in the various phases of Italian post-war development.

Development of state-owned industry in Italy

The origins of state-owned firms in Italy were: an interventionist ideology in pre-Fascist Italy in order to foster industrialisation; the nationalisation of major

---

[*]   Professor, University of Turin, Italy.

[**]   Professor, University of Milan, Italy.

banks controlling significant industrial sectors (steel, shipyards, etc.) in the 1930s by the Fascist government, which, however, provided neither the ideology nor the managers who run the state-owned firms.

After the Second World War, state-owned enterprises were maintained and consolidated by the democratic government and were part of the institutional pact among major political forces-Catholic, Socialists and Communists. Two articles of the Constitution of the Italian Republic are relevant in this respect: article 41 – which states the freedom of enterprise within the limits set by respect of basic civil rights – and article 43 – which envisages the creation of state-owned firms for essential public services, energy supplies and monopoly positions which are of significant national interest.

The theoretical premises of public entrepreneurship after the war – when the system was transformed and strengthened – can be summarised as follows:
-   state-owned firms are seen as the Italian version of a general tendency at that time toward state intervention in the economy aimed at sustaining economic growth and redressing market disequilibria;
-   a rigorous distinction is made between the government's role and the public managers' role, with no subordination of the latter to the former;
-   full respect of the rules of the market is recommended, not only as a pre-requisite of efficiency and competitiveness, but also in order to break monopoly positions (the main example was Mattei's ENI);
-   the national and social goals to be pursued – alongside profit – are the development of backward areas (the Mezzogiorno), the development of technologically advanced and high-risk production, restriction of foreign capital in strategic industries, the rescue of large firms which cannot be saved by private capital;
-   in order to cover the "unfair costs" of national and social goals, the state was pressed to supply additional financial means.

In the light of this philosophy, state-owned firms' strategies in the 1950s and early 1960s became real agents of industrial policy and contributed to developing basic industries, modernising industrial relations and introducing scientific management. Self-financing was the main source of investment funds.

However, after the mid-1950s, close personal ties between party leaders and state entrepreneurs were introduced. These links between public managers and party leaders eventually led to party management of the state sector, which contributed to a subsequent crisis of state-owned firms.

The major factor leading to this crisis was the 1974-75 recession of the Italian economy (rising costs of energy and raw material, the oil shock), which was worsened by high wages caused by labour unrest in 1969 and following years. As a consequence, state-owned firms became the targets of an overload of demands from several stake-holders and of increasing control by political parties and party fractions. Their goals and strategies became multiple and to some extent contradictory: rescue of firms in bad shape and acquisition of "dying branches" of private firms for "social" motives such as defence of jobs; anti-cyclical investments in recession. The result, in the second half of the 1970s, was a great increase in state-owned firms' indebtedness to the banking sector.

An objective and unintentional convergence of interests by different social actors took place, which put on the state entrepreneurs burdens that they could not bear. State-owned firms proved an increasingly vulnerable milchcow both for trade unions – who put forth contradictory demands – and for private entrepreneurs – who tended to socialise losses at the expense of state-owned firms. Moreover, political parties used state-owned firms for quelling social protest and for satisfying the demands of clients and particular groups.

In the 1980s, mostly under the pressure to reduce the huge Italian public debt, remedies for the state-owned firms' crisis were attempted by the new top management. IRI and ENI strategies aimed at restructuring and rationalising, through merging, take-overs and attempts at privatisation – only partially successful – inside each group.

In fact, the traditional functions of public entrepreneurship – sustaining growth and controlling social tensions – can hardly be maintained in an increasingly interdependent world with accelerated rates of technological change. What is needed now is international integration, flexibility and innovation. The role of the state is eroded. However, there are strong oppositions from political parties and from within the public sector.

In conclusion, the role of state-owned firms has been positive in Italy, whenever public managers have been able to keep a certain degree of autonomy from political parties and whenever they have formed a cohesive group with a distinctive approach, differing from both private entrepreneurs and political parties.

Morals for East Europe

Possible lessons for former centralised economies can be drawn from the Italian experience of state-owned firms. In spite of the fact that the importance of the public sector has diminished in the present world economy, the goals of a transition economy which we have outlined at the beginning of this paper cannot be achieved by relying only on the market and private firms. The public sector of the economy can play a positive role, subject to some basic conditions which can be drawn from Italian experience: first, the autonomy of public management, in order to avoid management of the economy by political parties; second, a viable compromise, in the short run, between the profit motive and the social goal of defending employment, with priority for profitability in the long run; third, the assumption that state-owned firms should be considered a temporary solution, useful to achieve the goals of the transition period, but subject to periodical reassessment of their role.

COMMENTS ON PART III:

András Inotai

Inagawa's (Ch. 10) study offers rich material on Japanese experience in the first quarter of a century after WW II. She puts competition policy into the framework of general industrial policy and deals with competition as an organic part of industrial strategy. She concentrates on the historical development of industrial policy and on a number of practical issues which certainly provide valuable information for the economic transformation process in East Europe. The paper is complemented by an impressive list of references and some instructive statistical tables.

Industrial policy is widely defined as "a policy of technical change, leading to change in industrial structure – the key factor in economic growth". Competition is considered an instrument of industrial policy and not a goal in itself. On the Japanese stage, the government has had a major role to play. First, there is a constant dialogue between government and industry to form a policy based on a concerted decision-making process. Second, although competition is generally allowed and even supported by the government, everyone is also aware of the costs of competition which, therefore, have to be controlled by government policy. Third, Japanese experience shows that government-led sectoral policies are needed during the early development stage, while they can be gradually withdrawn or downgraded once market mechanisms prevail. Fourth, if the government's sectoral policies to achieve scale economies (e.g. in the automobile industry) do not succeed because there is strong resistance from the main firms, or if the firms try to establish cartel-like agreements against government plans, it is still possible to mobilise smaller subcontractors to strengthen the competitive environment and enhance exports.

From these basic Japanese principles, various lessons can be drawn for East Europe. In the positive sense, short-sighted sectoral policies inherited from the centrally planned period should be replaced by strategy-oriented industrial and general economic policies. Also, the government has to opt for a high level of flexibility and should not consider opinions which differ from its own view as attacks on its economic policy. On the contrary, institutionalised dialogue between industrial lobbies and government policy-makers should be fostered. However, this cooperation presupposes that the government does not want to exercise its own entrepreneurial functions; nor does it consider privatisation as an instrument to maintain direct ownership control over at least a part of the economy. In the negative sense, it is doubtful whether industry-specific policies really work efficiently in a non-market environment, in which market signals are non-existent, weak or highly distorted, leading to inefficient investments. Once market signals work, it is less risky to select those industries which reveal the best chances for development and international competitiveness, and, accordingly, support them.

The breakup of the Zaibatsu, the traditional sources of Japanese economic power, is very instructive. Immediately after the war, political and ideological reasons and the US presence in, and pressure on, Japan made this feasible. In addition, the large domestic market and very low level of economic openness, not only in Japan but in most national economies, enabled companies to develop efficient economies of scale and to prepare the ground for international competitiveness in the second stage of industrial development. At present, East European countries are characterised both by small and shrinking domestic markets and increased international competition. As a result, the breakup of a number of

189

companies is accompanied by decreasing competitiveness and the loss of traditional markets. Across-the-board demonopolisation is a welcome development; but it may, at least temporarily, in a decisive stage of transformation, hinder international competitiveness and weaken bargaining power against powerful multinational firms and international organisations.

Successful industrial policy in Japan required substantial financial support from the very beginning. The fiscal surplus, the result of a tight monetary policy, did not remain with the banks, finance the state debt or fund the transfer of resources to abroad, but was rechannelled to the companies. In East Europe this fiscal surplus does not exist, for various reasons. The income centralising and redistributing role of the central budget amounts to between 50 and over 60 per cent of GDP, and the unexpectedly rapid decline of budgetary revenues (mainly due to the collapse of the CMEA), accompanied by rapidly growing expenditures (unemployment, social benefits, government consumption, politically motivated compensation, new subsidies, etc.) results in generally high fiscal deficits. Moreover, the servicing of foreign debt further limits the scope of a Japanese-type system of financing new and competitive industrial activities.

One basic pillar of the Japanese industrial policy was import protection and strict control on foreign capital. None of these two elements can be applied in the present situation in Eastern Europe. The world economy has fundamentally changed, and freer imports of goods, services and capital seems to be an unquestionable precondition of take-off, growth and successful transformation. This is particularly true for geographic and historical reasons. Geographically, Eastern Europe is not an island but a direct neighbour to prosperous Western European countries. Historically, the legacy of communism has created economic structures largely isolated from the international economy. The rapid overcoming of this national and regional (CMEA-level) autarky is absolutely imperative.

Japan/East Europe: comparisons

The paper summarises similarities and dissimilarities between Japanese economic development and current conditions for development in East Europe. Similarities include unsatisfied demand for consumer goods, need for an export push, technological renewal, low labour costs and highly educated manpower. The major differences are found in ownership structure, the banking sector, the

190

convertibility of national currencies and the international economic and trade situation.

This distinction makes several correct points, but also suggests unjustified parallels and deficiencies. Certainly, there is a large unsatisfied demand for consumer goods, although its size is very different in the individual countries of the area. More importantly, there is a fundamental difference in the pattern of unsatisfied demand. While, after the war, this demand concentrated on food in Japan, it is directed to high-price durable consumer goods and services at least in the more advanced countries in Eastern Europe.

The paper's suggestion that capital-intensive and traditionally competitive export industries should be developed in Eastern Europe, can hardly be supported by relative factor prices, the natural endowment, or, mostly, by past experience of industralisation. On the contrary, the erroneous and extremely costly specialisation on material- and capital-intensive goods based on a high share of imported inputs, and the collapse of just this trade as a result of the dissolution of the CMEA and the insolvency of the former Soviet Union, are expected to lead to fundamentally different development priorities in Eastern industrial policies. It is extremely uncertain that the main specialisation patterns in CMEA trade can be maintained (or reconstructed after a certain period) in the area's exports to OECD countries. Support for export industries by tax reductions can be strongly recommended, but the implementation of this measure requires financial resources, and the latter can hardly be made available without fundamental reform of the state budget. Here, immediate needs collide with medium-term possibilities. Uncontrolled liberalisation of wages is an ambiguous policy step when a large part of production is still state-owned, inflationary pressures are substantial, and unemployment is high and rapidly rising. Immediate wage liberalisation would lead to higher inflation and dramatic levels of unemployment, with unpredictable social and political costs.

The Japanese way of importing and upgrading technologies offers some possibilities. However, rapidly rising costs of technological development and international deregulation, accompanied by multinational production and distribution networks (subcontracting), have seriously limited the applicability of this experience. Astonishingly high costs of R and D and, more important, the rapidly shrinking time gap between the import of a ready-made (mature) technology and its modified (upgraded) version are the main limiting factors.

I share the author's view on avoiding an overvalued exchange rate. Also she is right in emphasising the vital importance of the commercial banking sector in making industrial activities competitive. At present, however, most of these banks in East Europe are not very healthy because of the large amount of non-performing debts in their portfolios. To manage their financial balance and cope with risky liabilities, they have to keep interest rates high. So interest rates are not lower (as in Japan), but higher than theoretical market rates.

Fierce competition among domestic (private) firms is another vital issue. In Japan, the government had been protecting the domestic market for decades (partly even today). In addition, this domestic market was rather large and rapidly developing. None of these criteria apply to East European economies, where protection is in most cases less than would be necessary even in the present conditions of international liberalisation. Domestic markets are small, characterised by declining growth and external competition. This environment is obviously making the rapid emergence and strengthening of new small- and medium-sized domestic firms even more pressing, but, at the same time, very much less viable.

Apparently, both Japanese and East European firms pursue a strategy of increasing market shares. Like Japan in the last decades, Hungary, Poland and most recently also Czechoslovakia could achieve surprisingly good export results in the last four years. However Japan's growing world market share was due to avoiding short-term profit maximisation; while the ex-socialist companies, to a large but hardly quantifiable extent, have been eating up their assets.

Obviously, flexible labour market policies are an important element in shaping competitive positions. In this respect, the different social and psychological patterns between Japan and the transforming economies should not be neglected. It would be easier to follow the Japanese example of consensus-building in a homogeneous society. This goal should be considered as probably the highest priority for success of the transformation process. Unfortunately, in most countries, governments (and also opposition parties) tend to atomise the society instead of working to strengthen the common foundation.

In recent years, Japan and other rapidly industrialising Far Eastern economies came to serve increasingly as reference countries to transforming economies. Evidently, both of them have one common feature, that of late-comers. However, this in itself does not imply that they have to take the same policy measures and go along the same development path. Differences arise, not only from the sometimes highly divergent economic, socio-political and psychological backgrounds, but also from the volatility of the international economy to which all of them needed, or will need, to adjust. Even more important, the political preconditions are fundamentally different. While the most dramatic economic and political transformations were initiated and implemented in Japan by the US Occupation authorities, Eastern Europe has shaken off foreign domination and dictatorship only very recently. If the ex-socialist economies happen to be as successful in the future as Japan and the Asian NICs in the last few decades, it would only prove that similar goals can be achieved by different economic development patterns. These patterns are expected to contain *also* Japanese experience, but their composition (factor mix) has to be "squeezed out" by the transforming economies themselves.

Ewald Walterskirchen[*]

In the paper by *Kramer* (Ch. 11) on Austrian development it was pointed out that Austria's policy since the war may be described as a gradual and stepwise opening towards integration in the world economy. In Austria, even twenty years after the war, 70 per cent of manufacturing output was still protected in one form or another (tariffs, import quotas). If liberalisation goes too fast, there is a danger of strong cycles between extreme opening and protectionism – as the Polish example reveals.

The Austrian experience commands a certain interest in that it was successful in keeping unemployment and inflation relatively low. This is usually attributed to the policy of consensus (social partnership and incomes policy). It can be agreed that macroeconomic guidance played a major role in the above-average development of the Austrian economy. Not only in Austria, but all over Europe,

---

Austrian Institute of Economic Research (WIFO), Vienna.

in the three decades after the war, economic growth and full employment had top priority for economic policy. This has changed only in the 1980s after GDP per head and personal savings had reached a rather high level.

In Austria, bureaucracy and the social partners were always inclined to act in favour of producers – even at the cost of consumers. Cartel legislation in Austria has been too permissive; but also the EC has tended to allow exceptions from strict cartel legislation if the cartel is a powerful weapon against Japanese or US competitors. Competition is absolutely vital in market economies. It may, however, have a different meaning at different stages of development. Japan has always tried to protect "infant industries" but to remove protection as soon as these industries reached their "maturity".

Competition was called the "moral principle" of market economies which everyone accepts in theory, but which everyone circumvents in practice. However, not only the market, but also organisation (in the enterprises and in the administration) plays an essential role in market economies. We are not living in the fully competitive world of economic textbooks where we just have to watch the market mechanism. We are living in a world where we have to bargain all the time and where evolution comes from activity and innovation.

In the paper by *Boffito* and *Martinelli* (Ch. 12), it was argued with special reference to Italy that state-owned enterprises may well play a positive role in the transition process. This is important because the speed of privatisation in Eastern Europe is slow, much slower than expected. Eastern European countries will have to live for some time to come in a mixed economy. Privatisation is absolutely necessary, but will take time.

It has been claimed that public enterprises could play a positive role in sustaining economic growth, restructuring production and checking social tensions, but on condition of an efficient management, largely independent of politics, and some control of prices and wages in monopolistic sectors, especially for strategic products. Reference is made to the Price and Wage Commission in Austria.

There was agreement that
–   an efficient management and a climate of competition are more important than the form of property;

194

–   transformation from public to private monopoly (under the same management) is not very helpful.

The examples of nationalised industries in Italy and Austria – and also of Volkswagen in the post-war period – show that state-owned enterprises may be run efficiently in a competitive environment, so long as political intervention is as low as possible and that restructuring and renewal are given high priority.

PART IV – A ROLE FOR INTERNATIONAL ACTION

Chapter 13

THE INSTITUTIONS OF EUROPE AFTER 1992

David G. Mayes[*]

During the last few years the pace of change in Europe has accelerated dramatically and the realistic scope for further change is also larger by an order of magnitude inconceivable even five years ago. Economic structures are changing rapidly not only in central and eastern Europe with the move towards market economies and the formation of new countries, but also in the West with the "completion of the internal market" in the European Community, through the 1992 programme followed by the move to Economic and Monetary Union set out in the Maastricht Treaty, the European Economic Area agreement effectively extending the EC internal market to EFTA and the applications by EFTA countries

[*] Professor, National Institute of Economic and Social Research, London, UK.This paper is produced as part of the UK Economic and Social Research Council's Single European Market Research Initiative: "The Evolution of Rules for a Single European Market". I am grateful for the helpful comments of *Simon Hausberger*. This chapter was written before ratification of the Maastricht Treaty on European Union was far advanced, in particular before the narrow "no" vote in the Danish referendum in summer 1992. Perhaps the whole process of European integration will now change; but this chapter focuses on the treaty as signed by heads of governments/states in February 1992.

to become full members of the EC. Adaptation to these new circumstances requires massive institutional, regulatory and behavioural change. However, the people and many of the institutions charged with achieving this have a history of 40 years of change which is very slow by comparison. Their development is based largely on a process of evolution, changing in response to experience in trying to increase efficiency and improve welfare. Step changes in intentions and expectations as we have seen recently leave a massive catching-up process to follow them. Inevitably experience leads to a reappraisal of both the intentions and the expectations.

Concentration at the early stages of dramatic change is on changing the explicit rules and institutions which govern behaviour. It is these which are set out in treaties and constitutions. However, the form of economic and social behaviour which evolves in the light of them involves a complex web of less formal rules or codes of behaviour, many of them unwritten (Shipman and Mayes, 1990). This is most obvious in the household, where who does what, where items are put, how people are likely to react are all known and acted upon – not necessarily co-operatively of course as this experience can be used to find a quick route to irritating others. When a new person enters the household many of the routines have to change. This may be the result of explicit discussion and agreement; people who do not know each other, sharing a flat for the first time, may actually write down some of the rules of behaviour, but in general they will be unwritten and even unstated.

Many of these unwritten rules form part of the culture of the society. The same sort of argument can be applied to the firm, which can also develop a culture. Some of the management literature which has become popular over the last decade, Peters and Waterman (1982) for example, emphasises the importance of taking positive steps to develop a culture which is favourable to the per-formance of the firm. However, the more normal experience in Europe is for the culture to be largely implicit even if the company has a written "mission statement" (Grinyer et al., 1989). This same cultural dimension extends outside the firm into doing business with others. Within the same cultural framework, even when dealing with new customers or suppliers, it is possible to anticipate a large proportion of the other party's expectations and reactions correctly. This is not true when it comes to dealing with foreign companies or markets. Even when language is not a problem misunderstanding is much easier. Japanese companies investing in Europe and the Western Pacific Rim for example have taken much trouble to explain to their suppliers what they require in terms of quality, delivery and response and have indeed sent managers into some of the companies to help them achieve those targets (Langhammer, 1989, 1991). Otherwise they have found it more efficient to bear the extra cost of importing from Japan despite more favourable local factor prices (Mayes and Ogiwara, 1992).

What we face within Europe is a twofold problem of both bringing different cultures of behaviour together within a common framework and, principally in the former Communist states, adapting to new internal cultures. Our understanding of how these processes work is very poor, not least because the problem runs across traditional disciplines, combining the economics of the behaviour of the firm and of regulation, the study of management, the politics of institutions and bargaining, the legal changes involved, and the social consequences and influences (ESRC, 1990). The problem of such sweeping change has clear spatial and environmental consequences – the list is very long. Moreover, this is a real and not an abstract problem, involving detailed knowledge of the structures within each of the European countries.

In the Economic and Social Research Council (ESRC)'s European research initiative (which I am coordinating) we are attempting to address the first problem: the integration of different societies. Some 20 projects involve around 80 researchers in the UK and other EC countries (the projects are listed in *Annex 13.4*). This research relates not only to the EC but to Europe as a whole. The current focus is primarily on the West, in part because the ESRC has a second "East-West" research initiative although that focuses primarily on political and social rather than economic issues. However, that is in the process of changing and I hope that we will be able to develop some new projects extending the scope firmly eastwards in the second phase of the research.

In this paper I seek to deal with only some of the problems, focusing in particular on the institutional changes already agreed as a result of the Single European Act of 1986, the Maastricht Treaty of 1992, the European Economic Area agreement and others implemented or in prospect over the rest of this decade in the Community. These changes are intended to help to increase integration in western Europe. By and large they are framed without regard to the problems of integration between East and West. Indeed we should ask whether they make that integration more difficult. It is arguable that the more tightly knit Western Europe becomes, and the more it focuses on evening out its own distributional imbalances, the greater the requirements for change imposed on the East and the smaller the help available. However, in framing the analysis this way round I do not want to imply that the Community's institutions are the only way of approaching closer integration in Europe. Indeed I expect that the evolution of the changes in central and eastern Europe will lead to a substantial rethink on the part of the Community.

I want to indicate how far the new institutions that have been created are transferable and how far they improve the prospects of economic transition. With some small exceptions these institutions relate to "competition" in the broad rather than the narrow sense. They are intended to regulate the framework within which market economies can operate closely together in open and fair competition. While the process of integration is also driven by many non-economic objectives, such as security, a fundamental tenet of the changes is that closer integration will enable a more efficient use of resources by removing unnecessary costs, increasing scale and enhancing competitive pressures, leading to an increase in the rate of economic growth.

13.1 Changes stemming from the Single European Act

The EC's institutions were drawn up in the 1950s. They were designed to deal with a Community of six, with a relatively limited range of competences and an initial emphasis on removing quotas and tariffs on trade in manufactures and establishing a common agricultural policy. Since then the organisation has grown in size and functions. With twelve members and new areas of focus, like the structural policies, decision-making has become more complex, and the size and the power of the Commission have increased. The ability of ministers to come to unanimous decisions in Council has been reduced.

Whether by consequence or coincidence the integration of the Community slowed even before the first widening to nine members. Indeed it is this widening of the Community which is probably the most significant feature of the period. Added to this, after the oil crises, was the slowing of economic growth. The Werner Plan for economic and monetary union agreed in 1970 rapidly came to nothing in the face of economic difficulty. Progress had been made with the development of regional policy and, mainly through the European Court of Justice, with the removal of some of the most obvious non-tariff barriers to trade, such as technical specifications. On top of this Europe found itself very obviously losing in the competitive battle with the Japanese. Many industries were becoming increasingly global in character, with firms addressing a wide range of markets and needing to organise their production on an international basis. The fragmentation of the Community into a lot of relatively small markets was increasingly seen by European multinationals as a source of competitive disadvantage. It was widely argued that the source of both US and Japanese success had been the existence of strong domestic competition behind effective external barriers. There was thus widespread industrial pressure for liberalising and harmonising European markets; the European Roundtable of industrialists produced a paper at the beginning of 1985 arguing for a single European market to be completed within five years (by 1990).

There was disagreement about whether this should be achieved behind a protective barrier, "the Fortress Europe" idea; but by common consent, when the White Paper on the Single Market came out later in 1985, its authors were pushing at an open door. In Mayes (1991) I attempted to classify the main proposals of the White Paper according to their correspondence with current business trends (*Annex 13.1*). The bulk of the measures and the trends were clearly pushing in the same direction. Thus although the single market programme and the Single European Act were major steps forward, they were not dragging along a reluctant industry but easing its path down a preferred route.

Thus there was already a culture for change and the legislative measures were following, not leading, it. However, it is easy to exaggerate the position. "Industry" as just described is very much the multinationals. Much of the rest of industry was either largely unaware of the proposed changes or felt that they were likely to be irrelevant. As a result, the 1992 programme elicited little popular support in its first couple of years. It required a major information campaign to change those attitudes. However, the campaign, conducted throughout the Community, was a resounding success. Most firms began to see 1992 as an important opportunity (Nerb, 1988) and felt they might suffer from increased competition if they ignored it. This Europeanisation of business thus became enshrined in the culture, even though there was considerable ignorance about what it might entail and many optimistic expectations may turn out to be ill-founded. (As with all deregulations there is likely to be overinvestment and a shakeout of less successful companies.)

The single market programme thus accelerated forces for change which were already present. However, the difficulties of the programme should not be underestimated. Although most of the dossiers have been resolved, many of the changes in the rules, let alone in behaviour, are still to come. In pharmaceuticals for example the arrangements for EC-wide registration and mutual recognition of national registration are expected in the middle of the decade. There is thus quite a long period of adjustment in total. In any case the measures on the whole permit change rather than compel it, with the exception of minimum health, safety and environmental requirements. Thus the permitting of free movement of labour does not appear likely to have much impact on actual labour movements among established Community residents. This will limit the extent to which market mechanisms can eliminate differentials. Indeed it is unlikely that the legislation would have taken the form it has if large migrations were expected, as can be inferred from current worries about migration into the EC from outside.

Some of the major mechanisms implemented by the Single Market Act are largely untried. Others involve a greater role for bodies outside the EC institutions, for example, the European standards institutions and Patent Office, which include countries outside the EC. Their operation is also voluntary; there are circumstances where national patents make more sense and where adherence to a particular standard is not necessary (see van de Gevel and Mayes, 1989 and EPO, 1992). There is thus no clear message yet to indicate whether and how far these institutional changes lead to increases in welfare and the enhancement of competition.

Community level regulation and EC rules for member state regulation

Two main institutional routes have been followed for regulating industry. One is to regulate at the EC level (as for large-scale mergers) and the other is to set rules for national regulation to avoid discrimination. In many areas there is a combination of both. In theory the choice over which to employ should depend upon the principle of subsidiarity. Subsidiarity in general implies that responsibility for executing policy should be allocated to the member state rather than to the Community if this is efficient and avoids any important spillovers. This institutional approach makes it rather easier to include new member states within the EC as it permits local variety; whether it greatly simplifies the implementation of the whole range of Community policies is more debatable.

As things stand at present there is a vast variety in regulatory mechanisms used for industry in the Community. In general it is not proposed to alter this directly although some have limits to their powers, both in terms of jurisdiction and equality of treatment of Community firms irrelevant of the particular member state where they are incorporated or the majority of their ownership lies. Clearly for the present discussion competition policy and the division of responsibility between the Commission and the authorities in the member states is the prime interest. As this is the explicit subject of other chapters (see especially Ch. 2) I only touch on it here and focus the discussion of institutions on the wider framework that is felt necessary to run a successful economic and monetary union in the EC.

The Treaty of Rome gives the European Commission sweeping executive powers under articles 85-94 to act against anti-competitive practices, whether perpetrated by private or public interests. In exercising these powers the Commission stresses its independence from the governments of the member states and indeed (as in the cases of Renault and Rover) has acted in a manner which they find uncongenial. Broadly speaking the Commission follows a procompetitive, German-style policy, based on rule, but with a degree of political sensitivity. In formulating its approach the EC has distinguished between antitrust policy and restrictive practices and the full range of activity is still to be sorted out. In particular the institutional framework of competition policy stands in clear contrast to trade policy which, under article 113, is decided by the Council and implementated by the Commission and to technology policy which is following an increasingly collaborative and interventionist route. Clearly the stage is set for clashes of behaviour where the boundaries of the policies overlap (Holmes, 1991). The form of regulation, at the national level, whether through statute or self-regulation, remains very much a matter for the local culture, although some instances seem to be more effective than others. That too has the potential for substantial clashes, both between member states and the Commission and among the member states.

However, it is largely up to the market and the national authorities to decide whether they wish to see changes in the structure of regulation, provided that they operate within the accepted EC framework. Michael Moran and his colleagues at the University of Manchester have observed that there has been quite a strong trend for the UK's regulation of doctors and lawyers to move towards a more statutory based system and one where there is greater independence from members of the profession. Although the recognition systems have had to be reorganised to enable qualified professionals from other member states to be allowed to practise in the UK, this has not had any particular implication for the structure of regulation as a whole. One therefore has to speculate whether the need for reorganisation in one respect led to a more general appraisal of continental systems, whether it is coincidental or whether there has been convergence towards the best system.

Competition among rules

While the focus is usually upon the regulation of competition among firms, the single market incorporates the concept of competition among regimes. Each state can follow its own rules subject to some minimum conditions and to equal treatment of all EC citizens or organisations. It is then for customers and firms to decide which rule system they prefer and then buy or locate accordingly. There is no clear basis in theory for expecting one outcome rather than another; but there has been a widespread fear in some parts of the Community that there would be a "rush for the bottom" (Hager et al., 1992) – a kind of "Delawarisation"[1] of Europe, whereby companies seek to take advantage of the weakest regulations in the Community after which member states in turn seek to lower their standards in a downward spiral.

This kind of fear was particularly expressed over the subject of social provision and the apprehension that "social dumping" might take place. The idea was that firms would move to where labour costs (apart from actual wages) were

---

[1]   Refers to Delaware, US, company law, regarded as less restrictive than the law in other States.

lowest, to the detriment of working conditions for the labour force in all parts of the Community. In practice this fear seems to be largely misplaced as other aspects of the attractiveness of low labour cost locations have tended to dominate and there has as yet been no rush to relocate. On the contrary there seems to have been some reinforcement of existing patterns of production. Many customers and employees might be expected to move towards the best not the worst. Some but not all competition is based purely on price. While quality may have fallen in some US examples, it has risen in international air travel; so there appears to be no single answer. On the other side of the coin there have been fears that the unemployed would tend to gravitate towards the member states which offer the best benefits. Thus those with the lowest nonwage labour costs would attract the mobile investment and those with the best benefits, the unemployed, thereby exacerbating the problem and increasing the chances of a general worsening in conditions for those not in employment.

In practice one of the major mechanisms of restructuring is that of merger and acquisition. Here differences in the institutional set-up have had an effect: acquisitions are easier in the UK, and to a lesser extent in the Netherlands, than elsewhere in the Community. Investment has also come from outside the Community. For both existing enterprises and greenfield sites, the institutional factors involved form one of the aspects affecting the decision to invest (see Stopford, 1992). Although the Community has rules about state aids which restrict what can be offered as inducements, the institutional structure is not similarly controlled.

The importance of these sorts of differences has been recognised in the Strategic Impediments Initiative between the US and Japan. In these discussions it is intended to identify how institutional differences affect the competitiveness of the two countries, and where this appears to offer an unfair advantage to discuss how it might be dealt with. Ironically, a similar approach has not been adopted within the Community: provided structures do not specifically discriminate against other member states, and firms from other states can operate within a given market on the same basis as the domestic industry, this is deemed to be acceptable. In part this is because the main areas of likely discrimination, like public purchasing, have been identified and dealt with directly. However, this cannot handle differences due to length of time horizon that investors adopt; it is argued (Hart, 1991, for example) that the structure of cross holdings and the

205

role of the major banks in Germany in the supervisory boards of companies and as holders of proxy votes enable companies to take a longer term view and hence ride out short-run difficulties and invest more than in some other parts of the EC, notably the UK. This sort of institutional difference again affects competition among countries.

Improvements in decision-making

Although the Single European Act is mainly remembered for providing the impetus to complete the internal market in the Community by the end of 1992, removing barriers to the free flow of goods, services, labour and capital, it also took a major step towards improving the decision-making of the Community through qualified majority voting (QMV). The role of the Parliament has also increased. Although the new rules may be clear, Holmes (1991) argues that the changes in practice are more fundamental. Although QMV officially has a limited range of policies to which it applies in practice it is much more generally used. The practice tends to be that member states in a small minority tend to back down. Indeed most decisions tend to be unanimous even though QMV can be applied, minority opposition being pushed to a vote only when there are political interests at home to be mollified. An agreement known as the Luxembourg compromise was worked out in 1966 in order to prevent particular countries being overridden on matters they find essential. In Holmes's view the Community has now reached the stage when that no longer seems to apply in practice. Indeed, there have been instances, as with the 1982 budget, where it appears that the European Court of Justice does not recognise the applicability of the principle.

In an enlarged and more complex Community, unanimity on most matters would be difficult and a more flexible approach would seem necessary. However, that flexibility is likely to have to take two forms, the one where those in the minority are prepared to acquiesce and the other where exceptions can be made from the general agreement. This latter approach has been used in the case of the Maastricht Treaty where eleven member states have agreed a protocol on special policy which does not apply to the twelfth, the UK.

Thus, although in some respects the Single Market was an inward looking attempt to improve the relative competitiveness of the existing European Community the form it has taken both opens the way to a larger grouping and encourages it, as is shown both by the pressure for the European Economic Area agreement and the subsequent applications for membership from some EFTA countries.

13.2 Maastricht and European Union

The Maastricht agreement produced a new treaty on European Union to replace the existing Community treaties, as amended by the Single European Act of 1986. Thus while the Treaty of Rome was able to cover the main issues for 30 years, the pace of integration has since proved so fast that the treaties have required amendment twice in six years. Originally, when the Hannover Council set up the Delors Committee in June 1988, it was expected that the new treaty would cover the necessary extra provisions to set up economic and monetary union (EMU). When the Madrid Council, a year later, decided to implement the first stage of the Delors Committee proposals on 1 July 1990 and to set up an intergovernmental conference to sort out the measures necessary for the subsequent stages, they referred only to EMU. However, largely as the result of a Franco-German initiative, the special Dublin Council (April 1990) confirmed its commitment to "political union" and set up a parallel intergovernmental conference on the treaty provisions necessary to strengthen the democratic legitimacy of the union. It also set a deadline for both intergovernmental conferences to complete their proposals in time for ratification by the member states before the end of 1992.

The result is the "Maastricht" *Treaty on European Union*, signed in Maastricht on 7 February 1992 by the Prime Ministers of member states, but subject to ratification by the Parliaments. Its major objectives are set out in *Annex 13.2*. It emphasises not just convergence to achieve EMU but cohesion and progress on other fronts and a determination to continue the process of creating an ever closer union among the peoples of Europe. EMU is a stage in the process, not just because of the potential for widening the Community but because of the intention of deepening it further. The treaty is much stronger on the economic and monetary aspects than it is on the political side of union. Nevertheless the Treaty does involve several new institutions.

The treaty sets out the nature, functions and constitution of the new central banking system which is to manage the single currency, monetary policy and foreign exchange in the new monetary union. It also explains how fiscal and budgetary policy are to be managed. Of most immediate interest are the principles for organising the transition to monetary union. Monetary union, as in the Werner and Delors proposals, is tended to take place in three stages. The first stage has already commenced with the freeing of capital flows and the integration of financial markets under the single market programme. That programme in itself provides a major plank in the establishment of what is described as "economic union". Stage 2 involves the creation of a new Community institution, the European Monetary Institute (EMI). The EMI is purely a transitional institution which will cease once it has been successful in bringing the Community to the start of Stage 3; it will be replaced by the European Central Bank (ECB). The ECB, together with the central banks of the member states, forms the European System of Central Banks (ESCB) from the beginning of Stage 3.

The role of the EMI is to oversee the transition when Stage 2 begins on 1 January 1994. It has planning, monitoring, and advising roles. In the transition, the member states' institutions have responsibility for the execution of monetary, exchange rate and fiscal policy and the EMI is intended to help with the process of increasing co-ordination among them. It is not until Stage 3 that the ECB takes over responsibility for exchange rate and monetary policy. How exactly the ECB will function is to be established during the transition. What has been set out in the draft treaty is its objectives, constitution and the nature and composition of the board which will run it. Indeed in this transition period all the institutions involved, the national central banks and the governmental and other bodies involved in fiscal, financial and monetary operation and regulation, will have to undergo a learning process in co-operation to prepare for Stage 3. National legislation for each central bank will have to be compatible with the statute of the ESCB, for example.

It is an interesting idea to have an institution managing the transition which is different from that which will operate at the end of the process. It emphasises that the process of change is difficult and requires special skills to achieve it. The analogy for the changes being undertaken in central and eastern Europe is to set up interim institutions also. However, this is bound up in the argument over the relative merits of gradual as opposed to immediate change. Although the Community is moving quite rapidly by contrast to its previous progress, these changes are still following a relatively slow process of evolution. Monetary union in particular will have taken nearly thirty years to achieve even if it happens on its first possible date, which in any case seems unlikely at present (Britton and Mayes, 1992).

However, institutional change is only part of what is required for a successful transition to EMU. For member states to participate in the monetary union they have to meet the four criteria of convergence set out in *Annex 13.3*. Then, in determining readiness for Stage 3, the Commission and the EMI must also take account of:

> *the development of the ECU*
> *the results of the integration of markets*
> *the situation and development of the balance of payments on current account*
> *the developments of unit labour costs and other price indices.*

The actual decision over whether to go ahead is a complex process. First of all the Council *acting by qualified majority* has to decide on the basis of the various recommendations we have just described:

(a) whether each individual member state fulfils the necessary conditions for adoption of a single currency;

(b) whether a majority of the member states fulfil the necessary conditions for the adoption of a single currency;

and then, in turn, recommend its findings to the Council, meeting as heads of state/governments (which will also have the benefit of an opinion from the European Parliament). If that meeting agrees that a majority of the member states meets the conditions *then* it must decide, *acting by qualified majority*, whether it is appropriate for the Community to enter stage 3 and if so to set a date. This meeting must take place before the end of December 1996.

If by the end of 1997 the date for starting Stage 3 has not been set then Stage 3 will start on 1 January 1999. The Council must meet, as heads of state/governments, before 1 July 1998 to decide which member states fulfil the conditions of convergence for participation. (The question of a majority is no longer relevant).

It is in Stage 3 that the full EMU will begin to operate, managed through the new institutional arrangements of the ESCB, the ECB and the Economic and

Financial Committee. This will generate all the requirements for the operation of a single monetary policy, foreign exchange policy and the co-ordination of economic policy. However, the treaty makes it clear that while the implementation of the ECU as the single currency of Europe is the objective, this will follow the irrevocable fixing of exchange rates at the start of Stage 3 and not occur right at the outset:

"*these activities shall include the irrevocable fixing of exchange rates leading to the introduction of a single currency, the ECU*" (Article 3a). Although it is stated that there should be a timetable for this transition, the treaty does not say when the single currency should be introduced during Stage 3. Most of the sections on Stage 3 focus on the constitution and operation of the new central bank.

In putting this structure together, therefore, the member states have tried to reach a compromise between objective conditions which are independently assessed and the political sensitivities. The net result is that uncertainty has been built into the system. We are not able to forecast clearly when EMU will be achieved, who will be included within it, nor when the ECU will become the single currency (we do however attempt that in Britton and Mayes, 1992, suggesting that it is indeed impossible for all the existing member states to achieve convergence in this century but most can enter EMU in 1997). This will have an adverse effect on the actions of business and the response of the market to the proposals (see Ernst & Young et al., 1990) as firms are unwilling to incur costs before they know that they are essential. Having the right institutions is not enough.

The form of the ESCB and the constitution of the ECB

It is the ESCB, composed of the national central banks and the European Central Bank (ECB), which has the objective of maintaining price stability. Without prejudice to that objective it has to support the Community's general economic objectives within a clear framework of free market principles. The ESCB has four tasks:
— to define and implement monetary policy,
— to conduct foreign exchange policy,
— to manage the member states' foreign exchange reserves and
— to promote smooth payments systems.

210

The ECB is the executive organisation in the system. It and all the national central banks are given independence from the institutions of the Community and member state governments in the exercise of their functions. The bank is run directly by a six man Executive Board of a president, vice-president and four other members, who are appointed by the Heads of state/governments after consulting the European Parliament and the Governing Council of the ECB, the period of office being a single term of eight years. That Governing Council is composed of the executive board and the governors of the national central banks. Voting is on a one man-one vote basis, acting on a simple majority, except where it refers to the bank's capital when votes are proportionate to the member states' sub-scribed capital, the executive board having no votes. The subscribed capital is determined by an equal weighting of the member states' shares of Community population and GDP at market prices (the latter averaged over the previous five years). The subscription is revised every five years.

The ECB is responsible for the note issue, open market operations, setting of minimum reserve requirements and other aspects of monetary control although they may be exercised through the national central banks. However, while the ECB can advise on prudential supervision of credit institutions and stability of the financial system, these functions remain the responsibility of the member states. The bank is subject to audit and is under the jurisdiction of the Court of Justice. Overdraft or other credit facilities by the ECB or national central banks to any Community or member state public body are explicitly prohibited.

The President of the Council and a member of the Commission may attend the Governing Council of the ECB. The ECB has to make an annual report on its activities which the President will present to the Council and the European Parliament. He and the other members of the Executive Board may be heard by the relevant committees of the Parliament at either side's request.

The transition organisation, the European Monetary Institute (EMI), has a Council composed of a President and the Governors of the national central banks and has the same guarantee of independence. While the primary tasks are to sort out the operating rules and procedures for the ESCB, the ECB and national central banks within it, and advising the member states on the conduct of monetary policy, it also has an important role in the operation of the EMS, administering the VSTF and medium-term financial assistance and the issuance

211

of ECUs to EC and third country institutions. The President is the executive officer; in his absence the Vice president, who is a governor of one of the national central banks, deputises. The EMI is subject to the same auditing and Court of Justice jurisdiction as the ECB and, on the day Stage 3 starts, transfers its assets and liabilities to the ECB, which will then liquidate it.

Economic policy

Matching these arrangements for monetary management are those for economic policy. The principle is that member states shall regard their economic policies as a matter of common concern and co-ordinate them within the Council. The Council, acting on a recommendation from the Commission, will set out broad guidelines for the economic policies of the member states and the Community. There will be multilateral surveillance of economic developments and the consistency of policies with the guidelines. Should a member state's policy be judged inconsistent by a qualified majority on the Council, the Council can make recommendations to the member state, which it may choose to make public. In particular, the Commission will monitor the member states' budgetary and debt positions on the basis of the planned or actual ratios of the deficit to GDP and debt to GDP using the same criteria as set out in the convergence criteria for entry into Stage 3. If the deficit is thought excessive after taking into account "relevant factors", including whether it exceeds government investment, then the Council can recommend action by the member state to remedy it. If the member state does not respond adequately to the recommendations then the Council can impose four sanctions:

– a requirement to publish further information before issuing bonds or securities;
– inviting the EIB to review its lending to the member state;
– requiring the member state to make a non-interest bearing deposit while the deficit remains excessive;
– levying a fine.

In order to take these sanctions and even make the recommendations for action the Council has to act on a two thirds majority of the votes cast – excluding the member state concerned – using the usual weighting system.

The Maastricht Treaty thus adds some formidable institutions to the structure of the Community, seeking to endow them with sufficient independence and power to be able to achieve economic objectives that several of the member states have been unable to sustain on their own. There are considerable constraints on behaviour as monetary policy is handed over to the ECB and fiscal policy is heavily circumscribed. It remains to be seen not just whether such a system can be made to operate but which member states can manage to adjust far enough to become part of the union.

Where the treaty is difficult to interpret is the question of how the system will work with some countries inside the union and some outside. Clearly there will be some form of continuing EMS but the system will be very asymmetric with countries inside the union dominating each of those outside. It does however open the way for other countries to join the system through a process of increasing convergence, like that already experienced by the existing members. A considerable degree of convergence is required for membership of EMU beyond the conditions for nominal convergence laid down in the treaty. Without substantial structural similarity, similarity of behavioural response, similar economic policies and a measure of convergence in real incomes, it is unlikely that countries will respond to shocks in a sufficiently similar manner for them to be able to hold to an exchange rate fixed within narrow bands. The period of adjustment for some European countries to a system as rigid as EMU could therefore be very long indeed. Adherence to the terms of the single market, or to a free trade area, represent easier steps of integration for states with considerable dissimilarity.

Other aspects of the Maastricht Treaty impinging on institutional change

The new treaty addresses the question of social and economic "cohesion" (i.e. reducing inequalities between member states and regions) in the Community and gives it high priority (articles 130A and 130B). A new cohesion fund is also established; a Committee of the Regions composed of representatives from the regions of the member states acts in an advisory capacity in the same way as the Economic and Social Committee. Explicit protocols set out these intentions. This focus is probably the most important for the successful development of the Community as a single unit (Begg and Mayes, 1991). As things stand there is a very considerable discrepancy between the richest and poorest regions in the

Community, far more so than in large nation states like the US or Canada. The poorest regions are also concentrated: Greece, Portugal, Ireland, Spain and Southern Italy. These states will have to be convinced that the benefits will be distributed sufficiently in their favour to justify incurring the short-run costs of trying to converge to EMU (NIESR, 1991).

These requirements will impose a considerable strain on the Community's ability to agree as the budget proposals for the years 1993-98, labelled Delors II, argue for a 30 per cent increase in spending in real terms, much of it going on structural support for the least favoured regions. Institutional changes alone are not sufficient for success; they need to be backed up by money and direct assistance. Some aspects of integration are not necessarily favourable; Nam (1991) suggests that the single market and associated legislation is on balance likely to worsen the relative position of the least favoured regions of the Community.

However, the chosen solution involves considerable local participation, increasing the importance of regional administrations. Combined with the Committee on the Regions and the enhanced role of the Parliament this could represent an important change in structure in the Community in the longer term. Given the pressures for decentralisation in various parts of Europe this form of change may have wider attractions. It may also act as a step towards a looser form of political union, which is one of the weakest parts of the Maastricht Treaty.

The nature of the new treaty and the compromises it involves

The Delors Committee report (1986) is very helpful in explaining the meaning of an economic and monetary union and hence what needs to be done to achieve it. *"EMU in Europe would imply complete freedom of movement of persons, goods, services and capital, as well as irrevocably fixed exchange rates between national currencies and finally a single currency. This in turn, would imply a common monetary policy and require a high degree of compatibility of economic policies and consistency in a number of other policy areas, particularly in the fiscal field."* The monetary union requirements are rather more straightforward than those for economic union, which it suggests are (1) the single market (2) competition policy and other measures aimed at strengthening market mechanisms (3) common policies aimed at structural change and regional development (4) macroeconomic policies including binding rules for budgetary policies.

This is *a* definition rather than *the* definition of an economic union: the role and nature of competition policy, the extent of the "single market" and the need for structural and regional policies represent choices rather than a requirement for all economic unions (as is shown by the existence of unions which involve them in varying degrees).

The Community has been rather good at meeting deadlines in recent years, as is witnessed by progress in agreeing the 279 measures to implement the 1992 programme; the completion of the agreement on schedule at the Maastricht Council was no exception. However, the eagerness to meet the timetable and the short notice for the proposals on political union have meant rather more loose ends and untidy features to the agreement than might have been expected. The most obvious of these relates to what is referred to as the "social chapter" of the treaty, to which the UK refused to agree and which hence has been adopted as a separate protocol by the other eleven members. Derogations have been common in the past to permit specific member states to delay implementation of Community rules which gave them particularly difficult problems, such as the final abolition of capital controls by Greece, Ireland, Portugal and Spain. However, this appears to be the first time that a country has been able to opt out entirely from an area of legislation.

The monetary union component of the new treaty has not been immune from such compromises as the UK is given the right to come to an explicit decision whether to participate in the final stage of monetary union, once the Community as a whole has decided to go ahead with it. The Irish Republic and Denmark must also hold referenda before they can agree to entering Stage 3. Introducing uncertainty into the eventual caste of participants and into the timetable of implementation substantially reduces the credibility of the process. Flexibility in the transition procedure to ensure that EMU is not introduced prematurely, and that the transition problems for those member states with the greatest difficulty are properly handled collaboratively by the Community, is eminently sensible, but this is not how the treaty reads – it reflects disagreement among the negotiating parties. The necessary ratification on the treaty by each member state may not be a formality if the sources of disagreement in the negotiations reflect strong views not successfully included in the final compromise agreed by the governments.

There are at least four main areas over which there was considerable disagreement of view over the form of the treaty over EMU:
the aims and accountability of the ECB;
the process of transition;
the extent of economic union required, especially in the social dimension;
the need for "cohesion" in the EC.

The aims and accountability of the European Central Bank

The basic problem which had to be resolved in determining what the ECB should do and how it should be controlled is the existence of the several aims of economic policy. An example is set out at the beginning of the Delors Report (para 16) *"Economic and monetary union in Europe ... would imply a common monetary policy and require a high degree of compatibility of economic policies and consistency in a number of other policy areas. These policies should be geared to price stability, balanced growth, converging standards of living, high employment and external equilibrium."* These policies inevitably conflict and within member states a compromise is reached as to which should be subordinated at any one time. However, the Bundesbank was very clear that a major contribution to the success of the German economy was the independence of the central bank and its unequivocal focus on the control of inflation.

Governments in other countries, e.g. France, held the view that while controlling inflation was all-important, there were occasions when other objectives should come first, particularly in the short run. In most member states the central bank is ultimately subordinated to the government; so while the bank might control the instruments of monetary policy and look after the immediate details, it was the government, usually through the ministry of finance, which set the objectives of policy and decided the fiscal and monetary stances. To some extent this was an argument over ideals: although the governors of the US Federal Reserve System operate with considerable independence, and the Bundesbank operates in a legal framework of independence, in practice a degree of compromise is reached. In the US this compromise is the result of 80 years of evolution. The Federal Reserve Board does not press its view to extremes and

216

so prejudice the integrity of government policy, although it could do so, while the Executive and indeed the Congress do not exercise their full powers of intervention. The compromise works through clear and understood objectives for the Fed and a system of accountability, both when the Chairman is appointed and in the reporting and justifying of the Fed's activities to congress. This particular balance between the executive, legislative and judicial arms of government is unique to the American constitution; any balance in the European EMU has to be both more complex because of the role of the individual member states, and more explicit because the system is new and at the beginning of a learning process.

If a European Parliament or European Council got to the stage of wishing to remove a President of the ECB, then the process of compromise would have failed. Like so many sanctions it is intended to work through the threat of its existence, not through its execution. We have already seen in the German case that there are limits to the independence of the Bundesbank, whatever the Constitution may say. The political imperatives of German unification were such that the government felt it had to take decisions on economic and monetary union, such as the one-to-one parity of the West and East German currencies despite undesirable inflationary consequences, because the alternatives might compromise the success of the exercise as a whole. Thus although the Bundesbank might protest and its President, Karl Otto Pöhl, (although a figure of international standing, tipped by many as the first President of the ECB) resign, the government's view prevailed.

The balance wanted by many countries was that the view of the Council of Ministers should ultimately prevail. From the German position, the new single currency had to be at least as strong as the Deutschmark if it was to be worth having and that this required a strong constitutional position for the ECB. In the end this latter view was accepted but there was considerable argument about the balance of power even within the ECB's structure. Each country needed to be represented on the board of governors but the same compromise which faces all EC representation had to be addressed: should representation be equal for member states, or related to population or to economic size? What sort of majority should be sufficient for action? Elaborate schemes were suggested but ultimately it became clear that if such a bank were to function effectively the executive committee must be able to act with considerable authority.

The resulting compromise falls, therefore, towards the extreme of independence, with policy narrowly focused on price stability, and a minimum of external controls from either the Council or the European Parliament. It remains to be seen whether the role of the Parliament in the appointment of the President of the ECB, and the periodic reports and examinations, in fact prove acceptable mechanisms of control and accountability. Whether the balance of the system as a whole functions satisfactorily can only be tested in practice when the first major price shocks rock the system. It is probable that the Council, in the form of the heads of state/governments, will sometimes come to short-run decisions about how to act, to which the ECB will have to adapt. Nevertheless, the signatories have taken the sensible course of agreeing a clear definition of powers and hence have defined a clear-cut, workable system based on existing central bank experience.

One example from outside the Community both illustrates the workability of the solution arrived at in Maastricht, and the tensions that can arise. The new Zealand government gave independence to its central bank, charging it to bring down inflation to 0-2 per cent within five years. The most recent inflation figures even show a slight fall in prices, largely as a result of the success of the bank's management and of a relatively consistent government deficit policy. But the New Zealand economy has not prospered during that transition and the government is now faced by a low rating in the polls and very considerable public pressure to ease its fiscal stance (much of the current unpopularity stems not so much from the stance itself but from the social expenditure cuts and healthcare charges used to achieve it). As the next election looms, the tension will be obvious. In New Zealand the government has to stand on its own. In EMU a problem of this nature, restricted to only some countries, can be eased by Community action. Short-term deficits can not only be condoned, without unleashing Community-wide inflation, but medium-term finance is available to let a member state ride out the period of difficulty.

The process of transition

The negotiations over the process of transition were clouded by the conflict between the wish of member states not be excluded at the outset from the benefits of EMU and the need to ensure that the terms of the EMU did actually

218

confer the benefits, particularly in the form of control of price stability. The approach of the Delors Committee and the Commission throughout was that the Community should pass from one stage of EMU to the next when it was fit to do so. Thus Stage 1 is entered when freedom of capital movements exists, Stage 2 is begun when the co-ordination mechanisms are in place but Stage 3 is not commenced until the member states have in some sense "converged". The alternative position put forward was that each stage imposes more effective sanctions on the member states because inflation and depreciation are no longer available routes to change and because a co-operative solution to individual problems becomes easier when all have a vested interest in the successful adjustment of the states with the greatest problems. This offers the potential threat that the difficulties of the weak could prejudice the whole system. In the agreed solution states with difficulties are excluded, the onus for finding solutions being very much their own responsibility.

In particular, it rapidly became clear that the conditions of convergence thought necessary to ensure that the new system would be stable and non-inflationary were such that many countries would bear heavy costs in trying to achieve them and that the likelihood of all twelve achieving them in the reasonably close future was remote. It was argued by some therefore (Spain, for example) that membership of the EMU would help to impose convergence and that budgetary compensation methods to less advantaged countries with budgetary problems in the transition would enable them to join from the outset. This would obviously imply a limited amount of extra inflation to the system as whole in the short run, but if the deficits were small by reference to the Community's rather than to the member state's GDP then the result would be manageable. If the criteria were absolute, either EMU would be put off indefinitely as convergence would be likely to elude one or another state at any particular time, or some would have to be left out. Once outside the system and having been shown to have failed to be able to achieve convergence, a state's credibility would be low and the costs of converging even higher, so that participation could be put off for a long period.

The convoluted compromise over dates for starting Stage 3 is an attempt to get round this. In the first instance the attempt can be made to try to get as many states as possible within the system. It is certain from the terms of the agreement, that the minimum number of participants must be at least a simple majority (7) but since the decision has to be by qualified majority in the Council a considerably higher number is likely, *if* the go ahead is to be given by the deadline of the end of 1996. After that date EMU will go ahead in 1999 (at the latest) with however many member states are deemed to have converged. As far as we can see from the technical conditions that union could consists of only one member state. That, of course, would be clearly ridiculous but EMU for even a small core of five or six member states, as in the initial Schengen agreement, could be a believable building block on the road to full EMU if other member states were clearly close to achieving convergence. Unlike Schengen, such an EMU must be established in Community Law not by intergovernmental agreement (O'Keeffe, 1992).

In effect, the main argument has been postponed. If a significant number of countries do not meet the criteria at the first decision date it is unlikely that some of those still experiencing problems will be willing to see the others go ahead with an arrangement which would be to their competitive disadvantage (assuming, that is, that the list of benefits set out in *One market, one money* and elsewhere is believed to be correct). Whether they would still be willing to see such a step even in 1998/99 is also debatable. Such a multispeed Europe might be thought undesirable; hence the scope exists for a compromise on the con-vergence conditions. In any case, we are unlikely to be discussing a Community of twelve in 1999, or indeed in 1997. The likely new members, Sweden, Austria, and Finland, are better able to achieve convergence than most member states and hence will increase the chance of both a simple majority of states meeting the criteria and of obtaining a qualified majority in the Council for going ahead at an early stage.

The extent of economic union required

The emphasis in presenting the need for monetary union has been placed on its importance for completing the single market and providing various micro-economic gains through a single currency. On previous occasions, a single currency had taken second place to locked exchange rates and the emphasis had been on the benefits to macroeconomic policy and the achievement of stability. The single market does not provide all the characteristics of economic union and the negotiating parties used this opportunity to argue whether EMU

220

required a wider collaboration in policy formation than under previous commitments. For example, it was argued that, to provide a proper union, Community competence should be extended to education, so that the Community's citizens could be assured of opportunities for high quality education wherever they chose to live in the EC. With anything less the free movement of labour would be impeded.

The same argument was extended to the "social chapter" which included wider proposals for social action both within the firm and outside. Should there be minimum levels for access to social provision? What minimum rights have to be offered for the wellbeing of people in the workplace, etc.? Here there were a number of objectors to the proposals, feeling that requirements would either harm their competitiveness or impose unsustainable budget deficits on member states which were already in difficulty. A blocking coalition was therefore established between the UK, Spain and Portugal. The Spanish and Portuguese were not unwilling to attempt more generous social provision, but just could not afford it. Hence when the cohesion fund was developed, and the commitment to greater emphasis on social and economic cohesion was emphasised, the Spanish and Portuguese ended their opposition to the social measures leaving the UK on its own. The price of that compromise is becoming clear as an element in the Commission's proposals for a 30 per cent real expansion in the Community budget over the next five years.

Since the social chapter in the treaty had to be resolved under unanimity, the UK had the power (and, it seems, the inclination) to block further progress until convinced of its benefits. This it did very effectively, despite the wishes of the other eleven countries. However, rather than letting the chapter lapse, which was the expected outcome, a last moment compromise was reached: the other member states would go ahead with the social chapter but it would be attached to the treaty as a separate agreement, rather than form part of it.

It remains to be seen whether the UK's point of view that a less regulated market in a number of respects does in fact permit more flexibility and hence ability to adjust more readily to shocks and pressures for change, or whether it merely tends to reinforce a lower cost position instead of forcing a transition to higher value added production. Thus far, the single market has not developed far enough to provide a test but, as Ermisch (1991) has indicated, the lack of

221

migration in the Community suggests that regulations which raise labour costs may increase unemployment in the less advantaged parts of the Community. The expectation at present is that it will be possible at some stage, perhaps not in the too distant future, to return to a policy acceptable to all member states through a combination of experience and changes of views.

The need for social and economic "cohesion"

A related part of the negotiations covered the need for action on the problems of the less favoured regions of the Community. Since these regions are concentrated in the lower income member states, one might be forgiven for suggesting that this was part of the price for getting those countries' agreement to EMU changes which benefit the more advantaged regions. A more charitable view is that increasing the equity in the growth process has been a feature of the EC treaties since the Treaty of Rome and has since been progressively strengthened. To a limited extent the rationale has been that the less advantaged regions represent an underutilised resource, particularly in so far as that lack of advantage is reflected in higher than average unemployment, but those resources are also underutilised in the sense that many of the activities can be performed more efficiently, hence releasing resources for further production elsewhere.

Against this it is argued that the strengths of the Community come from fostering what it does best and that putting funds into supporting the inefficient will reduce the overall rate of growth. There has therefore been resistance, in Germany and the UK in particular, to expanding the Community's budget and to increasing the structural funds. Their view has been that, if the Community as a whole is successful, then some of that success will tend to filter down to all regions. With freedom for capital and labour to move, resources can shift to where they can be most efficiently used. It is reasonably clear from the negotiations culminating in Maastricht that this view does not prevail in the Community as a whole at present, or at least that the mechanism for mobility is insufficient.

The policy which has been confirmed is that limited funds should be used to create an infrastructure in both physical and human capital, which will give the less advantaged regions an equal opportunity to compete with the rest in the single market. The size of the additional funds implied appears to be a matter of dispute. The Commission has asked for a doubling in real terms over the period

1993-98 in its recent budget proposal. Some of the member states have responded immediately that they had not intended an expansion in Community spending in total of the magnitude proposed. This promises a negotiation with the usual sparkle but it is already clear that, whatever the outcome, the Maastricht Treaty provides a clear gesture of support for the less favoured regions.

This support, in an effort to deepen the involvement of all levels of government in the Community's processes, has been extended to creating a Committee for the Regions. Since this is advisory (like the Economic and Social Committee) it does not represent an awkward commitment to an interest group with demands on funds, but is a pointer to the way in which the deepening of the union could go, weakening the relative position of the existing member states and focusing on regions with economic meaning (which may not coincide with previous political boundaries).

Taken together, the Maastricht proposals provide a clear indication of the way forward for European Union. On the one hand they represent a stage towards what is described as "ever closer union"; further work will be required on both the economic and political fronts if the internal market is to resemble, even remotely, the domestic markets of large federal states, like the US. On the other hand, several of the proposals have to prove themselves in practice, particularly monetary union, which is not only treading new ground but requires considerable effort on the part of many member states both to achieve it and make it work. Integration is an evolutionary process with steps both backwards and forwards. The Maastricht agreement represents an attempt to make a major step towards closer integration in which monetary union plays a major part. It presents a real opportunity to achieve a breakthrough which has eluded the Community for twenty years in making serious progress towards an economic and monetary union which can be expanded to include other European countries which wish to participate and can sufficiently adapt their economic systems.

13.3 The European Economic Area agreement and other institutional changes

Since the early 1970s a large proportion of the benefits from the Common Market had been extended to the EFTA countries through the free trade agreements (restricted to manufactures). With the next step in integration in the Community – the single market – a further agreement was required if the balance was to be maintained. This took the form of the agreement on the European Economic Area (EEA). To some extent, the EFTA countries could have got many of the benefits without an agreement, but would have been largely excluded from any of the decision-making on the subject.

In practice the EEA agreement is still one-sided. In effect, the EFTA countries have had to agree to accept the whole range of EC legislation and operate their markets as if they were part of the Community. There were problems even in trying to extend the operation of the European Court of Justice and add some EFTA justices to the bench (Brewin, 1992). It is therefore not surprising that several of the EFTA countries should have applied to become full members of the EC, since the EEA agreement involves taking on the obligations of the Community unilaterally. Of course, the EEA agreement does not cover all aspects of EC policy; full membership would involve taking on obligations beyond those relating to the internal market, such as the Common Agricultural policy. (For some aspects of EEA, see Rouam, Ch. 2 of this volume.)

Non-members may be disturbed by the Community's lack of interest in compromise and by the Community's willingness to exercise its economic bargaining power. This may also be reflected in the apparent stance in the GATT negotiations, even if the attitude of the US is also a contributory factor. The implication is that aspiring members of the EC, or those who want a looser association with it, will need to adapt to the EC's requirements rather than to look for forms of compromise.

Implications for institutional change in a wider Europe

On the whole, the current changes in the EC framework are designed to cope with the existing member states, although it is probable that several of the EFTA members that have applied or are likely to apply to join could be accommodated. Although it would complicate all the EC institutions, either increasing their size (or substituting new members for existing ones in some functions) the extension is not unmanageable. The countries concerned are small, of above EC average income, and highly integrated with the EC. There are problems to overcome in such areas as agriculture and fishing; however, in general the adjustment costs are likely to be relatively small and the adjustment periods relatively short. Indeed these countries are in the main rather better adapted to move to full EMU by the end of the decade than are several of the existing members (Britton and Mayes, 1992).

However, it must be expected that the inclusion of, particularly, Austria, Finland, Sweden and Switzerland will alter the balance of the Community, shifting its centre of gravity north and east, while previous commitments to neutrality are bound to have an impact both on foreign policy and on links with central and eastern Europe. Furthermore, these countries have not been particularly enthusiastic supporters of further common policies within EFTA, which suggests a question mark over their attitudes towards further integration in the EC.

Expansion of the Community beyond these countries – that is to countries in central and eastern Europe – cannot really be accommodated within the existing institutions. To get agreement in a Community of 20 to 30 members will often be very hard. A qualified majority would mean that quite a large number of countries could be outvoted. Effective action on some subjects may require smaller groups rather than representatives of every member state. The way forward in this respect has already been shown by the structure of the proposed European Central Bank. There is a strong feeling that the future will lie in a "variable geometry" Europe, where the number of member states involved in agreements on particular policy areas may be less than the whole membership (as exemplified by the Schengen intergovernmental agreement and the social protocol to the Maastricht Treaty).

Perhaps the greatest difficulties will arise from the real disparities between the possible ex-communist candidates and the rest of the Community. Extending the ideas of "cohesion" to them would put huge demands on the other members. However, unless there is a quite considerable transfer of resources it is difficult to ˙ee membership being possible for a long time. Without membership, there is still the problem of catching up. Internal institutions of the Community are not the prime obstacle. Other institutions, e.g. the European Bank for Reconstruction and Development (EBRD), have a role to play, although it is widely argued that the existing international institutions have not the necessary competence.

A further question is whether the institutions of the EC are transferable, or suitable for European countries in the process of transition "to the market" and whether there are lessons which can be learnt from EC experience. It is, however relevant that the EC institutions are largely based on arrangements that encourage integration, and operate on a regional rather than a bilateral basis. Wider use of regional institutions might be a route forward, particularly for payments imbalances (see Collignon, in Barrell, 1992). In general, however, the difficulty is not just a problem of institutions, but of the behavioural responses to them; and that is a subject well beyond the scope of this paper.

Complementarities and inconsistencies between the Internal Market measures and market trends

Trend	Complementary measure
New technology leads to reduction in minimum efficient scale through flexible manufacturing systems	Unified market enables greater access to new market areas but substantial differences in buyers' requirements are likely to remain
Japanese surplus looking for reinvestment abroad	Incentive for Japanese to invest in Europe to get inside external tariffs and reap full advantage of Single Market
R&D scale economies and advantages of collusion at the "pre-competitive" stage of R&D	Large co-operative R&D programmes in "pre-competitive" areas (IT, telecoms, innovation dissemination)
Scale economies, scope economies and competition incentives made available through cross-border ownership market	Capital-market deregulation and new legal framework making cross-border acquisitions easier
Growth of oligopolies within EC, prevent competition but unchallenged by domestic competition policy	European-level merger control to prevent anti-competitive concentration
Pressure for standardisation of technical/safety/environmental regulations, to reduce cost of modification before a product becomes exportable	Harmonisation, and removal of non-tariff barriers
Concern about the environment	Stronger environmental standards and regulations
Contracting-out and privatisation, as means to control public spending and increase revenue	Opening-up of public procurement, restriction of state subsidies to firms
Competition in concentrated markets requiring ease of entry/exit and reduced sunk costs (for contestability)	Single Market providing greater scope for potential entry and redeployment of fixed-cost resources to other uses
Fall in transport costs relative to production costs	Single Market allowing producers to locate in lowest-cost regions; infrastructure projects which further reduce costs

(continued)

Annex 13.1 (continued)

Complementarities and inconsistencies between the Internal Market measures and market trends

Trend

Shift to "knowledge-intensive" production requiring higher skilled more autonomous workforce

Increased external effects of national macro policies and interdependence of main macro instruments

Increased trade requiring exchange-rate stability to reduce costs of hedging/exchange risk

Trend

Use of product differentiation to reduce competition and achieve market power

Restructing/re-allocation/building-up of new sectors requiring state intervention

Innovation for competitiveness with non-European firms requires collusion to protect monopoly rents, or subsidy to compensate for their loss

Opening up of Eastern Europe as source of low production costs and direct investment opportunities

(In some member states) Return to "free" labour market with weak trade unions, flexible wages

Related measures

Social Charter and structural funds providing for vocational training, participation

Move towards common monetary and fiscal policies, economic union

Completion and "hardening" of ERM

Inconsistent measure

End to national standards as a basis for product differentiation

Restriction of state aid to industry

Competition promoted, collusion reduced, state subsidy restricted

Attempts to attract inward investment and achieve higher investment within the EC

Social Charter conditions for union power, minimum wages, etc.

Source: Mayes (1991).

The Preamble to the Maastricht Treaty on European Union

The signatories to the Treaty

Resolved to mark a new stage in the process of European integration undertaken with the establishment of the European Communities

Recalling the historic importance of the ending of the division of the European continent and the need to create firm bases for the construction of the future Europe

Confirming their attachment to the principles of liberty, democracy and respect for human rights and fundamental freedoms and the rule of law

Desiring to deepen the solidarity between their peoples while respecting their history, their culture and their traditions

Desiring to enhance further the democratic and efficient functioning of the institutions so as to enable them better to carry out, within a single institutional framework, the tasks entrusted to them

Resolved to achieve the strengthening and the convergence of their economies and to establish an economic and monetary union including, in accordance with the provisions of this Treaty, a single and stable currency

Determined to promote economic and social progress for their peoples within the context of the accomplishment of the internal market and of reinforced cohesion and environmental protection, and to implement policies ensuring that advances in economic integration are accompanied by parallel progress in other fields

Resolved to establish a citizenship common to the nationals of their countries

Resolved to implement a common foreign and security policy including the eventual framing of a common defence policy which might in time lead to a common defence thereby reinforcing the European identity and its independence in order to promote peace, security and progress in Europe and in the world

Reaffirming their objective to facilitate the free movement of persons, while ensuring the safety and security of their peoples, by including provisions on justice and home affairs in this Treaty

Resolved to continue the process of creating an ever closer union among the peoples of Europe in which decisions are taken as closely as possible to the citizen in accordance with the principle of subsidiarity

In view of further steps to be taken in order to advance European integration

Have decided to establish a European Union

Convergence criteria for Monetary Union

1 *"a high degree of price stability* ... apparent from a rate of inflation which is close to that of at most the three best performing Member States in terms of price stability." In the associated protocol this is defined as "price performance that is *sustainable* and an *average rate of inflation, observed over a period of one year* before the examination, that does not exceed that of at most the three best performing Member States in terms of price stability by more than 1.5 percentage points" (inflation to be measured by comparable Consumer Price Indices).

2 *a sustainable government financial position,* "apparent from having achieved budgetary positions without a government deficit that is excessive". The associated protocol defines this position in two respects: a maximum 3 per cent for the ratio of the planned or actual government deficit to GDP at market prices; a maximum 60 per cent for the ratio of government debt to GDP at market prices. (In this context the government is defined as general government, excluding commercial operations, the deficit is net lending and debt is total gross debt consolidated across the government sector.)

The governments of the member states have an obligation under this protocol to ensure that their policies achieve these targets.

3 *observance of the normal fluctuation margins provided for by the ERM of the EMS* for at least two years, without devaluing against any other member state currency.

4 *the reflection of the durability of convergence in long-term interest rate levels.* The associated protocol defines this as a divergence not exceeding 2 percentage points from the nominal long-term government bond rates of at most the three best performing member states in terms of price stability.

Annex 13.4

Projects and contacts under the Single European Market initiative

Coordinator: David G. Mayes, National Institute of Economic and Social Research, London (NIESR)

European Cohesion: competition, technology and the regions
Ash Amin, CURDS, University of Newcastle-upon-Tyne

Participation of Non-member states in shaping the rules of the EC's single market
Christopher Brewin, Department of International Relations, University of Keele

Competition Between Metropolitan Regions in the Single Euorpean Market
Paul Cheshire, Faculty of Urban and Regional Studies, University of Reading

The Legal Implementation of the Single European Market at National Level
Terence Daintith, Institute of Advanced Legal Studies, London

The Future of Public Procurement in Europe: rules, public choice and the single European market
Keith Hartley, Institute for Defence Economics, University of York

The Interaction of Trade, Competition and Technology Policy in the Single Market
Peter Holmes, School of European Studies, University of Sussex

Human Resource Regimes and the Single European Market
Robert Lindley, Institute for Employment Research, University of Warwick

A New Strategy for Social and Economic Cohesion After 1992
David Mayes, NIESR

1992: the stimulus for change in British and West German Industry
David Mayes, NIESR

The Implications of the Evolution of European Integration for the UK Labour Market
David Mayes, NIESR

The Harmonisation of EC Securities Market Regulations
George McKenzie, Centre for International Economics, University of Southampton

Regulatory Institutions and Practices in the Single European Market
Michael Moran, European Policy Research Unit, University of Manchester

The Free Movement of Workers and the Single European Market
David O'Keeffe, Department of Law, University of Durham

Environmental Standards and the Politics of Expertise in the Single European Market
Geoffrey Pridham, Centre for Mediterranean Studies, University of Bristol

Lobbying in the EC: a comparative study
Jeremy Richardson, Department of Goverment, University of Strathclyde, Glasgow

Regulation and Competition in the European Air Transport Industry
Paul Seabright, Department of Applied Economics, University of Cambridge

Rules for Energy Taxation in the Single European Market
Stephen Smith, Institute for Fiscal Studies, London

The Consequences of Finnish Membership of the EC for the Finnish Food Industries
Henri Vartiainen, The Helsinki Research Institute for Business Administration, Helsinki, Finland

The Evolution of Rules for a Single European Market
Helen Wallace, Royal Institute of International Affairs, London

231

References

Barrell, R. (ed.) (1992), *Economic Convergence and Monetary Union in Europe*, London, Sage.

Begg, I. and Mayes, D.G. (1991), "Social and Economic Cohesion among the Regions of Europe in the 1990s", *National Institute Economic Review*, November.

Bollard, A. and Mayes, D.G. (1991), "Corporatisation and Privatisation in New Zealand", paper for conference on privatisation at University of St. Andrews, Scotland (forthcoming in conference papers, ed. T. Clark).

Brewin, C. (1992), "The role of third countries in the evolution of the single market", paper presented at the ESRC SEM initiative seminar at NIESR, 26 March.

Britton, A. and Mayes, D.G. (1992), *Achieving Monetary Union*, London, Sage.

"Delors Report" (1986), *Report on Economic and Monetary Union* of the Committee for the Study of Economic and Monetary Union, Luxembourg, EC Publications.

Ermisch, J. (1991), "European Integration and External Constraints on Social Policy: Is a Social Charter Really Necessary?", *National Institute Economic Review*, May.

Ernst & Young and NIESR (1990), *A Strategy for the ECU*, London, Kogan Page for the Association for the Monetary Union of Europe.

ESRC (1990), "The Evolution of Rules for a Single European Market", Economic and Social Research Council, Swindon, UK.

European Commission (1990), "One Market, One Money", *European Economy* no. 44 (October).

European Patent Office (1992), "Results and Methods of Economic Patent Research with respect to the European Patent System", Workshop (March).

Grinyer, P., Mayes, D.G. and McKiernan, P. (1989), *Sharpbenders: the secrets of unleashing corporate potential*, Oxford, Basil Blackwell.

Hager, W., Knight, A., Mayes, D.G. and Streeck, W. (1992), *Public Interest and Market Pressures: problems posed by Europe 1992*, London, Macmillan (forthcoming).

Hart, P. (1991), "The Effects of 1992 on the external and internal growth of British and German companies", *National Institute Discussion Paper*, NS no. 2.

Holmes, P. (1991), "Trade, Competition and Technology Policy in the EC: Can they all rule OK? An initial view", paper presented at ESRC-NWO colloquium on the Single European market, Wageningen (November).

Langhammer, R. (1989), "Trade in manufactures between Asian Pacific Rim countries", *ASEAN Economic Bulletin*, vol. 6, no. 1, pp. 94-109.

– (1991), 'Towards Regional Entities in Asia-Pacific', *Asean Economic Bulletin*, vol. 7, no. 3, pp. 277-289.

Mayes, D.G. (ed.) (1991), *The European Challenge: industry's response to the 1992 programme*, London, Harvester-Wheatsheaf.

Mayes, D.G. and Ogiwara, Y. (1992), 'Implementing Japanese Sources of Competitiveness in the UK', NIESR (mimeo).

Nam, C. (1991), *The Impact of 1992 and Associated Legislation on the Less Favoured Regions of the European Community*, Luxembourg, European Parliament Research Paper 18.

Nerb, G. (1988), *The Completion of the Internal Market. A Survey of European Industry's Perception of the Likely effects*, vol. 3 in 'The Costs of Non-Europe', Luxembourg, European Communities.

NIESR (1991), *A New Strategy for Social and Economic Cohesion after 1992*, Luxembourg, European Parliament Research Report, no. 19.

O'Keeffe, D. (1992), *The Free Movement of Workers and the Single European Market*, Discussion Paper, University of Durham.

Peters, T. and Waterman, R. (1982), *In Search of Excellence*, New York, Harper and Row.

Shipman, A. and Mayes, D.G. (1990), 'Changing the Rules: a framework for examining government and company responses in 1992', *National Institute Discussion Paper* no. 199.

Stopford, J. (1992), 'Changes in European Multinationals' Competitiveness, Implications for Trade Policy', in Mayes, D. (ed.), *The External Implications of European Integration*, London, Harvester-Wheatsheaf (forthcoming).

Treaty on European Union (1992), ('Maastricht' Treaty), Luxembourg, EC Publications.

van de Gevel, A. and Mayes, D.G. (1989), '1992: Removing the Barriers', *National Institute Economic Review*, August.

LIST OF PARTICIPANTS

in the 14th international
Workshop on European Economic Interaction and Integration
Mariánské Lázně (Marienbad), CSFR, 27 to 30 April 1992

Stanislav Bělehrádek	Chairman, Czech Office for Economic Competition (AMO), Brno, CSFR
Alain Bienaymé	Professor, Université Paris-Dauphine, Paris, France
Carlo Boffito	Professor, University of Turin, Italy
Guy Charrier	Rapporteur permanent, Conseil de la Concurrence, Paris, France
Imrich Flassik[*]	Chairman, Czechoslovak Federal Competition Office, Bratislava, CSFR
János Gács	International Institute for Applied Systems Analysis (IIASA), Laxenburg, Austria
Ingrid Gazzari	Administrative Director, The Vienna Institute for Comparative Economic Studies (WIIW), Vienna, Austria
Simon Hausberger	Minister (retired) at the EC Mission, Brussels, Belgium
Miroslav Hrnčíř	Institute of Economics, Czechoslovak Academy of Sciences, Prague, CSFR
Nobuko Inagawa[*]	Special researcher, Federal Institute for Soviet and International Studies, Cologne, FRG

---

[*]   Author, but unable to attend the workshop

András Inotai	Professor, Director of the Institute for World Economics, Budapest, Hungary
Ivan Kalina	Czechoslovak Federal Competition Office, Bratislava, CSFR
Karel Kouba	Professor, Director of the Institute of Economic Sciences, Faculty of Social Sciences, Charles University, Prague, CSFR
Helmut Kramer[*]	Professor, Director of the Austrian Institute of Economic Research (WIFO), Vienna, Austria
Rikard Lang	Professor, Institute of Economics, University of Zagreb, Croatia
Kazimierz Laski	Professor, Research Director of The Vienna Institute for Comparative Economic Studies (WIIW), Vienna, Austria
Friedrich Levcik	Professor, consultant to The Vienna Institute for Comparative Economic Studies (WIIW), Vienna, Austria
Zdenek Lukas	The Vienna Institute for Comparative Economic Studies (WIIW), Vienna, Austria
Alberto Martinelli[*]	Professor, University of Milan, Italy
David Mayes	Professor, National Institute of Economic and Social Research, London, UK
Péter Pogácsás	Hungarian Competition Office, Budapest, Hungary
Philipp Rieger	Consultant, The Vienna Institute for Comparative Economic Studies (WIIW), Vienna, Austria

---

[*]   Author, but unable to attend the workshop

Dariusz K. Rosati	Professor, Division for Economic Analysis and Projections, United Nations Economic Commission for Europe, Geneva, Switzerland
Claude Rouam	Deputy Head of Unit, Directorate General for Competition, Commission of the European Communities, Brussels, Belgium
Christopher T. Saunders	Professor, Science Policy Research Unit, University of Sussex, Brighton, UK
János Stadler	Vice President, Hungarian Competition Office, Budapest, Hungary
Andrei Vernikov	Institute of International Economic and Political Studies, Academy of Sciences, Moscow, Russia
Dragomir Vojnić	Professor, Director of the Institute of Economics, University of Zagreb, Croatia
Ewald Walterskirchen	Austrian Institute of Economic Research (WIFO), Vienna, Austria
John Williamson	Professor, Institute for International Economics, Washington DC, USA
Ruben N. Yevstigneyev	Professor, Deputy Director of the Institute of International Economic and Political Studies, Academy of Sciences, Moscow, Russia

INDEX

competition 13-14
  and Treaty of Rome 20-3, 31
  competition-promoting policies 23-5, 42
    in a supra-national setting 27-38
  importance of 41-3
  policies and their role in forming a
    market economy 131-2
    instruments of 141-8
    objectives 133-41
  transformation of 44-6
  see also specific countries;
  specific types of competitive tendering
  21, 43
consumer goods 9, 15, 168, 190, 191
consumer welfare 13, 15, 45-6, 133
Cooperation between Member Countries
  on Restrictive Business Practices
  (OECD-1986) 35
cost function 17, 129
cost-price relationship 43-4, 56
Croatia 4, 101-4
  Agency of the Republic of Croatia for
    Restructuring and Development 112,
    113
  economic growth 104-7
  efficiency and markets 104-8
  market structure and competition
    114-20
  privatisation 7, 106-8, 123
    and transition 108-14
    shares 108-9, 112, 113
  prospects for development 120-3
  war damage 8, 118, 120-1, 123
  weakness of competition 105-7
currency convertibility 57, 58, 60, 62, 125,
  130, 132, 167, 172-3, 179, 191
current account convertibility 42, 62
Czechoslovakia 4, 8, 31n, 41, 50, 58, 61-2,
  70-1, 76, 94, 124, 125-6, 192
  agriculture 52-3, 61
  banking system 64, 65, 67-72

constraints on domestic competition
  62-7
creating a competitive environment
  49-54, 71, 74
entrepreneurship 50-4
Federal Office for Economic Competition 5, 73-4, 130
  case studies in competition control
    74-7
financial intermediation and competition
  67-71
foreign exchange 61-2, 68, 70, 71
incentive aspects of competition 55-7
inter-enterprise indebtedness 64-5, 71,
  72
macroeconomic stabilisation 57-60, 72
price liberalisation 50, 57, 79-80
private sector 5, 50-4, 60, 61
privatisation 5-6, 50-4, 57, 59-61, 71, 99
restructuring policies 57-61
role of foreign competition 61-7, 72

deflation 127, 128, 159
Delors Committee 207, 208, 214-15, 216,
  219
Denmark 197n, 215
distributors 10, 137-9, 144-5, 146, 175,
  191, 200
Domar, E.D. 104n
dominant position 3, 5, 21, 31, 54, 73,
  75-6, 79, 81, 86-7, 89, 134, 135, 141,
  145-6
Drutter, Izak 114n, 115, 118
Dublin Council 207

East Germany 126, 217
Eastern Europe 8, 12, 47, 83-4, 101, 124-7,
  128, 130, 144, 228
  lessons from Italian state-owned in-
    dustry 11, 188, 194
  privatisation 1-2, 4

240

relevance of Japanese industrial policy to 10-11, 49-50, 167-75, 188-93
see also specific countries
economic and monetary union (EMU) 200-1, 203, 207-13, 214-23, 225, 228, 229-30
Economic and Social Committee 213, 223
Economic and Social Research Council (ESRC) 199
economic growth 16-17, 44, 50, 104-8, 128, 194, 200
see also specific countries
economic progress 13-14, 16, 27, 134, 146, 147
economies of scale 3, 17, 23, 42, 125, 158, 168, 189, 227
economies of scope 17, 227
EFTA 4, 12, 22, 30-1, 33-5, 38, 47, 50, 179, 182, 197-8, 207, 223-6
energy 22, 111, 162, 187, 231
entrepreneurs and entrepreneurship 16, 45, 50-1, 62, 73, 74, 76, 79, 82, 84, 86, 88, 89, 125, 180, 186-7, 189
see also specific countries
Ermisch, J. 221-2
Ernst and Young 210
European Bank for Reconstruction and Development (EBRD) 225
European Central Bank (ECB) 208, 209-13, 216-18, 225
European Community 10, 12, 18, 21-2, 24, 27, 41, 47, 50, 74, 119, 140, 173, 179, 181, 183, 194, 197-8, 200-2
and European Economic Area (EEA) 223-6
banking system 207-13, 216-18, 225
community level and member state regulation 202-4
competition among rules 204-6
competition regulations 28-30, 33-5, 37, 143, 146
European Agreements 31-2, 38

Free Trade Agreements (FTAs) 3-4, 30-1, 223
improvements in decision making 206-7
US Agreement (Sept 1991) 32, 37-8
see also economic and monetary union (EMU); European Community Commission; internal market; Maastricht Treaty; Single European Act; Single European Market; Treaty of Rome
European Community Commission 3, 21-2, 28-9, 34, 46-7, 140, 144, 203-4, 209, 211, 212, 219, 221, 222-3
European Council 200, 203, 209, 211, 212, 217, 218, 220
European Court of Justice 3, 34, 142, 143, 201, 206, 211, 212, 224
European Currency Unit (ECU) 209, 210, 212
European Economic Area (EEA) 4, 12, 31, 33-5, 38, 46-7, 197, 199-200, 207, 223-6
European Monetary Institute (EMI) 208, 209, 211-12
European Monetary System 211, 213, 230
European Parliament 206, 209, 211, 214, 217, 218
European Roundtable of Industrialists 201
European System of Central Banks (ESCB) 208, 209-12
exchange rate 132, 172-3, 192, 208, 210, 214, 220, 228
Bretton Woods System 168, 180
Exchange Rate Mechanism (ERM) 228, 230
exports and exporters 8, 22, 41, 60, 63, 83, 84, 93, 107, 125-6, 128, 154, 158, 160, 164, 167-8, 180, 189, 190, 191

Far Eastern Countries 192-3
see also specific countries
Farnleitner, J. 179
Federal Reserve System (US) 216-17
Fiat 13, 31

suppliers 15-16, 17, 19, 39, 45-6, 60, 63, 65, 74, 83, 115-18, 136, 140, 145, 181, 199
surpluses 107, 108
Sweden 141, 182, 220, 225
Switzerland 182, 225

Tasmania 33
taxation 44, 49, 114, 127, 128, 136, 157, 160, 162, 165, 180, 191
technology 3, 6, 10, 16, 17-18, 20, 23, 25, 44, 49, 55, 81, 93, 104, 130, 133, 134, 151, 152-3, 154, 156, 159, 165, 169n, 175, 186, 187, 190, 191-2, 203, 227
gap 55-6, 62, 66-7, 167-8
Telser, L.G. 15
Thatcher, Margaret 41-2
Toyota 16
trade unions 19, 99, 180, 187, 228
Treaty of Rome 3, 36, 207, 222
and competition 20-3, 31, 143, 203
see also European Community
Tsuruta, T. 160n, 163
Turkey 104n

UNCTAD 35-8
unemployment 44, 58, 99, 132, 154, 185, 190, 191, 193, 205, 222
United Kingdom 107, 141, 199, 204, 205, 206, 222, 231
and social chapter 215, 221
privatisation 41-2, 61n
United States of America 22, 33, 96, 107, 108, 169n, 173, 174, 175, 189, 193, 194, 201, 204, 205, 214, 216-17, 223, 224
competition rules 29-30
EC Agreement (Sept 1991) 32, 37-8

van de Gevel, A. 202
Volkswagen 16, 195
wages 132, 153, 173, 174, 191, 194, 204-5, 228

Walrasian economics 43, 45, 130
Waterman, R. 198
Werner Plan 200-1, 208
West Germany 126, 217, 231
Williamson, O. 17
woodpulp case 30-1
workable competition 3, 16-20, 40, 43, 45-6, 56, 72
World Bank 24

Yasin, Y. 91n
Yeltsin, Boris 96, 97
Yugoslavia 1n, 4, 7, 99, 102, 103, 110, 114, 116-19, 120
economic growth 104-6

Zdunić, S. 111n
Županov, Josip 111n

245

RECENT PUBLICATIONS

of The Vienna Institute for Comparative Economic Studies (WIIW)
(as of December 1992)

BOOKS

Series: Studien über Wirtschafts- und Systemvergleiche
Springer-Verlag, Vienna-New York

Vol. 15   G. Fink (ed.): The World Economy and the East. Vienna 1989, 70 pp., AS 270.-, DM 38.-

Series: European Economic Interaction and Integration / Workshop Papers
The Macmillan Press Ltd., London and Basingstoke

Vol. 13   C.T. Saunders (ed.): Economics and Politics of Transition. London and Basingstoke 1992,
           421 pp, £ 50.-

Series: Statistical pocket books

COMECON DATA 1990
Statistical pocket book, in English; supplemented, extended and updated; The Macmillan Press Ltd.,
London and Basingstoke 1991, 449 pp., £ 50.-

FOREIGN TRADE DATA OF COUNTRIES IN TRANSITION 1980-1991
Statistical pocket book, in English. Orac Verlag, Vienna 1992, 416 pp., AS 960.-

Series: Yearbooks
Westview Press, Boulder, San Francisco, & Oxford

Yearbook I   H. Gabrisch (ed.): Economic Reforms in Eastern Europe and the Soviet Union. Boulder,
               San Francisco, & London 1989, 214 pp., US$ 29.50

Yearbook II   M. Friedländer (ed.): Foreign Trade in Eastern Europe and the Soviet Union. Boulder,
               San Francisco, & London 1990, 241 pp., US$ 32.00

Yearbook III   P. Havlik (ed.): Dismantling the Command Economy in Eastern Europe. Boulder, San
               Francisco, & Oxford 1991, 280 pp., US$ 34.50

Yearbook IV   S. Richter (ed.): The Transition From Command to Market Economies in East-Central
               Europe. Boulder, San Francisco & Oxford, 1992, 321 pp., US$ 35.95

in preparation:
Yearbook V   G. Hunya (ed.): Economic Transformation in East-Central Europe - Results, Lessons,
               Corrective Ideas

FORSCHUNGSBERICHTE (Research Reports)

published, under its own imprint, by The Vienna Institute for Comparative Economic Studies

No. 180   H. Gabrisch et al., Vienna: Depression and Inflation: Threats to Political and Social Stability. The Current Economic Situation of Former CMEA Countries and Yugoslavia. February 1992

No. 181   K. Laski, Vienna: Transition from Command to Market Economies in Central and Eastern Europe: First Experiences and Questions. March 1992

No. 182   Waltraut Urban, Vienna: Economic Lessons for the East European Countries from Two Newly Industrializing Countries in the Far East? April 1992

No. 183   A. Bhaduri, Calcutta – Vienna: Conventional Stabilization and the East European Transition. April 1992

No. 184   H. Gabrisch et al., Vienna: Advanced Reforming Countries Might Reach End of Recession. The Economic Situation in Central and East European Countries, ex-USSR and ex-Yugoslavia in Early 1992. July 1992

No. 185   R. Dietz, Vienna: From Command to Market Economies – an Exchange Theoretical View. July 1992

No. 186   D. Avramović, Rockville, USA – Belgrade: International Experience with Adjustment Programmes and with Lending for Adjustment. October 1992

No. 187   J. Fath, Vienna: Industrial Policies for Countries in Transition? November 1992

No. 188   R. Vintrová, Prague: Macroeconomic Analysis of Transformation in the CSFR. December 1992

CURRENT ANALYSES (since 1991)

Published, under its own imprint, by WIIW

No. 1   Recession and Transformation. The Economic Situation in Central and Eastern Europe and the Soviet Union in the first half of 1991 and Outlook for the end of the year. October 1991, AS 800.-

No. 2   Russian Federation: Economic Situation in Early 1992 and Western Financial Risks. May 1992, AS 420.-

No. 3   CSFR: Standing of Both Republics and Effects of a Separation. July 1992, AS 420.-

REPRINT-SERIE (Reprint-Series)

published, under its own imprint, by The Vienna Institute for Comparative Economic Studies. In this series the Institute reprints staff members' and regular co-workers' papers which had previously appeared in books or periodicals outside the Institute's own publication programme.

No. 139   H. Gabrisch et al., Vienna: Transformationskrise setzt sich fort. Die Wirtschaftslage in Osteuropa, in der ehemaligen UdSSR und in Jugoslawien 1991/92.
Reprint from: *Monatsberichte des Österreichischen Instituts für Wirtschaftsforschung*, 65. Jahrgang, Heft 5, 1992

No. 140   R. Dietz et al., Vienna: East-West Energy Trade. Recent Trends and Future Prospects with main focus on oil and gas.
Reprint from: *Seminar on East-West Energy Trade – Proceedings*. Seminar held in Vienna, on October 3rd-4th, 1991, co-sponsored and jointly organised by the Republic of Austria, the International Energy Agency, and the World Bank. OECD, Paris 1992

No. 141   Z. Lukas, Vienna: Die Landwirtschaft in den Oststaaten 1991. Tschechoslowakische Landwirtschaft am Scheideweg.
Reprint from: *Osteuropa Wirtschaft*, 37. Jahrgang, Heft 2, 1992, sowie *Osteuropa. Zeitschrift für Gegenwartsfragen des Ostens*, 42. Jahrgang, Heft 5, 1992, beide hrsg. von der Deutschen Gesellschaft für Osteuropakunde, Deutsche Verlags-Anstalt Stuttgart, 1992

No. 142   K. Laski, Vienna: Der aktuelle Stand der Diskussion über die Transformationsprobleme.
Reprint from: *Europäische Rundschau*. Vierteljahreszeitschrift für Politik, Wirtschaft und Zeitgeschichte, 20. Jahrgang, Nummer 4, 1992

No. 143   S. Richter, Vienna: Hungary's Changed Patterns of Trade and Their Effects.
Reprint from: *Soviet Studies*. A Journal on the USSR and Eastern Europe, University of Glasgow, Vol. 44, No. 6, 1992

Monographien / Monographs

Books:
W. Brus und K. Laski: **From Marx to the Market: Socialism in Search for an Economic System**, Oxford University Press, Oxford 1991

Brochures:
S. Richter/J. Stankovsky: **Die neue Rolle Österreichs im Ost-West-Handel**, WIFO-WIIW-Monographie, Vienna 1991